MAN OF STEEL

Man of Steel

The Career and Courage of Christopher Reeve

Adrian Havill

HEADLINE

First published in 1996
by Dutton Signet, a division of Penguin Books USA Inc

First published in Great Britain in 1996
by HEADLINE BOOK PUBLISHING

10 9 8 7 6 5 4 3 2 1

ISBN 0 7472 5611 X

Printed and bound in Great Britain by
Cox & Wyman Ltd, Reading, Berks

HEADLINE BOOK PUBLISHING
A division of Hodder Headline PLC
338 Euston Road
London NW1 3BH

This book is for
Amanda, David, and
always Mike.

CONTENTS

PROLOGUE

Christopher Reeve, a.k.a. Superman, was in the hospital, paralyzed, his pain deadened by morphine.

The comic book hero he had played hadn't needed courage. He was bulletproof, could see through walls, and fly. The actor who had portrayed him best was the one needing courage now, as never in his life before.

Only a handful of people knew Chris Reeve was there. Memorial Day weekend isn't the best time to alert the media. Like the rest of America, the press were basking in the sun at the beach or out on their decks charring steaks and burgers.

Besides, the first one-line wire reports weren't too alarming. There were one or two sentences that gave no hint of the severity of Chris' condition or why he was in a hospital bed in Virginia. Indeed, the Sunday papers of May 28, 1995, the day after his fall, revealed nothing. The words beginning to stumble out from the hospital's media spokespersons were few. No cause for panic, reasoned the skeletal staffs who had drawn the short straws and had to man the nation's newsrooms over a major holiday period.

"Could be cancer," speculated one scribe.

"Or AIDS," his associate responded.

At the epicenter of the entertainment industry, the *Los Angeles Times* broke the news near the end of its "Morning Report" column on Monday, May 29. The entertainment potpourri by Beth Kleid put the news under a "Quick Takes" sub headline at the very bottom of the page: *"Actor Christopher Reeve was in stable condition Sunday at the University of Virginia Medical Center after being thrown from his steed during a horse-jumping competition outside of Charlottesville, Va., on Saturday."*

That was all.

There were other, newer stars in Hollywood about whom to gossip these days. At the Polo Lounge and Morton's, the agents were poring over the surprisingly big box office numbers being chalked up by another comic strip character who had made it to the big screen. The movie-going public was about to make *Casper* the number-one film of the holiday weekend. The industry was also clucking over the surprisingly small numbers being posted by an actor thought to be as white-hot as Chris had once been. He had a similar last name—Keanu Reeves. His *Johnny Mnemonic* vehicle looked to be a flop, and the movie moguls were puzzled. They had always looked to "youngsters" like Reeves to replace a Chris Reeve when that star's luster was beginning to fade.

Christopher Reeve, the star of four *Superman* movies and hundreds of films, plays, and television shows, lay on a hospital bed motionless. He would soon be called upon to demonstrate the kind of courage one finds only in mythical heroes. But on that first weekend, few Americans knew of his plight.

It wasn't that way outside the country. There was no holiday in England. The tabloids of London, noted for their aggressiveness, had scanned the one-line reports and like sharks sensing blood, had six reporters in the air within hours. Armed with laptops, cameras, and road maps, the British press were invading Virginia by Sunday morning in rented cars, getting a lesson in tooling down the right sides of near-empty interstates and country roads, while the victors of the American Revolution slept late.

On Monday, while the *L.A. Times* and others offered their benign one-line bulletins, one British tabloid would scream: SUPERMAN BREAKS HIS BACK! and
quote a nurse as saying that the injury had happened
"in the worst possible way." By Tuesday the American newspapers were quoting the English dailies,
and more than fifty reporters were streaming into the
Virginia university town.

Thursday, the *L.A. Times* "Morning Report" made
the story its first item of business, and the word was
not good: *"Actor Christopher Reeve is paralyzed and
cannot breathe on his own after suffering a broken neck in
a riding accident, his doctor reported Wednesday. Reeve
suffered 'multiple fractures' to the top two vertebrae in his
neck and injured his spinal cord. The 42-year-old 'Superman' star may require surgery soon to stabilize his upper
spine, but his doctor refused to speculate on Reeve's long-
term prognosis. Reeve was taken to the University of
Virginia Medical Center in Charlottesville after he fell
headfirst off a horse during a jumping competition Saturday. A statement issued by the family said, 'Christopher
deeply appreciates having received expressions of goodwill
from so many people. As the medical statement indicates,
we do not know what is ahead for him.' "*

In truth, Christopher Reeve was close to death. He
lay as stiff and as still as Superman would have if
Kryptonite itself had been injected directly into his
veins. The people of the world were finally learning
of his condition. They would quickly show how
much they cared. And Christopher Reeve would in
turn demonstrate what mythic heroes with infinite
strength rarely have to display—the qualities of character and courage.

PART ONE

*The essence of courage is not that
your heart should not quake but that
nobody else should know it does.*

—E. F. BENSON

1

> *"We don't know what lies ahead."*
>
> —BENJAMIN REEVE

The Memorial Day weekend of 1995 hadn't started out particularly well for Christopher Reeve. He had piloted his plane south with Dana and Will. The destination was Culpeper County Airport in Virginia, a rural airstrip. Located about six miles from Commonwealth Park, a privately owned equestrian center, he was scheduled to compete there on a recently purchased roan gelding.

The mature California thoroughbred, named Eastern Express, had experience in these types of events. The three-day meet was part of a circuit in which riders compiled points that led to rankings and, beyond that, eligibility for the 1996 Olympic trials.

Culpeper County sits at the foot of the Blue Ridge mountain range. At certain times of the year it is frequently enveloped in early morning or late evening fog which shrouds the area with a silvery mist, making visibility under one hundred feet almost impossible.

That was the case this day, diverting Chris to another airport in the Shenandoah region some fifty miles away. The alternate airport was used to celebrities, and the fact that most of them simply landed and walked to a rented limo, bypassing the terminal, meant even the controller wouldn't know that he had just been visited by one of the rich and famous. It had been leaked that Princess Di had once landed there. She had wanted to avoid the horde of reporters who had staked out the closer-in commercial airports when she visited Washington. But the manager had gotten wind of the super-deluxe aircraft that swooped down on the runway. It was the kind of flying machine that would have the armchair pilots who hung around the hangars talking for weeks.

Still, the chiseled features of the six-four movie star turned more than one head as he strode to his waiting car. By now Chris was in a hurry. There was a horse he wanted to see—perhaps to purchase—and he had planned to meet its owner at a truck stop outside of Opal, Virginia.

The drive along the old highway, with Shenandoah's soft, round-topped mountains on both sides of the road now verdantly green, is always pleasant. The handsome couple couldn't help but notice the apple orchards—hundreds of acres of them—that line the highway as they descended. They had just finished blossoming, and their scent continued to fill the highways, transfixing drivers if their windows were down.

Life had never been better for the forty-two-year-old actor. He was in the prime years of his life, and neither flab nor wrinkles had diminished his still boyish good looks. One could quibble and find a few gray hairs or crow's-feet forming around the eyes, but he could still melt a female's heart at forty paces.

His three-year-old marriage to Dana Morosini may have been the best personal decision he had ever made. Their son, Will, who was born two months after the ceremony (Dana joked that she'd worn a "maternity wedding dress") was a joy.

"I didn't expect to really fall in love," Dana had said of Chris. But she had and he had.

"She is my life force," was how Chris assessed Dana.

He was finally beginning to shake the specter of Superman. Oh, sure, with a more directed career he could have had the type of action career—spiced with a few light comedies—enjoyed by a Sly Stallone or Arnold Schwarzenegger. But that was not for Chris Reeve. Truth be told, he considered himself more of a stage actor, not a movie star, though public perception still defined him as an actor of star presence, just below the first tier of tinseltown's pecking order.

The facts said otherwise. By 1995 he had appeared in more than one hundred fifty plays, some seventeen feature roles on the big screen, and starred in a half-dozen or so TV movies. He had done jobs that most major stars wouldn't touch—narrating audio books and TV documentaries. And he was still very much in demand. He had just been part of an "inside" joke by playing an agoraphobic radio listener, calling Kelsey Grammer on his hit TV sitcom, *Frasier*. A week from now, he was slated to narrate Tobias Picker's *Encantatas* with the Houston Symphony. After that he was scheduled to begin filming a miniseries for Francis Ford Coppola based on Robert Louis Stevenson's *Kidnapped* for cable's Family Channel and Hallmark Cards. Next he was scheduled to direct a movie for the first time—a romantic feature called *Tell Me True*.

"I've done second-unit work, but this will be my first time directing," Chris had enthusiastically told the *New York Daily News* on the night his friend Kathleen Turner's new play, *Indiscretions*, opened the month before. He refused to talk more about the project that night, protesting that he didn't "want to jinx it."

He was also near the end of an hour-long documentary he was producing on the life of the giant gray whale, a joint project of the BBC and PBS. And in a month the first of a trilogy of western movies he'd already filmed was set to run on CBS. They were nineteenth-century westerns—each title began with the name *Black Fox*. The movie had him on horseback in several scenes as Alan Johnson, a former plantation owner battling the Commanche Indians for land in Texas. One can't get further away from the image of Superman than that.

His life was finally in balance. Family, career, the athletic adventures, and making a difference—or at least trying—was what it was all about. Chris and Dana checked in with Will at the Culpeper Holiday Inn, taking two rooms.

There were so many causes. He was a big part of Amnesty International, Save the Children, the Starlight Foundation, Special Olympics, Child Hope, Asthma Research, the Creative Coalition—an organization he cochaired that fights on many fronts, particularly on funding for the arts—and virtually any group trying to clean up the environment.

"I don't want to think of my career twelve months a year," he had recently told a Boston newspaper. He no longer did. If someone had forced him to prioritize at this point in his life, the career would not be mentioned first.

Flying, skiing, sets of strenuous singles tennis, sailing, windsurfing, racquetball, bicycling, figure skating, soccer, scuba diving, gliding, parasailing, mountain climbing, horse jumping—they filled in some of the blank spots. He tried to do most of his movie stunts himself.

"Horse jumping is the most dangerous thing I do," he had just told the Associated Press. He knew from firsthand experience. In 1993 in Calgary, Alberta, he'd been thrown from a horse during a jumping competition.

"The horse shied at a ditch. He stopped, I didn't, and I did like a field goal through the horse's ears. He put on the brakes very suddenly, but I kept going and went head over heels and landed on my knees and was none the worse for wear, but a number of people watching went 'Ooh!' "

Why had horses become such a part of his life? He was drawn to it, he said, by the bonding between man and animal.

"You are the brains and the horse is the power. You put that package together and it's wonderful."

He had fallen in love with horseback riding in 1987—so much in love that his first thoroughbred was named Valentine.

Chris was far from a Superman. He had been sickly as a child, hospitalized in 1986 for an emergency appendectomy during the filming of *Street Smart*, and in 1993 had caught malaria while scouting film locations in Kenya for a movie he wanted to make, *The Hunt*.

Because of this he sometimes overcompensated. Chris' way of escaping from the pressures of his acting life was rushing alone to a New Jersey airport at daybreak and flying to Vermont. In the summer months he'd take a racing bike out of his plane at the little airports and would pedal and sweat through Vermont's Green Mountains for fifty miles. He'd then jump back into his aircraft, zooming through the skies as the sun descended, and be back in the city by dusk. In winter he would repeat the exercise, skiing at various resorts.

He rarely revealed to friends that he was allergic to horses. It was his secret. He took Dimetapp decongestant pills to keep his eyes from getting watery. He was allergic to many substances—the polyester cape he wore in *Superman* had given him a rash. He had long worn glasses for reading but tried not to be photographed in them.

Rashes and malaria were small prices to pay for the thrills he got from his pursuit of what others called extreme sports. He had crash-landed a plane just the past year in the village of Watlington, England, in bad weather. Calmly walking to a cottage near the field in which he had landed, he asked the woman answering the door if he could use the phone. When she asked him why he looked so familiar, he was said to have answered, "I'm Superman."

It wasn't the first time. He had crash-landed a glider in a strange British airfield in March 1980 after it ran out of hot air currents while filming *Superman II*. The landing strip turned out to be a secret defense base, and two policemen had taken him into custody.

"They were very nice to me. We had tea and biscuits, and I wound up signing autographs. The newspapers heard about it and suggested I was a lousy pilot. That upset me," he said.

In 1984 he had cheated death on Martha's Vineyard. Parasailing, his chute had broken loose, plunging him more than a hundred feet into shallow water. He walked away from that one with bruised ribs.

"I raced down to the beach to see if he was okay. I thought no one could take a fall like that and not be injured or dead," was the eyewitness report of local artist Dennis Widdis.

In a 1983 special for ABC-TV on stuntmen, *Celebrity Daredevils*, Chris had a small plane roar straight at him and pass over his head, inches from his face. He had the crew reshoot the shot because its members had screamed in fear during the first fly over. Then he played turnabout by piloting a glider straight toward game show host Bert Convy. A gust of wind had made it too close, and Convy was quoted as saying, "It's the closest I've ever come to seeing death stare me in the face."

Chris had insisted that the producers destroy the tape of Convy because he thought it made him look irresponsible.

"A little danger adds up to a lot of excitement. What good is it to go through life without ever taking risks?" he had once said. Years of walking away from brushes with mortality, virtually unscathed, may have made him feel omnipotent. Certainly it would be easy for one to call these incidents a death wish. But Chris was always careful to train for these events before putting his life on the line.

Chris was well aware of the consequences of a serious accident. He had just played a paraplegic cop in an HBO movie, *Above Suspicion*. His character spent most of the film confined to a wheelchair. The actor had argued to the moviemakers—unsuccessfully—that his character should never walk again. It was unrealistic, he told them. People with severe spinal injuries never walk again, he had maintained. Chris told the TV tabloid show *Hard Copy* about a research visit he'd made to a spinal cord trauma unit.

"You see how easily it can happen. You think, God, it could happen to anybody," he said.

Commonwealth Park seemed to offer good fortune to riders. It had never had a serious accident in the nearly ten years it had been operating—the worst injury was a broken arm by a teen who'd fallen off her horse, landing on it.

Chris had begun to love the lifestyle of people who traveled the horse circuit. He was more than willing to spread the equine gospel to others by letting them use his name. In 1994 he had ridden with celebrated jockey Julie Krone in Gladstone, New Jersey, with the U.S. equestrian team. It had drawn national coverage. He had just posed for a poster while riding his Irish thoroughbred, Denver. It was to promote equestrian safety by urging riders to wear helmets.

"In films I play an invincible hero. But in real life I wouldn't think of riding without a helmet," the copy read. The poster would never be distributed.

Commonwealth Park is halfway between Washington, D.C., and Charlottesville—the home of Thomas Jefferson's Monticello and the University of Virginia. Its 210 acres are owned by entrepreneur Johnny "Monk" Reynolds, a colorful character who had bought it as a farm in 1976. Monk had spent years making it a mecca for horsemen and women. Celebrities have abounded here. Sissy Spacek, Robert Duvall, Linda Blair, Dickie Smothers, and the fifties' heart throb, Tab Hunter, have been here many times. The children of Paul Newman and Charles Bronson have ridden here in competition. It was surprising, then, that this was Chris' first visit to Commonwealth. He had been to the Culpeper area often, visiting Mike Bowman's Aroda Farm and Sally Lamb's Oakland Heights Farm in search of better horses. He had dined several times with the local horse breeders at a nearby German restaurant, the Bavarian Chef. Chris was looking for thoroughbreds—the ones that are seventeen hands high—to keep for competition, or ones which he could ride and jump through the woods and streams of the pastoral central Virginia countryside.

Chris was one of nearly three hundred riders—from children to seniors—who had paid $85 to enter the three-day competition, according to Emmitt Turner, the meet's organizer. There were boarding fees for horses of $60 added to that. When those costs are tallied up and added to the dollars needed to maintain and board the animals, it's easy to understand why the "horsey set" are, by and large, made up of the country rich.

Chris' arrival at Commonwealth Park met with the usual swivel of heads, but there was no stampede of autograph seekers, no mobbing by fans. Horse people—particularly here—consider themselves above that.

The Reeve colors were blue and silver—the same as the prep school he had attended. With his navy jacket, cream breeches, black leather boots, and velvet-covered helmet, he was an imposing figure. For additional safety he wore a padded vest when he rode.

Many would say he was a mediocre rider, and in fact, he had just moved from "advanced beginner" or "novice" and was struggling to compete at the "training" level, a step up in the ladder of rankings given out by the organizations that rate a rider's proficiency. Given his height and the more than two hundred pounds he carried, Chris acquitted himself well. He rode with passion and total concentration. Yet he had one consistent riding fault—he tended to shift his weight forward when he jumped his mounts over obstacles.

"When you jump that way, there is always a risk of going over the horse's head," horse trainer Kristen Hyduchak would say.

In August 1994 he had actually won a novice event at Huntingdon Farm in South Stafford, Vermont. A month later, at the New England novice championships, he had placed third. The win-and-show had given him the courage to move up to the next rung, the so-called "training" level.

On Friday, May 26, he had certainly ridden well enough during the dressage phase. This is the part of the competition which puts the rider and horse into concert, its master guiding the animal through a series of intricate steps, like ballroom dance competition. The purpose is to demonstrate the mount's obedience and agility. His efforts had placed him near the middle of the standings, an achievement of which he had every reason to be pleased.

Saturday was the kind of day in late May that makes one utter the phrase "glad to be alive." Blue skies, a few puffs of cumulus clouds, and a small breeze made for a postcard-perfect day at the Commonwealth competition. It was time for the most arduous part of the competition—cross-country jumping—a circuit of eighteen different jumps and hazards over a course of several miles. Three of them were considered "double efforts"—a barrier that required horse and rider to make two quick leaps to be successful.

Participants liken it to the running of a marathon. It would be the most demanding of the three events. The barriers of stone or wood—placed randomly apart in woods, near streams, or in fields—are immovable.

"It's a test of heart for both a horse and its rider," was how Liz Hoskinson, the spokesperson for the American Horse Shows Association, described it.

The final day would be devoted to show jumping, inside a ring. The purpose of the last event was just to show the horse and rider could come back from the day before. It wasn't simply getting over the jumps that counted. Each event would be timed and judged by senior members of the Commonwealth Dressage and Combined Training Association.

It's hard to appreciate the difficulty of guiding an animal that weighs more than a half ton over fixed barriers more than three feet high. The trick is to be perfectly balanced, relaxed, with soft and supple hands holding the reins. If the reins are held too tightly, the animal won't feel enough freedom to jump to its ability. If they're too loose, it encourages the steed to refuse the jump and shy away. The legs of the rider play a part too. There must be pressure on the horse. A rhythm between the rider and animal needs to be established. And the rider needs to approach each jump consistently—one normally can't gallop at one and trot toward the next. Riders say that when everything comes together, it becomes euphoric—akin to a golfer hitting the perfect drive that lands on the green or a tennis player slamming the ball with the soft spot of his racquet and scoring an ace.

Dana, who had opted to stay with their two-year-old toddler, would have been proud of her husband's first two jumps. Chris aced them cleanly and headed for the third, a series of zigzag timbers three feet three inches high. It was considered an easy barrier—a three on a scale of one to ten. What followed next is still a matter of speculation.

Monk Reynolds at first told the press that "something spooked the horse." The rumor was that a rabbit had run in front of Eastern Express and caused it to stop dead in its tracks.

A friend of Chris', Lisa Reid, told *People* magazine that she had seen the accident and described it thus: "The horse was coming into the fence beautifully. The rhythm was fine and Chris was fine and they were going at a good pace. The horse put his front feet over the fence, but his hind feet never left the ground. Chris is such a big man. He was going forward, his head over the top of the horse's head. He had committed his upper body to the jump. But the horse—whether it chickened out or felt Chris' weight over its head, I don't know. But the horse decided, 'I can't do this.' It backed off the jump!"

Reid said that Chris hit his head on the rail fence and then landed on the turf directly on his forehead. He lay there, still. A judge alerted the medic team on the premises with the phrase: "Superman is down."

Local newspapers recorded a slightly different version of Reid's remarks and were more definitive: "Chris made a novice mistake—he leaned too far

forward—making the horse stop dead. He hit his
head on the fence under the rim of his helmet. . . .
He smashed forehead first onto the ground. The rest
of his body continued to flip over, out of control,
snapping his neck backward."

Another witness to the event—an attorney—wrote
a letter to Reynolds. It seemed to seek in a lawyerly
fashion to indemnify Commonwealth Park . . .

My daughter was a participant in, and competed
in the Junior Training portion of the Horse Trial.
She and I were sitting on the ground directly in
front of fence #3, the fence where Mr. Reeve fell,
observing the various competitors ride the course
in preparation for her ride.

We were in such a position as to observe fence
number three, the site of Mr. Reeve's accident,
as well as the option in and out fence, which we
were particularly interested in seeing how the
various riders would ride that fence. . . .

I watched a rider whom I later found out to be
Mr. Reeve take jumps one and two and approach
fence number three at what appeared to me that
the horse came at the fence at a gallop, could not
see a spot for the jump and stopped abruptly,
immediately in front of the fence. When the
horse stopped, it naturally ducked its head and
nose over the fence. Mr. Reeve pitched forward
over the horse's neck, slid down the neck, and
landed directly on top of his head on the opposite side of the fence from the horse. The
horse then backed away and ran back toward
the start box.

Mr. Reeve did not appear to me to take a
particularly hard or fast fall; it was more of the
typical front fall that I have seen many times in
many competitions where riders essentially slide
down the neck of the horse when the horse

comes to an abrupt stop. I distinctly remember that I had the time to say to my daughter, 'Refusal, fall, oh, my God that rider landed right on his head.' Obviously, Mr. Reeve was unable to make an effort to get his arm out in front of his body to break his fall.

Contrary to newspaper reports, I saw no evidence that anything startled, or "spooked" the horse; rather, the horse just did not see a spot to jump the fence and came to an abrupt halt. I noted that the on grounds crew arrived within about a minute or a minute and a half after the fall. I also noted that the technical delegate for the competition was on site with a radio walkie-talkie almost immediately after the arrival of the EMT.

Obviously the jump judge was also on the scene almost immediately. My daughter and I debated between ourselves as to whether we should go forward in the early minutes after the fall to render assistance. Not being trained in emergency medical procedures and based on my observation of the fall, which as I have stated appeared to be right on the head, I determined that we should leave the assistance to trained personnel.

Chris' only recollection, as told to TV broadcaster Larry King and others, is that somehow his hands became caught either in the reins or the bridle of his mount, and because of that he was unable to put his hands out to break his fall.

Regardless of what others say happened, Chris lay on the turf, motionless and not breathing. His lips were turning blue. The blood drained from his face, giving it a funereal pallor. Eastern Express cantered away, uninjured.

"The life had gone out of him," Helmut Boehme, one of the first to arrive, would say.

The emergency medical technician who pumped air back into Chris' lungs saved his life. He wouldn't be the last. In the days and weeks ahead, several others would bring him back from the brink of death.

The ambulance carrying Chris sped to Culpeper Memorial Hospital. The emergency room's young doctor in charge, Bill Maloney, made a quick decision—chopper him out on a Pegasus helicopter to the University of Virginia's Medical Center in Charlottesville, some forty-five miles away. The medics had Chris in the air an hour after his fall.

The university teaching hospital was the premier institution for difficult illnesses and accidents in central Virginia. It was the learning arm of the university's prestigious medical school—the college that Thomas Jefferson had founded some two hundred years ago. In the emergency room, Mohan Nadkarni, the doctor heading the department that weekend, had Chris taken to an intensive care unit on the sixth floor in the west wing of the building. He was given morphine. It would be enough to deaden his pain for days.

Dana was notified. When she arrived with Will, Nadkarni baby-sat the toddler while Dana was rushed to her husband's side. As he lay unconscious, she began singing to him. It was an environmental song they had taught Will, "This Pretty Planet." She began repeating the lines about "spinning in space" and "your holy place" over and over.

The medical center had had experience with just one other major personage. In 1972, while visiting his daughter and her law student husband, Chuck Robb (now a U.S. senator from Virginia), former president Lyndon Baines Johnson had suffered a heart attack and was rushed to the hospital. But never a movie star.

The British press invasion began arriving to begin

its siege virtually in tandem with Chris' family. The medical center's spokesperson, Marguerite Beck, began to take precautions.

"I put security at three different points," she said. "One was seated by the door of the ICU, another was at the back stairs entrance, and another was near the elevators."

That didn't stop the more aggressive members of the press. The local paper, the *Charlottesville Progress*, would soon describe a "mischievous scribe from *People* magazine" as trying to "infiltrate" the emergency room. Tabloid reporters staked out the parking lot and attempted to pay cash to departing nurses for information.

The people who were closest to him began to arrive. Chris' former lover, Gae Exton, flew to Dulles International Airport near Washington from England with the two children she and Chris had had during their ten-year relationship, Matthew, fifteen, and Alexandra, eleven. All three had been unable to stop the tears from falling unchecked as they hurried through London's Heathrow Airport on the way to their flight.

At Dulles, Exton met Chris' sixty-one-year-old mother, Barbara, and the two women drove with the children to Charlottesville together. Chris' mother had always been close to Exton—the two had bonded some fifteen years ago. But surprisingly, it would be the two look-alikes, Dana and Exton, who would stay together in the days ahead—showing no animosity between them.

Chris' father, Franklin, sixty-six, came in separately from Connecticut. The two parents had divorced with great bitterness when he was four. Their common concern united them now, and they dined together the next night for the first time in years. His younger brother Benjamin, forty-one, once a budding writer and professional photographer but now a suburban Boston lawyer, soon arrived. The family booked a block of rooms at the Omni Hotel, the best Charlottesville could offer.

The hospital would initially say only that Chris had "a cervical injury and is under close observation." It listed him as "serious but stable."

Chris' press agent in Los Angeles, Lisa Kasteler, seemed even a step behind those reports. The reporters wondered while they waited. Was it just Hollywood hype? Just how serious was it? Ever cynical, some even suspected it was manipulation for publicity reasons. With the dearth of information, no one in the press would have been surprised at that point to have heard the announcement, "Chris Reeve was apparently stunned and is mending nicely now."

The British press, up against deadlines, began making Sunday phone calls to their editors. Their version of the released statement—"He's paralyzed and on a respirator"—was the blunt assessment. It would turn out to be chillingly accurate. Alerted, a line of local TV reporters was on the scene by late Monday afternoon in time for the evening news. All of them sought the same space—a high vantage point that placed the hospital and mountains in the background. The number of them doing stand-ups soon approached that of the Rockettes. The hill crest on the hospital's grounds contained silhouettes and cameras of anxious media. Inside the facility, the walls featured the backs of British writers composing stories verbally while they talked to their editors transatlantically. Sometimes one would be silent in order to listen in to another reporter to see if any information had been missed.

When Dana saw Chris paralyzed, unable to speak and attached to a respirator, she was devastated. Told that Chris could face a lifetime of being paralyzed, she went into a brief phase of denial.

What can we release to the press? she was asked.

"Nothing yet," she responded in a soft whisper.

The press were all referred to Kasteler, who stone-walled them. She answered each question with an "I don't know," even to questions that asked *how* he was injured.

Not until five days after the accident would the gravity of Chris' condition be confirmed. Lisa Kasteler would bear the brunt of the press criticism, accused by several of withholding vital information. But Kasteler was simply acceding to a traumatized family's wishes. When asked by a reporter if she represented Chris Reeve or Dana, Kasteler answered, "They're one and the same right now." Ironically, her attempts to withhold information only resulted in increased coverage.

Chris' mother would be the first to break the family's silence. She told National Public Radio that "he was confused" when he regained consciousness, "mouthing but not speaking words" that "the doctors understood better than I.

"He was asking what had happened. It was tough. You could see him struggling."

By Tuesday morning there were three dozen members of the print press in Charlottesville. The silence by the family and the presence of every family member, including an ex-lover, fanned the flames of speculation that death was imminent. A rumor spread that he was brain dead and Dana was debating whether she should "pull the plug." Gae Exton was seen leaving the hospital in tears. The lack of concrete information eventually drew one hundred ten reporters flying in or phoning from around the world—as far away as Japan and Australia. A Chilean news crew was one of several South American teams on the scene. Chris had once stood up to the Pinochet regime years ago, the Chileans explained, and was a national hero in their country.

"He's an international star and he's been injured," a woman from the British tabloid *Today* explained.

"It's particularly pointed because of his role as Superman. He usually plays strong, fit, athletic characters. And now he's been injured, apparently seriously, which is very tragic," Peter Hitchins of the *London Daily Express* said.

The British press also pointed out that Gae Exton was British and that the *Superman* films had been filmed, for the most part, in England.

Besieged by the press, Marguerite Beck would only say, "The bottom line is, I have to respect the family's wishes. If they don't want to give out information, that's their call."

The lack of information then led to "death watch" reports. The grim news making its way around the world finally forced an afternoon news conference on June 1. It confirmed everyone's worst fears.

"Mr. Reeve currently has no movement or spontaneous respiration," neurosurgeon John Jane said, explaining that Chris had an odontoid (tooth-shaped) fracture of both the first and second cervical vertebrae, known as C-1 and C-2. The news was ominous. The lower the number, the more serious the injury.

"He's alert but cannot make sounds because a breathing tube has been inserted into his windpipe. It's premature to speculate about his long-term prognosis. He cannot control his expiration, so what he has to do is to say words in an exaggerated fashion and use local breaths to make a sound, and it doesn't work badly. It's not good for back-and-forth rapid conversation, but it's good enough to communicate."

He also admitted that Chris was "fighting for his life."

Dr. Jane said that Chris also had pneumonia in one lung, but it didn't seem to be much of a concern to him.

"Pneumonias come and go in these kind of cases, and it's going now, but I am sure it will come back."

He also had some good news.

"The spinal cord definitely has not been severed at C-1, an initial fear. He may require surgery to stabilize the upper spine."

This didn't prevent *USA Today* from reporting the next day in the first paragraph of its story that "few survive the kind of spinal cord injury that actor Christopher Reeve suffered when he was thrown from a horse over the weekend."

Reeve's brother, Ben, stepped forward to read a prepared statement on behalf of the family.

"Our thanks to the fans and all the people who are part of his life's work and who have sent their good wishes. Christopher deeply appreciates having received expressions of goodwill from so many people." (Fans and friends had sent nearly two hundred bouquets of flowers already, and the family had distributed them throughout the hospital. Soon nearly every room in the hospital would have a Chris Reeve floral arrangement.)

Then he paused and looked concerned.

"We do not know what lies ahead," he said.

A hospital employee watching the conference muttered, "Pray for a miracle."

2

"Everything went well."

—JOHN JANE, M.D.

Perhaps one reason Christopher Reeve's plight first captured the attention of the world was the unfortunate fact that his family suppressed the news for so many days. This heightened speculation in the daily press and raised questions with the public and among his fans. A secondary part of the equation was that he will forever be identified as the all-powerful comic book hero Superman—a character who can both deflect bullets and even turn back time, by *flying* super-fast to reverse the earth's rotation. Certainly, it was just playing a part, but the sculptured jaw on the frame of Chris' muscular body had made him a god of good and justice in the minds of millions, and besides, gods don't get hurt, do they?

The story of Christopher Reeve's tragic accident and recovery is much more than that, however. The optimism and courage he has shown throughout this life crisis has won admirers from members of the public who have never seen him on stage or in the movies.

"I can tell you that he is lucid, that he has a sense

of humor, and it's his kind of humor. Clearly, it's a difficult time, but it's lightened by moments of grace," Ben Reeve said a few days after the fall as Chris lay paralyzed.

If laughter is the greatest medicine of all, then a surprise visit by comic actor Robin Williams must have brightened Chris' first weeks in Virginia. Williams was one of Chris' oldest and closest friends. (Chris' kids call him Uncle Robby, and Chris is the godfather of one of Williams' sons.) The comic entered Chris' room wearing a blue scrub cap, a surgical mask, and a yellowish green physician's jacket complete with stethoscope. He began his conversation by impersonating a Russian proctologist.

"I'm goink to haff to, just go down, hold on . . ." Williams later told *Premiere* magazine he had said to Chris in a fractured Russian accent. "Then he realized who it was, and his eyes lit up, and he started to laugh."

Williams said he asked Chris what was going on, and Chris told him there was a debate in progress as to whether or not to "pull the plug." Chris told Williams that after seeing Dana and Will, he had "decided to stick around."

The comic clearly lifted Chris' spirits. And the timing by his former roommate from his Juilliard drama school days was impeccable. Days before, on the first of June, Chris had indeed contemplated suicide.

"When I was first coming out of, you know, unconsciousness, you have the thought, 'Maybe it's not worth everybody's trouble,' and I had that thought for maybe ten minutes," Chris would later tell Barbara Walters.

"That you want to die, pull the plug, whatever?" Walters asked.

"Yeah, I suggested, 'Maybe I should just check

out.' And then Dana said to me, 'You're still you and I love you.' "

Dana told him that since there was no brain damage, the "essence" of Chris remained. She also, surprisingly, told him that it was his decision, but she was there for him no matter what it turned out to be.

Chris said he made the decision not to have Dana "pull the plug" when all three children walked into the room together as he lay there paralyzed and still speechless, able only to mouth words.

"I could see how much they needed me. What happens to me when I have a problem is that I get embarrassed. I go like, 'Oh, I don't want to cause you people trouble' and 'I don't want people to have to be burdened to take care of me,' you know? That was my thought that afternoon, but the minute they all came in and I could see the love and feel the love and know that we were still a family and that we're great, and how lucky we all are that my brain is on straight, that thought vanished, and it has never come back."

One magazine would report that in the first days following the fall, Chris tried to spit out the ventilator tube which gave him air several times in an attempt to end his life. The Reeve family denied the story. But Dana began sleeping in his room so that when he awoke in the middle of the night, he wouldn't feel despondent during what Chris started to call "the demon hours."

John Jane, sixty-four, was as qualified as any neurosurgeon in the nation to make the attempt to fuse and stabilize the fragments of bone that were floating in Chris' neck. Jane had spent nine years at the University of Chicago as an undergraduate and in its medical school, graduating *cum laude*. He had gone back in the sixties to get a Ph.D. in biopsychology. Afterward, he practiced in Canada for years. At the

University of Virginia's medical center, Jane saw a lot of "roadkill"—brain-trauma victims who had been choppered in from the site of auto smash-ups on the interstates near Charlottesville, and spinal surgery was another area in which he had extensive experience.

"He's experiencing no movement but no pain. The spinal cord is damaged, but not cut in half. I'm encouraged. If it were totally severed, we could say with certainty that there is no chance of recovery," Jane would say on May 31.

The surgery was scheduled by Jane for 8:30 A.M. on Monday, June 5. Normally, he performed seven to eight operating procedures each day. This one, he estimated, would take five hours, dropping the daily average nearly in half. In fact, Chris' operation would take nearly seven.

Jane said Chris' surgery would attempt to "keep the bones in line" so the spinal cord wouldn't be damaged again. "We have a ninety percent success rate, and if it fails, we'll simply try again. The mortality rate is four percent."

If the operation was successful, Jane said, Chris would be able to sit up soon. His pneumonia was now in check, and no impediments were expected.

The outpouring of sympathy from the public and celebrity colleagues soon threatened to overwhelm the medical center.

Metropolis, Illinois, a small town of 6,700 on the Ohio River that had made the most of the Superman legend for decades, prepared an eight-foot postcard of plywood. It was put at the base of the Superman statue in the center of town and left for people to sign as they arrived for the annual Superman festival, held each June. The local paper—the *Planet*—said organizers stopped counting at 5,000. Filled within days, a four-foot sheet of butcher paper was added.

The card was signed, "From your super fans in Metropolis."

Another "card" with 3,000 signatures on it was signed by fans and stars alike in Los Angeles. Celebrity names on it ranged from Fay Wray to Victoria Principal. The cards were wheeled in and out and then displayed for a short time in the lobby.

"I've never experienced anything quite like this," an overwhelmed Liz Courain, who headed volunteers at the hospital, would say. The cards, letters, gifts, and faxes—arriving by the thousands—far exceeded those for Lyndon Johnson according to hospital officials. By the end of 1995 there would be more than 300,000 expressions of sympathy and support from every corner of the world.

Chris' celebrity well wishers included Margo Kidder, his Lois Lane costar from the *Superman* series. Ironically, Kidder herself had once been paralyzed in a 1990 car crash, her head slamming into the steering wheel. She had spent the next two years in a wheelchair. A doctor then discovered a nerve blockage in her spine and corrected it in the operating room.

"You can't give up, no matter what," she said. She also said she reminded Chris that one could always beat the odds and walk again.

Geena Davis, who had just costarred in *Speechless* with Chris, had a poignant tribute.

"One of my favorite images of Chris was a scene where he runs and catches a moving train. He didn't want to use any tricks or stunt doubles; he just said, 'I can catch it.' And he did. He ran like the wind."

Jane Seymour, his costar in the 1979 lushly romantic time-travel epic, *Somewhere in Time*, and an accomplished horsewoman herself, offered perhaps the most generous gesture of all. Three months pregnant at the time of the accident, she would name one of her twin sons after Chris when she gave birth on November 30. John Barry's musical score from their film was played in the delivery room as the two children came into the world.

"It's hard to imagine that something this awful has happened to him," she said when informed of the accident. "Riding horses is potentially lethal. You can be the best rider in the world . . . but anyone who sits on a horse knows the risks he or she takes."

In Houston, Lou Gossett, Jr., replaced Chris in *Encantantas*. Armand Assante got the *Kidnapped* miniseries role with Hallmark. The directing job was said to be "waiting for him, whenever he's ready." The whales were put on hold, rescheduled for an undetermined date by PBS. William Shatner took over the narration of an equestrian video for Chris, who had begun the project months ago.

"We've gone from super to out-of-this-world," the producer said, referring to the *Star Trek* veteran. It was still show biz, no matter how questionable in taste the producer's statement. And the show went on.

Every day Dana walked little Will up to the seventh floor, where there was a playroom. While he played there, she watched television with her husband, mostly sports events. On sunny days the nurses wrapped Chris in a blanket and wheeled him out to the hospital's sun room ("looking like a little old man," Chris said later), where Dana would read to him some of the more interesting letters he was receiving.

His mother flew in and out from Princeton, New Jersey. She was a newspaper reporter in the college town for the half-century-old publication *Town Topics*.

For Chris, the most difficult times before the operation were always the hours between midnight and dawn. He later told ABC television: "The demons would get me in the middle of the night. The hours between two A.M. and seven A.M. were the worst. . . .

I'd lie awake and I'd think, 'What's going to become of me? Woe is me. . . . In my dreams, I'd be whole, riding my horse, playing with my family. We have a beautiful boat that Dana and I worked on and built together. We'd be making love, we'd be doing everything. Then suddenly I wake up and it's two in the morning and I can't move and I'm on a ventilator. . . ."

Chris was awake at six for the eight-thirty operation Monday morning. Before he went into the operating room, he mouthed to his mother, "It's not over yet."

John Jane had assembled a team for Chris' surgery which included neurosurgery associate Scott Henson and anesthesiologist Christopher Shaffrey. Before operating, he told his patient that afterward he should be able to move "if only a little." Chris gave him a rare smile.

The surgery was difficult and took much longer than expected. Jane used soft wires to fuse Chris' first and second vertebrae. Then he wired the construction to a titanium ring that was connected to the base of the skull. They took bone matter from Chris' hip and placed it between the first and second vertebrae so that "when we squeezed it, it held solidly in place," Jane said. In essence, he was reattaching Chris' head to his spine.

The reason the surgery took several hours longer than estimated was because many small fragments of bone were found in the C-1 vertebra. It had been shattered.

"The phrenic nerve is intact. It has not been damaged. He does not have conscious control of his respiration, but the mechanism is there. The second thing is that the nerves in his trapezius are working quite well on his right side. So both pieces of information combined with a third thing, namely that he has a sensation, an impaired sensation, on the left side of his body and he has quite good sensation . . . over his thorax. All of that together tells us that the injury to his spinal cord was not complete—his spinal cord has not been severed. That's confirmed by the MRI, which shows the damage is mainly on the left side of the spinal cord . . . so that is good news."

Jane said he had drilled holes into Chris' skull and passed wires through to get a solid fusion. He looked weary, but seemed pleased with the result of his work. Then, in a rare lapse from the formal medical information he was imparting, he offered this aside: "He's come this far against all the odds, so as far as I'm concerned, he really is Superman."

They put Chris' neck in a brace and raised him to a semi-upright position. It was the first time he'd been other than prone since the accident. He drank some tea. He started eating solid foods again. He could speak slowly when exhaling after the air from the respirator was pumped into his lungs. Two of Charlottesville's better restaurants volunteered to deliver gourmet meals. The family accepted the donations— "Superman" had long been a connoisseur of food and wine.

"Testing. One, two, three," were his first words after the operation. Dana also joked with the press for the first time. She had begun to smile again.

"He's been visiting daily with the children and other family and watching hockey on TV—I think his spirits might be better if the Rangers were in the playoffs. . . . Much of his day is spent listening to messages from well-wishers. I can't begin to express how important these are to him."

"Never, never give up," said one telegram from boxer Vinny Pazienza. The fighter had broken his neck in an auto accident in 1991 and was told he'd never walk again. Releasing his telegram to the press, he reminded everyone that he'd be fighting the super-middleweight title in just two weeks.

Will's third birthday took place two days after Chris' operation. Like most other days, it was spent in the hospital, partly in the seventh-floor playroom area. At the Omni hotel, the kitchen staff baked Will a birthday cake with three candles, decorating it with a drawing of Mickey Mouse in icing. Will asked why his father wasn't there for the cake cutting.

Chris had begun to move his head, but he still couldn't breathe on his own. Hospital orderlies transferred him to a chair for thirty minutes a day. He was allowed to go outside into the sunshine for brief periods. Therapists also had begun manually exercising his arms and legs to prevent atrophy.

Knowing that a move from Virginia was imminent, Dana thanked everyone from "President and Mrs. Clinton" to the "Hollywood and theatrical community" for their good thoughts during the initial crisis period. She said that Chris was particularly touched by the letters he'd received from people with spinal injuries.

"Almost three years ago a spinal injury not much different from yours left me hospitalized," one read. "It was the darkest moment of my life. I've come miles since that moment, and life is every bit as enjoyable and worthwhile as it ever was."

Particularly affecting were the messages sent by schoolchildren, often written in pencil or crayon and accompanied by crude drawings that showed a caped figure flying. Many of them ended with the prediction: "Don't worry, Superman, you'll fly again."

When his daughter, Alexandra, learned that the entire third-grade class of a local elementary school had sent her father dozens of cards and letters, she wrote them a thank-you note.

"My dad's very sick and that's why I'm writing you, not him," she wrote. "But I have told him about your letters and he is very grateful. It is nice to know you are thinking of him."

Family snapshots of the children were placed at bedside where his eyes could rest on them. Somewhat surprisingly, a photo of Chris aboard Eastern Express was added to the mix.

A fan sent Chris a photograph of a Buddhist temple that he asked to be put on a wall where he could see it. The temple had many steps going up to it, and above that there was blue sky. Chris took it to be a metaphor for his recovery, imagining himself climbing the steps to the temple.

"I can visualize that," he told his mother.

"His spirits are high," was the latest word from a hospital spokesperson a day after the operation. Perhaps the public expected Chris simply to get up and walk out of the hospital. Certainly the updated reports making their way into the daily papers gave everyone hope that it was a possibility.

A headline bannered REEVE REGAINS SOME FEELING IN CHEST and it was followed days later with REEVE HAS SOME FEELING IN SHOULDER followed by REEVE REGAINS SOME FEELING, SHOWS IMPROVED STRENGTH. Though true, they gave hope of a quick recovery.

"The phrenic nerves, which travel through the neck and chest to the diaphragm, are indeed not disturbed, indicating that the paralyzed actor has the mechanism to breathe on his own," said an optimistic Marguerite Beck.

But recovery was years away, if ever. Benjamin Reeve testified before a U.S. Senate committee, lobbying for more research money on June 27.

"There's a certain helplessness, lying flat on your back, strapped to a bed in intensive care," he told them. "Medical breakthroughs in the neural sciences are my brother's only hope."

He was right. Research was promising in drugs that would seemingly regenerate damaged spinal cord nerves for which there wasn't enough funding from federal or private sources.

"There's an incredible amount happening, and it's being partially dampened by what's happening in Washington," a neurosurgeon at New York University would say.

"Substantial progress is taking place with animals, including drugs, transplants, and gene therapies." He said prospects were brightening for victims of spinal cord injuries.

Chris was about to become the poster patient for spinal cord injuries. As Mickey Mantle had done for liver transplants, as Ronald Reagan has for Alzheimer's, and in much the same way that Lou Gehrig brought attention to ALS (the disease became synonymous with his name), Christopher Reeve and spinal cord injury were about to mean one and the same to most people.

As a longtime social and political activist, Chris would embrace the cause and fight for a cure rather than shrink from it. There are 7,800 spinal injuries like his every year, but this doesn't even count the 5,000 who die on the way to the hospital. Spinal injuries have been particularly prevalent in professional sports. Recent injuries have created a long list of paraplegic players. Some of them in pro football include Dennis Byrd of the New York Jets, Mike Utley of the Detroit Lions, and Darryl Stingley of the New England Patriots. Triple Crown winner Ron Turcotte became a paraplegic after a spill at Belmont Park in 1978, and soul singer Teddy Pendergrass became a quadriplegic after an auto accident in 1984. Yet no one would ever focus attention on the plight of spinal cord injury victims like Chris Reeve.

Dana and Barbara began looking at institutions that specialized in the rehabilitation of spinal injury patients in mid-June. The National Spinal Cord Injury Association gave them a list of five that it believed offered the best treatment for upper spinal cord patients. They were the Mount Sinai School of Medicine in New York, the Shepherd Spinal Center in Atlanta, Texas Medical Center's Institute for Rehabilitation and Research in Houston, Craig Hospital in Englewood, Colorado, and the Kessler Institute for Rehabilitation in West Orange, New Jersey. *Newsday* reported that Chris was headed for Colorado, and the *Atlanta Journal and Constitution* reported that he was considering Shepherd. Location, though, was paramount, and a facility near New York where most of his family lived was always a primary goal.

Chris was released from the University of Virginia Medical Center at nine in the morning on June 27. He was strapped onto a gurney and attended by a nurse who manually squeezed air into his lungs with a plastic pump. An ambulance drove him to the Charlottesville Airport, where a flying ambulance was waiting. The specially equipped plane then flew to Morristown, New Jersey, a forty-minute flight. It was an airport into which Chris had flown as a pilot many times. Another ambulance and a police escort took him to the Kessler Institute for Rehabilitation. Dana and Will had gone there earlier and were waiting for him when he arrived.

It had been foggy and raining when they left Virginia, but they landed in New Jersey under blue skies and a bright sun. Dana took this to be "a very good sign." She was wearing a chain around her neck that Chris had been wearing when he went down in Culpeper. The hospital attendants had given it to her. The chain had a single word on it, "Faith." She would wear it continuously.

"We've taken the first steps and today have taken the first steps of what is certain to be a long journey," Benjamin Reeve told reporters that morning.

"We are looking to the time when Christopher

Reeve again has a public career. In order to do that we are going to need the goodwill of many people."

The acute-care portion of his recovery was over. The rehabilitation phase would now begin. It would tax their financial resources severely. The cost of his treatment would be nearly $2,000 a day—about $250,000 for his stay at the Kessler Institute.

Chris described that next phase as being "a little bit like boot camp."

PART TWO

*Nothing can come out of an artist
that is not in the man.*

—H. L. MENCKEN

3

"He was a solemn child."

—BARBARA JOHNSON

In the literary enclaves in picturesque New England college towns, the name of Franklin D'Olier Reeve is far better known than that of his actor son, Christopher. Franklin Reeve is one of America's foremost poets and renowned as a translator of Russian and Slavic literature. He has seen few of Chris' films.

"The last movie my father probably saw was *Casablanca*," Chris told an interviewer in 1979. His father's lack of interest in films didn't seem to bother him.

When Chris was twenty-four, he told his father he had just been chosen as the lead in a film about Superman. His father took him out to dinner and ordered champagne.

"He was ecstatic," Chris said to Gene Siskel, "and I was glad he was so excited."

The euphoria ended when the misunderstanding was cleared up. His father had assumed his son was going to be in a revival of George Bernard Shaw's *Man and Superman* and had gotten the lead role of Jack Tanner.

"Ah, Jack Tanner, it's a great part, a great part,"

Franklin said. He then wanted to know who was going to play the character of Ann Whitfield, the principal female part.

"No, Dad, it's Lois Lane we're looking for," Chris told his disappointed father. Franklin Reeve didn't know what a Lois Lane was.

"The kind of theater my father is interested in is political, activist theater . . . outcast theater, the theater of revolt," Chris told a writer years later.

Franklin D'Olier Reeve was born in Philadelphia in 1928. His boyhood was spent in a posh section of Morristown, New Jersey, as a child of privilege and wealth—his grandfather, Colonel Franklin D'Olier, was the president of the Prudential Insurance Company between 1938 and 1946. Franklin's great-great-grandfather Michel was born in Montauben, France, but had moved early in life to County Mayo, Ireland, marrying there. Michel's son William then migrated to America. It was William who began the family fortune in Philadelphia by founding a number of cotton mills in 1869.

Chris' lineage is so distinguished that it has been traced back to the year 1214. One direct descendent was a noted ambassador to Constantinople under Louis XIV. Others were titled members of the French nobility, and more recently, Franklin D'Olier—Chris' great-grandfather—was one of the nineteen founders of the American Legion and its first national commander. A flyer, he journeyed 25,000 miles over every city in Japan just after the end of World War II, assessing the bombing damage.

By the late 1940s, though, Franklin D'Olier Reeve had become estranged from his family. Shortly after the falling-out, he entered Princeton University, living on campus at Blair Hall. A photo taken of him in those days could easily be mistaken for that of his actor son. About the time of his 1950 graduation from Princeton (with a B.A. in English), he married Chris' mother, Barbara Pitney Lamb, a distant relative who was attending Vassar.

Franklin spent the fifties working on a Ph.D. at Columbia University in New York. During those years he worked his way through school by doing a variety of jobs—waiter, longshoreman, and also as a part-time actor—before becoming an associate professor at Columbia, teaching Slavic languages in order to pay part of his tuition costs. His wife would sometimes write human-interest feature stories for weekly newspapers. The marriage of the academically inclined intellectual and his teenage bride was doomed to part ways.

"He [my father] reacted against all that privilege by cutting himself off from it," Chris once said, explaining why his father turned his back on the family fortune. "He's never made a dime in his life. He's always lived at the subsistence level, because the place he had to be was on the outside looking in."

Before Franklin and Barbara separated, the couple produced two sons. Chris was born—blond hair and blue-eyed—while his parents lived on East Eighty-eighth Street in Manhattan on September 25, 1952, residing, as the *New York Daily News* would aptly phrase it, "so close to the East River he could smell it." Franklin chose the distinguished British educator Frank Kermode, best known for his biography of D. H. Lawrence, to be Chris' godfather.

Benjamin was born a year later. His mother now had two children, and she was barely twenty.

"[It was] unthinkable," Chris would tell a reporter years later. "I sometimes wanted to say, I'm so sorry for being born when you were only a baby, a teenager."

Chris and Ben were always close. In preschool they acted out fantasies together, pretending they were pirates of the Barbary Coast by standing on top of grocery boxes. "To us they became ships, simply because we said they were," Chris recalled to writer Margery Steinberg.

Chris was nearly four when the divorce came. The permanent separation was as rancorous as a breakup can get. Chris found himself volleyed back and forth between the two parents throughout childhood.

"I felt torn between them," he told writer Sara Matthiessen, "They had the tendency to use me as a chess piece."

Chris once spent a month writing a play about his childhood as therapy. Revealingly, he called actors "misfits."

"You're not really sure what's expected of you, where your allegiances are," he would say of their divorce. "My parents remarried, and for the next fifteen years they never spoke. My father would drive my brother and me back and stop the car just before he reached the edge of my mother's property. I resented being shuttled back and forth.

"My father and mother were always fighting over me, and therefore canceled each other out. Consequently, I grew up not wanting to depend on them or anybody else. That's probably the key to my personality," Chris confessed to one interviewer.

"The difficulty was to know what was expected in each house."

Chris' father would go on to a distinguished career teaching writing and poetry at the University of Illinois, Yale, and presently, Wesleyan University in Connecticut. In 1962 he accompanied poet Robert Frost to Russia, serving as his interpreter. The trip with Frost resulted in two books: *Robert Frost in Russia* (1964) and *The Russian Novel* (1966). He has since written more than a dozen books of poetry, several literary novels, a history of the Russian symbolist movement titled *Between Image and Idea*, and has translated and edited a collection of five novels by Turgenev.

One literary work, his 1968 novel *The Red Machines*, is about midwestern migrant farm workers. To write the book, Franklin Reeve spent the summer driving a truck to ferry migrants to and from wheat fields so he could experience their lives. Today he is nationally known in academic circles for his critiques of nineteenth- and twentieth-century Russian novelists. That Chris greatly admires his father is evidenced by an interview he gave the *Los Angeles Times* in 1979.

"You have to remember that twenty years ago, my father was both a professor of Slavic languages and a laborer unloading banana boats in Hoboken at night. He did it to make ends meet and also as a political involvement. He was very leftist, intrigued by the labor movement. He felt himself a worker in the masses," Chris told interviewer Wayne Warga.

Chris also praised his father's versatility. "He can do everything—from playing Parcheesi to translating Dostoevsky."

Benjamin was also scholarly. At the age of thirteen he invented a computer language that was used at Princeton University for decades. Benjamin's childhood was equally as difficult—"He had no easy time," Chris would say. Ben would go on to renovate office buildings in New York's SoHo district, write nonfiction books on the sources of energy, and dabble in photography before becoming an attorney. He got his law degree from Northeastern University in Boston, and made Massachusetts his home. Chris has called his brother a "part-time genius."

In addition to the angst brought on by the family breakup, Chris was a sickly child. He suffered from asthma, allergies and alopecia areata, a disease of the nervous system that once caused his hair to fall out (the affliction would reappear during the early 1980s, after coloring his hair for *Superman II*. It caused him to be seen in public with patchy bald spots). He was also an early klutzy Clark Kent.

"I was very tall and physically awkward," Chris remembered in 1980. "I had [another] disease called Osgood Schlatter's disease, which prevents your tendons from keeping up with the rate of growth of your bones. You have a lot of fluid in your joints, and you don't move terribly well. As a result, I was very, very awkward. And enormous. I used to stand with my legs locked all the time. I was six-two by the time I was fourteen. And I moved like a building. Even though I was attractive, I lacked self-confidence. The theater was a nice place to go to solve those problems."

His mother's memory is that Chris was "a solemn child." She moved back to Princeton, and in June 1959 married Tristam Johnson. As is often the case, her new husband was the opposite of Franklin Reeve. A quintessential WASP, the rich investment banker managed a series of national brokerage houses—Kidder Peabody and Hornblower, Weeks. The stockbroker banned television in their large, comfortable Princeton home, calling it "the boob tube." Chris was called upon to sing in the church choir but would later say, "I wasn't interested in God, just music."

With the marriage came two "scholarly" stepbrothers, Mark and Brock. The former would study archeology at Harvard, the latter, the classics at Yale. Tristam and Barbara Johnson then had a daughter, Allison, who would later study medicine at the University of Connecticut. In addition to raising five children, Barbara was hired to write feature stories and cover local government for *Town Topics*.

Princeton, New Jersey, was and still is an idyllic small university town, cloistered halfway between Philadelphia and New York. Its residents have the highest education level of any incorporated city in the country. In music and theater, Princetonians support the classics. Shakespeare and Bach are favored over slick Broadway musicals by its citizens.

The new family wealth brought a return to privilege. Chris was taken out of the public school system and enrolled at Princeton Day School, said to be one of the most expensive prep schools in the country. Chris excelled in academics and activities. He was a boy soprano and a madrigal singer—no stigmas were attached to that kind of vocal expression in Princeton. He learned to ski during weekend excursions to the Pocono Mountains in Pennsylvania, beginning at six.

When he was eight years old, a teacher suggested that the school have him skip a grade—from the third to the fifth. A school psychologist spoke to Chris about it and then vetoed the jump. His diagnosis: while Chris had the intelligence to handle the increased difficulty of the curriculum, he wouldn't be able to accept being anywhere except at the top of his class.

Most of Chris' pursuits were solitary, a pattern he would follow throughout his life. He learned to play Ravel and Debussy on the piano (his mother gave him a Steinway grand when he was sixteen). His sports included fencing and hockey, in which he won a varsity letter. Unsurprisingly, his position was goalie, the spot on the team that requires the least interaction with others.

In the fourth grade, a drama teacher walked into his classroom asking if anyone could sing. The class was studying dinosaurs at the time, which bored Chris. He recalled raising his hand and singing out, "Mi, mi, mi." This led to a role in Gilbert and Sullivan's *Yeoman of the Guard* and later, *Little Mary Sunshine*, playing Captain "Big Jim" Warington. His music teacher, Frank Jacobsen, allowed him to direct the school orchestra, and Chris was elected to head the drama club in his senior year. He didn't miss the classroom structure.

"Everybody else in school would be sitting there working on some test in third period, but I'd look at my watch and excuse myself and go to the theater," Chris remembered.

"He always had the imagination, the knack for capturing an adventurous character's spirit and projecting it," his drama coach at Princeton Day, Herbert McAneny, would say in 1977.

Chris usually played a mature man, and nearly always the lead in the school productions. Once he played a seventy-two-year-old Scottish woman, complete with brogue. McAneny would stage a spring musical each year with Chris always as the character on whom he relied to carry the show.

"Being someone else took me away from a lot of things I was not prepared to deal with," Chris would later explain to *People* as one explanation of why he became an actor. The broken home, the illnesses, the awkwardness he felt—he once told a reporter about a friend Roger "who regularly beat the hell out of me"—all pushed him into acting.

Chris discovered that in the thespian world one could be another person. He told writer Margery Steinberg: "Well, on Fridays, [when] I'm down at the theater playing a part—I'm not me, I'm him. I'm the boy in *Our Town*. That got me through a lot of turmoil.

"If you look at pictures of me when I was a kid, I never cracked a smile. Acting was a way to help me loosen up, expose myself, and relax," he would amplify to *Newsweek*.

"It [the theater] solved the problem of Friday and Saturday nights," he said of his acting as a teenager. "I didn't have to worry about how I was going to ask little Suzy out for a date, because I was too busy in the theater. I would think, if I'm really lucky, she'll come to see the play, think I'm terrific, then I'll have a better chance."

He later recalled: "That whole dating game was painful. It really was, because I was a very serious kid, and a lot of girls weren't ready for that. I don't mean serious about 'I love you' but about World War III and the latest article in *The New Statesman*. I was not a lot of laughs. The girls I dated were never the ones I [liked]. I always ended up with dates who were not quite the girls I wanted."

Chris was closer to Franklin than his mother. His intellectual personality had always been influenced heavily by his father, in spite of his living with Barbara and her new husband after the divorce. On New Haven, Connecticut, weekends, when his father was teaching at Yale, Franklin taught him to sail, and later began entering Chris in sailboat races.

"I would win a lot," Chris said years later. "But it was at a certain cost. I would terrorize my crew. I was really aggressive, demanding, and critical of myself and other people. If I didn't win, it would set me back for days."

Evenings were spent in university literary salons populated by his father's intellectual cronies—Robert Frost, Robert Penn Warren, and Daniel Moynihan—heady company. It was definitely a group able to discuss the latest article in *The New Statesman*.

"I adore my father," Chris once said. "[He's] more like a contemporary—he looks ten years younger than he is. It's a struggle to remember being fed applesauce by this man."

Chris became a regular at the age of eleven with the McCarter Theater, a prestigious regional company that once had a close affiliation with Princeton University. It was within walking distance from the family home on Campbelton Circle. He began with child roles in *The Diary of Anne Frank* and *Our Town*, and as he became taller, he graduated to adult parts in classics such as Sean O'Casey's *Plough and the Stars*. Veteran stage actors like John Lithgow (Lithgow's parents managed the playhouse) and Katherine Walker "practically adopted me," he said later.

He would expand on those remarks in *Playboy*, adding: "The people I really owe my upbringing to are the repertory actors at the McCarter Theater in Princeton. In that atmosphere I learned to think for myself.

"I knew very early on that I wanted to be an actor. I was saved a lot of soul searching—who am I, what am I going to do with my life. Acting is what I do best.

"The luckiest thing that happened to me was that my parents let me take responsibility for my own life from the time I was thirteen."

His mother would agree: "He had drive. He was self-directed; he seemed happy only when he was in a play. Nearly everything he's done has been to improve his acting," she told the *Washington Post* in 1977.

It was during the McCarter years that Chris began to dress the part of the stereotypical Eastern elitist. His daily uniform would generally be unpressed cords topped with a plain oxford cotton shirt under a crew sweater, and loafers without socks. He would continue the classic style into his adulthood.

"I'm extremely meticulous about my clothes," he would tell *Gentleman's Quarterly* years later. "I still wear khakis, button-down shirts, and crew-neck sweaters—Ivy League clothes like Princeton in the sixties. I appreciate people who dress well, but I tend to stick to basics."

At McCarter, Chris tried to find a part in virtually every production—whether it was on or offstage. In *Ah, Wilderness*, he played the piano in the orchestra pit; in *Finian's Rainbow* he was in the chorus.

"I remember a director I worked under named Milton Lyon," Chris recalled years later. "I had just been in a production of *Finian's Rainbow*, which he directed. He said to me, 'You better know what you want, because you might get it. I think you might be the one in ten thousand who really has the potential to go a long, long way.' That encouraged me; handed to me at age fourteen, it made a lasting impression."

Chris' summers as a teen were spent learning the acting craft. June and July between his ninth and tenth grades were spent taking stagecraft and theatre makeup courses at nearby Lawrenceville School. He regularly passed up trips to the New Jersey shore with his family in order to stay in Princeton and learn more about the acting craft. There were soon daytrips by bus to New York, auditioning for everything from commercials to off-Broadway roles.

In 1968, still three months shy of his sixteenth birthday, Chris began what would be a lifelong theatrical love affair. He apprenticed at the Williamstown Theater in northwestern Massachusetts (the area would eventually become his home). The summer of 1969 found him at the Loeb Drama Center in Cambridge, where he got his first major role in Turgenev's nineteenth-century Russian classic, playing Beliaev in *A Month in the Country*. That was followed by other classics: *Death of a Salesman*, *The Hostage*, and *The Threepenny Opera*. He got more experience with the Boothbay Playhouse in Maine (*Private Lives*) and at the San Diego Shakespeare Festival (*Troilus and Cressida*). By sixteen he had an Actor's Equity card. When he became seventeen, he had gained a theatrical agent.

"I paid my dues," Chris later told the *New York Times*. "I acted in summer stock, off-Broadway at the Manhattan Theater Club, all sorts of roles, like Aeneas in *Troilus and Cressida*, MacHeath in *The Threepenny Opera*."

As soon as Chris got his high school diploma, he joined the national touring company of *The Irregular Verb to Love* with Celeste Holm. It would be the first of several parts where he would play a young male ingenue opposite a mature female star. That fall he entered Cornell University in Ithaca, New York. Chris' decision broke a tradition that ended several generations of Princeton men in the family.

Chris said he chose Cornell both for its theater arts department and its academic program. His major would not be theater—he wanted a well-rounded education—but rather English and music theory. But not that well rounded. A tryout for goalie on Cornell's hockey team—the puck whizzing toward him at ninety miles an hour—convinced Chris that "my future was in the theater."

"I believe in the old-fashioned kind of education," he would tell a writer years later. "Studying science and math gives you the discipline to take on challenges." He also took advantage of Ithaca's snowy winters by becoming an expert skier, later joking to an interviewer, "Come to think of it, it could be said that in the years I spent at Cornell I majored in skiing."

Still, acting was the way most hours were spent away from his classes. He acquired a 1970 Fiat to get to auditions. He largely skipped the Vietnam War protests, where students occupied the Cornell school buildings in protest. Instead, he helped establish a residence hall for acting majors. He learned to smoke and drink his scotch and vodka straight—"never messed up with water." His summers were spent doing plays like *Forty Carats* opposite Eleanor Parker or flying to Paris, where he was allowed to be a backstage observer at the Comédie Française (weekends in France were filled with skiing in Switzerland). He also spent part of a summer in London, where he not only wrote a college thesis on the British repertory theater but his agent got him paid a stipend for being the dialect coach on the Old Vic's production of *The Front Page*.

"I was hired as a 'dogsbody,' " Chris recalled in an interview. "[That's] a glorified errand boy. I also worked on the first British production of *Equus*." He termed it "a grand time."

He earned his bachelor of arts in 1974. He failed to attend the graduation ceremony because he had an acting role away from the Ithaca area.

"I managed to continue working as an actor during Cornell because I had an understanding agent who'd set up auditions around my class schedule. Somehow I managed to balance the academic and professional sides of my life," Chris later remembered.

Following Cornell, Chris drove the little Fiat to New York. It was soon vandalized, the radio stolen and the wires on the dashboard ripped out, though Chris would boast to friends that "the doors still close and the engine is in good shape." He enrolled in advanced drama studies at the highly selective Juilliard School in New York. It was a bumper year for actors who would go on to make names for themselves. William Hurt, Kevin Kline, Patti LuPone, Mandy Patinkin, David Ogden Stiers, and Treat Williams were just some of the students attending class with Chris. Members of this soon-to-be distinguished group of Juilliard alumni would roar around New York in vans doing everything from Moliere to mime, giving inner-city children their first taste of live theater.

"It was great," Chris once recalled to a writer from the *Los Angeles Daily News*. "The kids ate it up, and crazy things happened. Sometimes we'd put shows on in school basements with pretty low ceilings. Once in the Bronx I was supposed to draw a sword and flourish it, so that's what I did—and I knocked out four light bulbs. The kids just loved it."

"We formed a 'rag-tag' basketball team," a former schoolmate told the author. "I mean we were really 'rag-tag.' Chris played center. Finally, the administration called us in and laid down the law. We were told we had to dress more appropriately if we were going to represent Juilliard."

John Houseman, the distinguished actor and director, was one of his teachers. Houseman once lectured Chris with this wisdom: "Mr. Reeve, it's very important that you become a serious actor. Unless of course, they offer you a load of money to do something else."

Chris developed a rapport with another Juilliard classmate who would become an important lifelong close friend, Robin Williams. He later said that one reason they got along so well was because they were such opposites.

"You see, I didn't try to do bits with him. I was just my old boring self," he told Us magazine.

A few years later when Williams had his TV hit sitcom *Mork and Mindy*, and Chris was Superman he would comment on their common extraterrestrial backgrounds as, "He's the one from Ork, and I'm the one from Krypton."

To finance his Juilliard studies Chris landed a small part on the CBS television soap opera *Love of Life*. His character, tennis bum Ben Harper, became so popular his part was increased and he had to drop out of school. Chris welcomed the lightweight project "if only for the challenge of making something out of bad material. In college you perform the masterpieces, the classics. It isn't like that in real life.

"At first the character was set to appear just once or twice a week, and I could study the rest of the time. But he caught on and I was in almost every episode after a while. The guy was a scoundrel—no moral scruples whatsoever. He was married to two women at the same time, and one was pregnant. The Mafia had a contract out on him," Chris remembered about his two years on the show.

For the first time he would learn the power of

acting and how some of the public confuses the actor with the character he plays on the screen.

"I was sitting in a restaurant one day, and a woman came over and whacked me over the head with her purse. 'How dare you treat your poor pregnant wife that way!' she screamed. Needless to say, I was stunned.

"There are women who are both attracted to and repulsed by monsters," Chris summarized. "When you play that kind of role, you don't have to hang around just being yourself."

Determined to improve his acting abilities, Chris studied under various New York drama coaches after his daily stints on *Love of Life*. There were small parts with off-Broadway's Circle Repertory Company. He also got the lead in a 1975 Manhattan Theater Club production of *Berkeley Square*, playing Peter Standish.

After Juilliard, Chris moved into a fourth-floor walk-up apartment on West Eighty-third Street which he would describe as "a hole in the wall" that "looks like downtown Calcutta." He furnished the place with cast-off furniture picked up off the streets of New York—stuff that people had thrown out with the trash. Book shelves were divided by bricks. Empty wine bottles stood along the headboard behind the "bed," a mattress on the floor.

In those days Chris was part of the seventies singles scene. He once told *Mademoiselle* he batted .220, or "roughly two hits for every ten tries.

"I used to get bad attacks of cold feet. I found it difficult—and I still would—to approach some girl at a bar, minding her own business. Making that opening line is like swimming across the Hudson River— you have to cross an incredible gulf.

"That phase of my life was exciting, to a point, but it's also embarrassing and vaguely disappointing to wake up with someone and literally not know what she likes for breakfast. You make love and *then* try to communicate, which is all backward."

When asked by writer Susin Shapiro if he shared platonic friendships with women at that time, he gave the flip answer, "Oh, sure, all the ones I couldn't get lucky with," before addressing the subject seriously.

"When a man and woman meet, the first question that needs resolving is the issue of romance and sex. But expectations and promises not fulfilled are very exciting. That's why the early stages of a relationship are such fun. It's that anticipation."

Although Chris wasn't in many long-term relationships in the early seventies, he did begin a love affair that has endured for more than two decades. As a toddler he had become enamored with flying when he lived on East Eighty-eighth Street in New York. He would watch planes take off from nearby LaGuardia Airport from his bedroom window and dream of guiding the planes skyward. In 1975 he took his first flying lesson.

"I started . . . with a guy named Robert Hall—same name as the clothes store—he's one of the really tough, grouchy, chain-smoking, coffee-drinking, nail-biting instructors who's worth his weight in gold. I had my first forty hours with him," he told *Flying* magazine.

"He wouldn't let me solo until after twenty-six hours, after which I'd had five hours under the hood—I mean, he really believed in getting you ready, not these eight-hour wonders where you go up and battle around and get scared to death. The excitement of getting it right and flying the airplane—of course, I missed my first approach here today, but never mind! Doesn't mean you're flying it wrong."

After his first flight lessons, Chris continued his training at Teterboro Flight Academy in nearby New

Jersey. He got his private pilot's license soon after. Chris immediately purchased a used Cherokee 140 that had been flown five thousand hours for $8,000. He would describe it as a "Volkswagen engine with wings." It was to be his escape from the pressure of trying to make it in the uncertain world of acting in New York.

"I used to go everywhere in that little airplane and camp out. I went to Burlington, Vermont; London, Ontario—all those little towns on the way to Chicago—then down to New Orleans. I parked in grass fields every night and camped out with a sleeping bag."

In 1978, he took some of the money he'd earned from *Superman* and purchased a new A36 Bonanza. He soon moved up to a fully pressurized Baron, which he likened to driving a BMW, a far cry from the "Volkswagen" with which he'd begun his flying days. For this latest plane he had to go to Wichita, Kansas, for special training. And said Chris, "It's a great way to see the country." The twin-engine aircraft seated six.

He told *Gentleman's Quarterly*: "My idea of relaxing is flying 12,000 feet over the Grand Canyon at sunset with the radio playing Mozart.

"I always put down in places that I would never see otherwise. Who's going to go to Amarillo? I get a big kick out of dropping into Amarillo, or wherever, and meeting some waitress who has an accent and a pencil in her hair. I wouldn't run into these people normally. I just love coming down after three or four hours in the sky and being someplace else. It still amazes me. I'm not yet caught up in twentieth-century technology. I still think it's all pretty impressive, particularly because in acting, I'm dealing with the past a lot, old-fashioned things. I mean, films and plays tend to be about old ideas like love and romance, adventure . . . it doesn't deal too much with the future and technology—the real world," he said in the *Flying* interview.

There were close calls even then. Once, flying from San Diego to Los Angeles with a friend, his passenger said, "What about the jet?" Chris looked up to see a National Airlines 737 coming directly toward him. Chris said he swerved and used "the see and avoid method of not getting killed."

Chris also became heavily involved with gliding, a motorless and certainly more dangerous kind of flying that relies on only air currents and the skill of a lone pilot to stay aloft. He purchased a Schleicher AS-W19 sailplane and once told an interviewer, "I go all over the place in search of new highs."

One of Chris' "new highs" was gliding at 31,000 feet in a sailplane above Pikes Peak in Colorado. Chris said he would have gone higher, but his glider didn't have oxygen. He also said that because of the air currents in the area it had been too easy—"that's kind of cheating. Your grandmother could do that.

"I think there are as many moments of religious or near religious experience in a glider at 31,000 feet as there are struggling in a pew," Chris would tell *Cosmopolitan*.

That his pursuit of flying was another way to escape from the pressures which he would face in real life was never more evident than the statement Chris gave to the *New York Times* in 1979: "I love the air and the water. It's the land I have a problem with. When I'm on a boat or I fly my plane or my glider, I'm forced into immersion into something besides me. I defy you to be 12,000 feet in a glider above the Mohave Desert in a glider and worry about your divorce or your bank balance. The air only lets you stand up if you understand it. You're set free."

In the fall of 1975, Chris got the biggest stage role of his life. He was cast as Nicky, the grandson of Katharine Hepburn in Enid Bagnold's *A Matter of Gravity*. Clearly a project that was tailor-made for the some-times prickly Hepburn, Clive Barnes in the *New York Times* would describe it as "not so much starring Katharine Hepburn as enshrining her." In spite of having had parts in several dozen professional plays, beginning in childhood, it was Chris' first Broadway role.

Working with Hepburn would become a sort of advance degree in theater studies for Chris. The legendary actress soon took him under her wing and gave him daily tips on both acting and theater manners.

When they first met prior to going out on a pre-Broadway tour that was to include Washington and Philadelphia (Chris was still doing his soap opera and would have to fly to New York early in the morning to film his *Love of Life* lines), Hepburn told him to "shine your shoes."

"Only later did I understand what she meant. She was really saying that I didn't care about my appearance," Chris told Gene Siskel.

He would also say, "The thing I like most about Hepburn is her passion as a person. The world seems to have a structure and a value when you're around her. When we started rehearsals I came on like a wooden Indian. There I was, playing the grandson of a star I'd seen on screen since childhood, and the whole work process became one of trying to relax and meet her halfway.

"I'd always thought of acting as a way to lose yourself, disappear into a part, and thus find a kind of freedom. She taught me that quite the opposite is supposed to happen. You must really bring your own convictions, things you really love and hate to the character, and adjust after that," he told *Newsday*.

The opening night of the Broadhurst Theater on West Forty-fourth Street turned out to be a landmark evening for Chris' family. The new Broadway actor threw caution out the window and mailed tickets to both his mother and her second husband and also to his father's new family. Franklin and Barbara were seated side by side, even though they hadn't spoken to one another in fifteen years.

"I thought, what the hell. And they buried the hatchet. Afterward we all went out and got bombed!" Chris told a writer.

Chris had memorized the entire script long before his first audition so that he'd be comfortable enough to improvise when asked to read for the director. Still, he would confess to being unprepared for its New York premiere on the evening of February 3, 1976, intimidated by being onstage with the great Hepburn.

"I can remember her in the wings just before I was supposed to go on—I was twenty-three, on Broadway, and scared to death—and she's leaning on a cane, smiling and telling me, 'Be fascinating, now, be fascinating.' Fascinating? I was trying not to pass out!" Chris remembered.

When Chris did walk out onstage that night, he received a smattering of applause usually reserved for major stars. His mother had told most of Princeton about her son's debut, and nearly two hundred former Princeton Day School students were in the audience. Chris would later tell an interviewer that Hepburn noticed and "shot me a look."

Chris' lessons in both how to act and behave like a star would continue with Hepburn for the duration of the run—nearly a year including the pre-Broadway tour.

"You, standing on that stage, are more interesting than any fictional character, because you live and breathe. She said, 'Don't disguise yourself, let us see you.' The character you saw onstage was both

Katharine Hepburn and the character she was playing."

Hepburn later began improvising and inserting "bits of business" into her part as the months on Broadway slipped by. It confused Chris at first. It also hurt him physically.

"Three performances a week I would make an entrance and get a hug and a kiss from her. The rest of the performances she would raise the cane she was using to appear old, and stab me right in the solar plexus," Chris told *Newsday*.

Chris also told a writer he felt a little smothered by Hepburn's attentions.

"She's wonderful, she loves people, and she cares desperately, but boy, is she a nosy parker. She's into everyone's business as well as her own. The first thing she does when she comes to the theater is open all the doors so we all get some fresh air. So we breathe. She asks everyone what they'd had for dinner, and if it wasn't steak and ice cream—her idea of the essence of nutrition, you were ordered to go out and have them."

When Chris was in pre-Broadway tryouts in Washington, Hepburn's limousine would show up at his hotel with instructions to take him to certain museums and then have him join her for lunch.

"You just wanted a little elbowroom," Chris said, summarizing how he felt about Hepburn's attentions.

In separate interviews Hepburn had no reservations in her praise for Chris. "A hell of a nice person," she said. "A very sweet fellow, absolutely charming and lovely to look at. He's honest and true; you can see it in his eyes. You *believe* him."

In the end, it became a love affair of mutual admiration. Hepburn would tell him he was going to become "a big movie star" that "will support me in my old age" (Chris' adroit answer: "I can't wait that long").

The two would go on to exchange monthly letters for years.

"She lets me know what she thinks of what I've been doing, in no uncertain terms," Chris told the *New York Daily News* years later. "She called me once to tell me about a role I had done. She didn't like the actress I was working with at all—didn't approve of her, I think was how she put it."

When the newspaper pressed him on the name of the actress, Chris would only smile enigmatically.

He was once asked, if he could go back in time and seek out any woman in the world to romance, who would it be? Chris immediately claimed it would be a young and feisty Kate Hepburn.

"If I could have been in my early twenties when she was in her early twenties, I would have traveled a long way to get to meet her. And I would have had a tremendous crush on her. Just a *tremendous* crush," he confessed to an interviewer.

A Matter of Gravity was a Hepburn vehicle all the way. The play's title referred to her search for self-levitation. The comedy was as eccentric as that sounds. In the *New York Times*, Chris was dismissed by Clive Barnes with the line, "Of the rest of the cast I was not duly impressed." He had fared better during the pre-Broadway tour, particularly with the Washington critics.

"Katharine Hepburn and Enid Bagnold are smartly matched in the latter's new comedy at the National," Richard Coe would gush in the *Washington Post*. "*A Matter of Gravity* is a play literate, questing, and evanescent. It's a joy to hear their words levitate."

Near the end of his review Coe had this line: "I admired Christopher Reeve as Nicky."

"David Richards, who was then the theater critic of the *Washington Evening Star*, also had nice words for Chris: "None of the supporting actors gives the impression of having much of a handle on his character, although Charlotte Jones, as the cook bewildered by her aeronautical skills, is fitfully amusing, and Christopher Reeve makes a nice transition from playboy grandson to browbeaten husband."

Immediately following what he would later describe to *USA Today* as "my B.A. in drama," Chris flew to Hollywood. His agent had gotten him a small part in Universal Picture's action movie about the rescue of a nuclear submarine, *Gray Lady Down*. Starring Charlton Heston, and with a supporting cast that included David Carradine, Stacy Keach, and Ned Beatty, the film was considered by one of his agents (he then had a total of nine who claimed to represent him—four in New York and five in Hollywood) as a fine way to break into film work.

Maybe it was, but the movie about a submarine colliding with a freighter off the coast of Connecticut turned out both to be a critical failure (a critic called it "a disaster about a disaster" and another as "Airport '77 played underwater") and a failure at the box office as well. It disappeared after a short run in March 1978. Chris' role as Officer Phillips was relegated to stock lines like "Stand by!" and "Looks bad, sir." He was mentioned in one review. *Playboy* wrote: "Nice work in a minor role by Christopher Reeve." Considering the notices the film got, it was just as well. Years later, it would be summarized by Leonard Maltin in his *TV Movies* annual as a "tired drama" with the final line, "Look for Christopher Reeve as one of the officers."

Perhaps a letdown was to be expected after working with the likes of Katharine Hepburn and Charlton Heston. The catalyst was Chris' rejection for a major role in an NBC-TV miniseries drama (the lead was won by Richard Jordan) called *The Captains and the Kings*. The loss of the part cast Chris into a depression that lasted several months.

"I was twenty-four years old and being very hard

on myself," he told *Cosmopolitan.* "I felt, I'm really not very good. I felt tense and unhappy. I went to L.A. and sat on the beach for a while. Whenever my agent tried to find me for a callback, I'd be gone [flying a plane]. It didn't seem to matter, which is one of the signs of depression."

He escaped into the air, flying his little "Volkswagen engine with wings" north and following the TransCanada highway from west to east. He was a hobo inside a flying boxcar.

"I sat on the beach at Santa Monica—not even Malibu—for five months. I absolutely wrote myself off. I was sponging off friends, sleeping on couches, turning into a vegetable, and then one day I said, 'This isn't right,'" he told *People.*

Chris said his depression was "the only time I've been out of work in my career. But you can only thrash around like that for so long. My father helped. My agent helped, and one day I was able to say to myself, 'It's time to stop flying off into the sunset.'"

Returning to New York City, Chris hit an actor's trifecta. He landed an important supporting part (Juilliard classmate William Hurt was the lead) in the Circle Repertory Company's off-Broadway production of *My Life.* The play was almost Freudian in the role Chris played—a grandfather reviewing his life to determine how he had become that way, albeit a much older character. His salary was a not-so-grand $85 a week. The *New Yorker's* Edith Oliver wrote that she "admired" Chris, and *Back Stage* called him "gifted and appealing."

He also became seriously involved with a young woman about whom he would later say, "I was absolutely smitten." Turning down the lead in what would be a short-lived TV series, *The Man from Atlantis* (playing a half man, half fish), he had another breakthrough in January 1977. He was chosen to be Frank Langella's understudy in the Broadway pro-

duction of the commercial hit *Dracula.* After two days
of rehearsing the Transylvanian classic, he was in
another casting office trying out for a Woolite TV
commercial. (He was turned down.) There he got the
call that would change his life.

The black cape he would have worn as Dracula was
about to be exchanged for a red one.

4

"He lives for the part!"

—RICHARD DONNER

Russian-born film producer Alexander Salkind, with his blue-rinsed white hair and diminutive stature, looked like a old munchkin escaped from Oz. His twenty-nine-year-old son and partner, Ilya, except for his dark long mane and thick mustache, was a clone.

Salkind was a second-generation moviemaker who had migrated from Russia to Germany (Salkind's father had worked with Greta Garbo), and when Hitler came to power, the Salkinds escaped to France. After the fall of France they flew to Mexico, where they stayed in hiding until after the war.

It was these somewhat mysterious movie men together with their French partner, the bearded Pierre Spengler, to whom Warner Brothers had just handed some $25 million for a project many movie industry observers believed impossible. The task—to convince a mass audience that a man could really fly—was daunting.

The Salkinds and Spengler were not without credentials. In 1973 they'd hired British director Richard

Lester to create yet another version of Alexandre Dumas' *The Three Musketeers*. Lester's film went off into so many tangents that there were miles of footage left on the cutting room floor. The resourceful Salkinds were able to piece together a second movie from the remnants, titling it *The Four Musketeers*. On a $5 million budget for one production, the two films eventually grossed $120 million worldwide, delighting its distributors but infuriating the actors. They believed that they had been taken since there was no talk of *two* motion pictures being made while undergoing the rigorous production schedule. This led to the Salkind clause—a now standard contractual insert in film contracts which stipulates how many films are to be made from an actor's efforts over a period of time.

The idea for *Superman* was Ilya's. He had been strolling alone down the Avenue Victor Hugo in Paris when he passed an old movie house showing the Tyrone Power version of *Zorro*. The film's poster started him thinking about heroes with two identities and their popularity. It was then that doing a big-budget version of *Superman* occurred to him. He faced a hard time selling it to his father. Alexander Salkind had never heard of the man of steel. Neither had many of the Salkinds' European bankers, from whom they would need an additional $15 million. The superhero was a distinctly American tradition.

"We agreed from the beginning that the only way to do the film was to play it straight. That way it would be believable. Humor was important, but we wanted the audience to laugh with Superman, not at him," Alexander told the press in 1978.

They also needed to quickly find a scriptwriter, a director, and a star for the title role. The three priorities were deal breakers—Warner had veto power over each choice. In order to get bank loans guaranteed by the British government, the movie had to be made at England's Pinewood Studios, just outside London.

The Salkinds immediately chose William Goldman, but the writer who had authored the screenplays for both *All the President's Men* and *Butch Cassidy and the Sundance Kid* declined. They next went to Mario Puzo, believing him to be even more bankable because of the success of *The Godfather*. Puzo delivered a four hundred-page manuscript in two months, enough for two movies totaling six hours.

"We were thrilled with Mario's ideas, and much of Mario's story stayed. But when we asked for rewrites, he wasn't interested," the younger Salkind would say.

One idea of Puzo's with which they weren't thrilled—Clark Kent updated to be a TV newsman and Lois Lane as the station's weather girl.

The two then hired Robert Benton and the husband-wife writing team of David and Leslie Newman, who had written *Bonnie and Clyde*. The trio compressed the Puzo script and added more of their brand of humor (two outrageous examples: the villain Lex Luthor lived on a diet of Kleenex and in his subterranean hideout kept as pets all the alligators, rats, and snakes that had been flushed down the toilets of Metropolis). When it was still deemed too long, they hired yet another A-list screenwriter, Tom Mankiewicz—he was synonymous with the success of James Bond—for more script doctoring. Mankiewicz's contribution would be to unify the first two efforts and eliminate some of the campy humor that tended to denigrate the character of the superhero.

The choice of director was yet another series of false starts. The Salkinds and Spengler had gone to see a movie by a first-time director entitled *Sugarland Express*. Then after viewing a TV movie, *Duel*, directed by the same newcomer, Steven Spielberg, they had become convinced he was the right man for their film.

"He wanted to direct *Superman*," Spengler said in 1977, "but his price was high, so we decided to wait until a new movie he was making came out. It was something to do with sharks.

"Let's see how his fish movie does," was the way Alexander Salkind put it at the time.

The answer soon became emphatically clear. With *Jaws* established as the number-one grossing film ever by the end of 1976, Steven Spielberg's price became very, very high indeed. The Salkinds started looking elsewhere. Most directors were reluctant to take on the project because they feared it was impossible to make. The Salkinds offered the job to seven directors, getting turned down by each. Guy Hamilton had the job for a short time, but had to decline because of British tax problems. Finally they settled on Richard Donner, a Bronx-born action expert. He was thought at the time to be a second-tier choice, having made his reputation in television directing the *Kojak* series and made-for-TV movies. But Donner had just scored on the big screen with *The Omen*, a surprise blockbuster. After screening the horror opus, the Salkinds offered him the job.

Donner was considered to be one of the swaggering new breed of Hollywood action directors—no turtleneck or beret for him. He would soon be pacing the set wearing a black leather jacket, purple-tinted aviator glasses, jeans lowered to the hips, and white socks with Bass Weejuns. He carried two walkie-talkies with him everywhere, into which from time to time he barked orders.

"The story is bigger than life and it has humor," he said after reading the script. "But to the actors it has to be total reality and they have to play it dead straight. We're a new country. We've got the American Indian, we've got Superman. You don't fuck with either one of them."

Donner had signs made, which he posted around the set. They read: THINK VERISIMILITUDE!

The producers had no doubt who would be their Superman. They felt that Robert Redford in a wig and the right makeup was perfect for the part. When Redford turned them down, the trio was crushed.

"Redford would have just been Redford playing Superman. No one would have ever believed he *was* Superman," a Hollywood producer would sagely say later.

Undeterred, Ilya Salkind went directly to Paul Newman, offering the fifty-three-year-old star a part for a man in his twenties. After Newman refused, Ilya inexplicably offered him the part of Lex Luthor, Superman's nemesis. Newman turned him down once more. The part would go to Gene Hackman at a salary of $1 million.

These contracts were made in 1975. After that a wide-open search began for the title role, with nearly every male actor in Hollywood scrutinized. Clint Eastwood, Nick Nolte, Burt Reynolds, and Ryan O'Neal were approached, but eventually were rejected because they couldn't be made up to resemble the superhero. Casting directors and agents sent up trial balloons on long shots, ranging from Lyle Waggoner and Kris Kristofferson to James Caan and David Soul. Eventually the long list became a running joke, with even Elton John and Howard Cosell mentioned by the press as the new Man of Steel.

The producers then decided that a young newcomer with a name could fill the bill. Ilya said, "How about the biggest name to come out of the 1976 Olympics, Bruce Jenner? He has the looks, the build."

But on film Jenner looked *too* young. And as one

production assistant stated candidly, "Jenner is not an actor. He lacks the assurance that comes with acting experience."

The failure of Jenner killed the chances of another athlete, a young bodybuilder named Arnold Schwarzenegger. Now the filmmakers began to panic. Shooting was due to begin in three months, and the lead had not been found. Their financial backers were nervous. Millions of dollars had been spent for preproduction work, and many of the epic's characters had yet to be cast, let alone the lead.

In order to placate their bankers, Spengler and the Salkinds took another tack. They decided to hire an actor—*the* actor—who they believed had more stature than anyone in Hollywood. They believed that a star who commanded serious respect and who could guarantee some sort of box office returns was worth paying a fee totaling several million dollars. They agreed there was only one actor who fit that bill. That actor was Marlon Brando. They offered him a tiny part—Superman's father Jor-El—and promised he would have to work only twelve days for $3.7 million or a percentage of the gross box office—whichever was higher. Alexander Salkind took the offer to Kurt Frings, a Hollywood super-agent who agreed to act as a go-between.

"My job was to get Marlon to do the picture. He said the price was too good to turn down. It's the highest salary ever—who could turn it down?" Frings said. Still, Brando forced the Salkinds and Donner to visit him in his California home. Brando rambled on for more than an hour discussing his home in Tahiti, American Indians, and his hydraulic water system before signing.

Brando's hiring created one problem. They had hoped to shoot a scene with him at a studio in Rome, but there was a standing arrest warrant waiting for him in Italy. When he had made *Last Tango in Paris* there, his sex scenes with Maria Schneider had run afoul of the Italian censors. The thought of their multimillion hire being led off in handcuffs caused the Salkinds to quickly cancel Brando's Roman holiday.

With Brando on board, the producing team began to scramble to sign what was beginning to give Ilya some of his father's gray hairs. Shooting was scheduled to begin in March 1977—it was 1977 *now* and there was no narrowing of candidates. In fact, there were no candidates.

"Why can't things happen like they do in the movies? Why can't he walk through the door and be discovered?" Ilya was said to have complained to the casting team.

Months before, Ilya had gone through the photos in the Screen Actors' Guild directory sent to him by casting director Lynn Stalmaster and circled the picture of Chris Reeve. He liked his look and was impressed by the New York stage credentials. Now that Brando was in the fold, the younger Salkind flew to New York with director Richard Donner to interview the twenty-four-year-old unknown. The three met at the Sherry Netherland Hotel.

Chris would later say he had been unimpressed with the idea of playing Superman. He would tell friends that he had to catch a train at Grand Central Station anyway and the hotel just happened to be on his way. If the hotel had been in another location, he said, he'd have skipped the interview.

Donner and Salkind were unimpressed with Chris as well. At first glance he looked far too young, too thin, and too green for them to trust handing him the part of Superman. It was midway through their meeting when an epiphany occurred. Donner asked Reeve to don a pair of Clark Kentish horn-rimmed glasses and impersonate Superman's alter ego. After he did so, the two became very excited.

Chris would say later, "I alter my body to fit the part by controlling my spine. As Clark, I shorten myself, round my shoulders in a slouch, hold my head differently. With Superman, you change all that. How you carry yourself is ninety percent of the impression you make on other people. The other ten percent is mental attitude."

Chris then added a little method acting as to how he saw his part: "Kent's attitude is, 'What's going on?' Superman's is one of relaxed control. Clark is his puppet."

With Donner and the younger Salkind in his camp as the choice for what was being trumpeted as the part of the decade, Chris was flown to London for a screen test. He didn't need it. Spengler's wife, Monique, picked Chris up at Heathrow, and became immediately convinced that this was their Superman. She began lobbying her husband before any test cameras turned.

Chris' dead-on impersonation of Clark Kent, his sandy hair blackened and slicked down, the piercing blue eyes, the body encased in a deliberately ill-fitting gray flannel suit, sealed his fate. It was a masterpiece of awkwardness with just the right touch of projected sincerity. And when he donned the cape and boots, albeit heavily padded, he jumped off the screen (the test was the "getting-to-know-you" scene on Lois Lane's balcony). A week later, Chris was startled when the then doyenne of dish Rona Barrett announced on *Good Morning America* that he'd been selected. A phone call was made to London for confirmation. Ilya Salkind was only too happy to oblige—the search was over.

Chris called his mother and told her: "It was just another audition, but this time I happened to land a big one—a tuna instead of a minnow."

* * *

"Bring him in," said Dick Donner to the handlers worrying over every nuance of the February 23, 1977, press conference in the Belasco room up on the third floor of Sardi's restaurant in New York. Chris walked in. He looked as if he'd stepped off the pages of a prep school brochure: gray crew-neck sweater, blue blazer, sand-colored Hush Puppies.

Donner, the most skeptical of the principals who'd chosen Chris for the part, now said, "If there's a God in heaven, he sent me Christopher Reeve."

"We're paying Chris a good salary for someone just launching a motion picture career," Ilya Salkind claimed. "We want him to feel like a star. And don't forget, his salary has an escalator clause for each additional picture."

The good salary was $250,000 for what was scheduled to be eleven months of work. Chris' agent had a clause inserted which gave his client an additional $5,000 per week after fifty-two weeks of shooting. After eighteen months of devoting his life to the film, Chris would call the overtime, "No fortune."

Will he be believable?

Donner jumped in before Chris could answer. "I've no worries on that score," he said. "Chris is really good. And highly disciplined. He lives for the part. He calls me in the middle of the night to say I finally figured out how to play such and such. You know, a year from now every chick in America is going to have his picture on her bedroom wall."

Perhaps it was Hollywood hyperbole, but the press was ready to buy it. Flash cubes popped and there was a smattering of applause.

"Chris will attack the American fable of Superman head-on. There will be no parody, no tongue in cheek; he will be a Superman, born on the planet Krypton but raised in a wholesome American family, who fights for truth, justice, and the American way," Donner said with a straight face.

Chris let the press know he was a serious actor.

Using rehearsed lines of which he would use many variations in the days ahead he said: "Like a lot of teenagers I never had a problem deciding what I was going to do with my life. I've never gone through any self-searching to decide what I can do best. Acting is what I do best.

"I haven't been acting this long to be typecast as Superman. Once this movie is out, I'll play neurotics or weaklings. But right now Superman is not a bad role for me."

He would later say how much different the story was from his expectations: "When I read the script for the first time, I thought *Superman* was a romantic comedy. I didn't see the blue suit and the special effects. I saw Superman and Lois Lane exchanging one-liners on the balcony over a glass of wine. And the scene where he takes her flying is so original, so charming. This was right out of a Preston Sturges movie, and the part was exactly what I always wanted to be, a romantic leading man, a light comedian. So I was sold on doing the movie."

The part of Superman was as much physically challenging as it was mentally for Chris. He was put on a diet of four multivitamin-laced milkshakes a day, fed buckets of chocolate-mint ice cream, and forced to eat double lunches and dinners. Two one-hour sessions per day were allotted to supervised weightlifting. He was first trained by a British Olympic coach. The Olympian was followed by David Prowse, a bodybuilder who'd filled the costume of Darth Vader during *Star Wars*.

"I looked at it like sketching," Chris said. "I was designing a body. I always worked looking at myself in a mirror, and not because I was in love with myself. I started out straight as a tree and gradually worked into a wedge shape, always keeping in mind that Superman had wide shoulders and no waist."

Ilya Salkind was still casting key roles. Lois Lane was yet another search that had gone through the gantlet. Barbra Streisand was a first choice, but wouldn't submit to a screen test and eventually was considered all wrong. The producers then went to Jill Clayburgh. But she was booked for years after making a strong impression in the sleeper hit *Silver Streak*. After giving tests to the likes of Stockard Channing, Anne Archer, Deborah Raffin, and Liza Minnelli, the Salkinds settled on Lesley Ann Warren. They felt she was not only right for the part, but because she wasn't a well-known star, she wouldn't overpower Chris. Dick Donner then vetoed her, feeling she had the wrong "look."

It was the script doctor Tom Mankiewicz who steered the Salkinds to Margot Kidder, the eventual Lois. He felt she had been overlooked and asked the Salkinds to call her at the Montana ranch she shared with her soon to be ex-husband, writer Tom McGuane (she had become romantically involved with Harrison Ford).

"What is this, some kind of joke or something?" was Kidder's first response when she was asked to fly to Los Angeles to test for the part.

After reading for the role, the actress was asked to go to London for further screen tests. Playing it coy, she told them she had to go back to Montana to mother her toddler daughter, Maggie, to whom she had given birth while married to McGuane. After letting them plead for two days on how urgent the matter was, she let herself succumb to their implorations. Then, after being told she had the female lead, she gave this reaction: "I never read a Superman comic until the day of the screen test. So what I'm bringing to the part is myself—manic and disorganized!

"I saw my screen test and couldn't figure out why they cast me. I played it straight, and the director was in stitches. My friends always told me I was funny, but I always thought I should be doing Russian tragedy. It's weird, because in this movie I'm showing the side of myself I reserve for friends—plus they dress me like Daffy Duck—and everyone loves it."

The chain-smoking, hazel-eyed Kidder celebrated by going shopping at a London lingerie boutique and dropping $500 on underwear. It was the largest part she'd ever landed. She was an unusual woman. Tough as nails, and a hang-glider enthusiast, Kidder would wind up doing all her own stunts during the shooting.

Most of the gossip by the press during the *Superman* filming focused on what the writers would do with Superman and Lois Lane to create romantic tension. Would they sleep together? Screenwriter Robert Benton put it into perspective a month before the opening: "You could say that the romance is something warmer than a handshake but considerably less than *Deep Throat*." And though the moviemakers would save the bedroom sex for the sequel, one scene between Chris and Kidder in the script became a classic exercise of soft-core eroticism.

LOIS: Can you see through anything?
SUPERMAN: Yes.
LOIS: Okay, what color underwear am I wearing?
SUPERMAN: Pink.
(Lois blushes and becomes flustered but is interested.)
LOIS: Do you like pink?

For her part, the always candid Kidder seemed to be anxious for the sequel to hit the screen.

"We get to make love in that one, but he doesn't take his tights off. I don't know about the cape. Rightly or wrongly, there's something about sex on

screen which makes someone into a star. And there's
something about no sex that doesn't."

The producers quickly filled in the other principal
players—an international Who's Who of screen
names. Susannah York was chosen to play Brando's
wife and Superman's mother. His adoptive parents
on Earth were interpreted by Glenn Ford and Phyllis
Thaxter, who just happened to be Ilya Salkind's
mother-in-law. The bawdy Valerie Perrine was selected to be a key villainess. Ned Beatty (with whom
Chris had worked in *Gray Lady Down*) was chosen as
a comic foil for Hackman. A galaxy of other veteran
British and European stars—Trevor Howard, Terrence Stamp, Maria Schell, and Sarah Douglas—filled
key roles.

The part of Clark Kent's editor, Perry White, became more of Keystone Cops caper than by-the-book
casting. A long list of "usual suspects," including
Jason Robards, Eli Wallach, and Walter Matthau were
considered before deciding on Jack Klugman. Two
days before Perry White's first scene, Klugman,
who'd verbally agreed to play the part, turned down
the job over a misunderstanding over how much
money he was to be paid. Eddie Albert was then
signed, throwing the costume department into high
gear, since he had totally different body measurements than Klugman, whose costumes had already
been made. He too attempted to renegotiate his salary, sending the producers into a snit. Ilya Salkind
frantically phoned another actor, Keenan Wynn, directly, eventually reaching him in his car and getting
a commitment. Wynn hastily flew to London, had
his costume measurements done, and then col-
lapsed. The sixty-one-year-old actor was rushed to a
hospital complaining of chest pains, and thus lost his
job. After more panic, particularly by the costume
department, former child star Jackie Cooper was
signed. The joke among the crew during the week

was that getting a part in *Superman* was now a lot like smoking—dangerous to one's health.

Chris was still trying to define his character, applying the techniques he had picked up from more than a decade of acting.

"A hero shouldn't know he's a hero. If he does, he's boring. Someone once said: 'You can't play the king; the people around you play to you being king.'

"What makes Superman a hero is not that he has power, but that he has the wisdom and maturity to use it wisely. Superman doesn't know all the answers. He's not always secure. Part of being human is having doubt and conflict and worry and struggle. Even though he's from Krypton, that needs to be in *Superman*. There are elements of Superman in Clark Kent. Sometimes he'd like to be a normal person with normal responsibilities. And Clark would like to let Lois know who he is so that she'd care for him more.

"When Superman flies in to Lois' apartment, he should just say hello as if he walked in off the street. He shouldn't stand there and pose all full of himself—she'd send him away."

And as for the mind of Superman? Chris went directly into his own psyche.

"I decided Superman would represent the side of me that would be everything in life I'd like to be. And as Clark Kent I'll take all my insecurities and exaggerate them for comic effect."

Chris said he had gone to the creators as well. There were two points the creators of the comic book hero, Jerry Siegel and Joel Shuster, told him were important in understanding his character. The first was: "He's an orphan, and that governs his emotional behavior," and the second: "He's an alien, and what makes him super is he's got the wisdom to use his powers well."

In addition to his exploring the soul of a comic

strip hero, Chris was having difficulties that were more physical than mental. He had already gained more than forty pounds, boosting his six-four frame up to more than 235, most of it muscle. His biceps had gone from 12 to 15 inches. His chest had gone from 41 to 45 inches while his waist remained at 33 inches. He could now bench-press 350 pounds. When he started he couldn't lift fifty. No padding would be needed for any shots. He had once been described as Jimmy Stewart viewed sideways. He was now anything but that.

Yet Chris still hadn't gotten the hang of flying. Encased in a leather harness, he was required to hold his body, including his legs, rigidly straight for ten minutes or longer while suspended in midair by an overhead crane. The wires holding the harness were at first coated with black felt. The effect didn't work in test shots, and the felt was stripped away. Chris would eventually claim his thighs had grown calluses from the ordeal before the shooting was over.

At one point, shooting a scene that had Chris and Kidder in a harness together, the contraption began to come apart. He instinctively grabbed Kidder as if he could really fly away with her in his arms.

The crew was quick to have him change Superman costumes. The wardrobe department would eventually sew together forty of them as well as six capes. The slightest evidence of sweat, wrinkles, or snags found Chris changing into yet another suit. Unlike the black-and-white serials of the forties and fifties there would be no frames in *this* film with a baggy look.

Superman was a forty-year-old franchise whose integrity had been compromised many times but never destroyed. Conceived by Siegel and Shuster when they were teenagers in Cleveland fantasizing their way through the Depression, the first Superman story premiered in Action comics in 1936. The two once said that they had modeled their character's appearance on Douglas Fairbanks, Sr., and his alter ego, Clark Kent, on Harold Lloyd. An instant hit, the legend of an indestructible hero from another planet (except for that old bugaboo, Kryptonite) soon had its own ten-cent comic book and spawned a newspaper strip, a radio series, records, animated cartoons, a TV series, and a 1966 Broadway musical. (Surprisingly, Chris would claim never to have read Superman as a child, saying he had preferred the Daffy Duck and the Punch-and-Judy combination of Tweety and Sylvester.) The movie serial which starred Kirk Alyn in the title role and Noel Neill as Lois Lane had cost just $200,000 for all fifteen episodes. As one of hundreds of intellectual properties owned by the Warner Corporation (it had purchased the rights from Siegel and Shuster for a mere $130), it was an institution in need of enhancement. Thus Warner was going all out, leaving no opportunity unexploited. Besides flogging the movie via ads and publicity, Warner was licensing everything from Superman sneakers to telephone booth–shaped cookie jars, and would eventually take in $30 million in profits from licensing.

Donner was adamant about establishing the reality of the flying sequences. He had begun to accept what he was doing as fact rather than fantasy.

"Krypton, Metropolis—I find myself believing this. That's why the whole thing about Superman is he'd better fly and you'd better believe it. Otherwise, it's not going to work."

Donner concluded with a straight face: "There is a little bit of 'God Bless America' in it. There is a purity and a fantasy in it that is right for our times."

On a lighter note, much ado was made of whether Chris "dressed" left or right. Dick Donner was concerned that when his star wore the costume with the bright red tights that the protruding part of Reeve's anatomy be in the same place for each shot. To make sure, he assigned a script girl to keep track. After a conference it was decided that a true Superman would be neither left nor right—but dead center. A plastic codpiece was found which not only centered the appendage, but in effect, enhanced its apparent size—much to the delight of the filmmakers.

Chris told *Time* about his flying methodology. On landings: "Superman usually came in sideways the way a hockey player stops. But if you land from seventy-five yards in the air, it takes some practice. You come in at about the same speed as a parachute jumper."

On takeoffs: "I want to convey the feeling that Superman was slightly dull on the ground, like a fish out of water. But as soon as he takes off, he's at home."

The British tabloids reported every "Superman" sighting at Tramps, the London nightclub of the seventies, but Chris claimed to do little partying.

"I'm not here to have fun," he said in an interview, sounding defensive. "I'm here to put something on the screen that's going to entertain people. If you go to a party on Friday, by Monday nobody remembers whether you were there or not. But they'll remember what you put on the screen whether it's good or bad. It's my job to see that it's good.

"I go home from work each day, sometimes in agony because I feel that a scene wasn't one hundred percent. Will they fix it with music or play it off Brando or Hackman—perhaps they'll save me. I guess I'm driven. So that's why I can't take visitors or screwing around. It drives me nuts because I'm so rigidly forward."

Chris' response was somewhat disingenuous. He had already met and was about to begin living with Gae Exton, his lover for the next decade. Their torrid romance was played away from the press—for the moment.

Though forbidden to indulge his passion for piloting planes and gliders during filming, Chris did so anyway. He worked on his multiengine rating and spent several free weekends alone in the air, gliding through the English countryside.

As a young actor with little screen experience, Chris' first scene in the film must have caused trepidation. It was opposite Marlon Brando, the only scene in the film where the two were on-screen together.

"What's my motivation?" Brando had asked the Salkinds when he accepted the part. "How do we know that Jor-El doesn't look like a green bagel and that people on Krypton don't speak in electronic beeps?"

Alexander Salkind tried to hide the churning he was feeling in his gut. He tried to reason with his star.

"Everyone knows the legend, Marlon. You can't tamper with something as sacrosanct as Superman."

Brando then wanted to know if he could play his character as a suitcase, with the bag actually being placed in the middle of the room and his voice projected from inside it.

Brando eventually did his scene with Chris dressed in what could be called a futuristic toga and reading from cue cards—somewhat galling, considering the salary he'd been paid. Chris evidently acquitted himself well. Hours later, Brando sent caviar and champagne to his dressing room. He would later try to give Chris advice after learning that his costar was doing his own stuntwork.

"Why are you risking your life?" Brando asked. "It's just a movie."

The filming of *Superman* would eventually employ more than one thousand. Location shooting moved around the world. Prairies near Calgary, Alberta, were used to approximate the wheatfields of Kansas. Margot Kidder, who had been born near the town of Yellowknife in Canada's Northwest Territories just south of the Arctic Circle, had a moment of smug satisfaction at ordering dinner in a swanky restaurant where she once had worked as a waitress.

"I got a great kick out of walking into the dining room of the posh Banff Springs Hotel with Gene Hackman, Valerie Perrine, and Tom Mankiewicz. The last time I was in the dining room, I wore a short tartan kilt, carried a silver tray, and was madly in love with the room-service waiter. I worked for tips and not much else. Now I was back as a movie actress!"

New York City doubled for Metropolis—it has always been the comic book's obvious alter ego. The shooting for that sequence took place during the unusually hot summer of 1977.

Mayor Abe Beame was determined to bring more film shooting into Manhattan, and he took a personal interest in making sure the crew's requirements were met, attending the first scene's filming in front of the *New York Daily News*, which had been renamed the *Daily Planet* for the duration of the crew's stay. Its film critic, Kathleen Carroll, was given a cameo appearance, as was movie reviewer Rex Reed. Despite Beame's presence, the initial shooting of exteriors, shot on the evening of July 13, 1977, was a disaster. The steamy heat caused a blackout that enveloped most of Manhattan *except* for the *Superman* set, which had mobile generators roaring away. The production went on while Harlem was burned and looted.

Two days later, several thousand New Yorkers turned out to watch the filming of Chris' scene at the Solow building, a glass and steel skyscraper on West Fifty-seventh Street. Chris was fastened into his harness and hung with invisible wires from a giant crane some two hundred forty feet above the street. The crowd began cheering as he was suspended and spotlit, his body rigid against the summer sky. Ilya Salkind said later that that was the moment he knew the movie would be a hit.

Perhaps it was inevitable that friction between Dick Donner and the Salkinds would surface. With so much at stake and the production weeks behind, millions of dollars had already been lost. The film's scheduled opening for the summer of 1977 had become impossible.

Donner's directing attempted for perfection, shooting retake after retake. This grated on the Salkinds. They leaked information to the trades that he was in violation of his contract by being so far behind schedule. As a warning, they hired Dick Lester in mid-production, giving him the title of producer, but clearly to look over Donner's shoulder.

"If they're going to fire me, why don't they just fire me?" Donner shouted at one point.

Lester tried to calm him down, telling Donner that the Salkinds owed him a chunk of cash from *The Three Musketeers* and he was on the payroll only because of their debt to him.

"I'm just here for the money," he told Donner in order to calm him down.

Donner was clearly nervous. At one low point during the shooting, a story was published by a Canadian magazine that he had taken to wearing a Superman suit and cape in private, standing in front of a mirror with it on and talking to his reflection, repeating over and over, "I'm going to finish this fucking movie and I feel great!"

Lester suggested to the Salkinds that any shooting which would be used in a sequel should be halted in order to save money and time. The Salkinds agreed, but their summer of 1978 dreams were soon gone.

The movie was rescheduled for a pre-Christmas opening.

The Salkinds made several statements to the press about their desire to establish a *Superman* dynasty of five to ten films. This clearly rankled Chris.

"I read somewhere that Ilya Salkind said, 'Chris Reeve is going to make five *Superman* movies and be famous and work for me forever and be miserable.' Well, as far as I'm concerned, I'm finished when I've done the sequel. There may be some disagreement about that on the part of the producers, but the way I see it, I don't have an agreement beyond the first two."

He also seemed to be unhappy with his $250,000 salary, saying, "I'd have made more money doing TV soap operas . . . it's no fortune. They're nice guys, the producers, and on a personal level I'll go out to dinner with them anytime. But we've had our disagreements. I keep reading about how much the movie cost; ridiculous figures like $65 million. The truth is, it probably cost about the same as *Close Encounters of the Third Kind*—between $18 and $20 million. Why exaggerate? Bragging about the budget serves no purpose at all. All this talk about this being the most expensive movie ever made and how much Brando got—people resent it.

"As I get closer to the film's opening, the more nervous I get. Dick Donner's a basket of Jell-O. We're both thinking the same thing—what if we miss? All that work, all that money, all that care. This movie could be the biggest pratfall of the century.

"We're right to be anxious."

5

"You've got me? Who's got you?"

—LOIS LANE

During the first week of October 1977, Chris was standing in line at Pinewood's studio commissary getting a quick snack. According to reports, he was in full Superman costume, and stepping backward—in more of a Clark Kent move than a super one—he crushed Gae Exton's toe with his heel. Exton would be his companion for most of the next decade and the mother of two of his three children.

"The first thing I noticed were his blue eyes—he has those incredibly piercing blue eyes. But it wasn't love at first sight," Exton would tell the fan magazines. She also said she was attracted to him because he reminded her of her brother.

"She just thought I was a large American person with black hair and wore red boots," Chris would say. "That's one of the things that attracted me to her—she was and is singularly unimpressed by celebrities."

Exton was British. Tall, with straight ash blond hair and a model's face ("and great legs," Chris would remind the press), she worked in management for a modeling and casting agency in London that would later have branches in New York and other world capitals. Her father, Clive, managed London hotels and restaurants, and Exton had worked in them as a teen, later managing her own bistro, where she learned to be a gourmet cook. She had been educated by nuns in convents before becoming a model herself. Like Chris, she had been sickly for much of her life and had been in and out of hospitals. She moved into the management side of the modeling business after several years, and on the day she met Chris, she was at Pinewood attempting to place some of her clients on British television programs.

Exton, who is eight months older than Chris, had just become separated from her husband, David Iveson, a former coal miner turned businessman, running an engineering firm. After he married, Iveson had turned to cocaine smuggling. On October 12, 1979, he was sentenced to three years for having been responsible for more than a million dollars worth of cocaine smuggled into England. He served sixteen months before being released.

"I was looking for somebody who wasn't pitching something at me, or sponging in some kind of way," Chris would tell an interviewer years later. "I felt a little exploited on the party circuit [in London]— here's this new hero. . . . Gae wasn't disinterested, but she wasn't fawning over me. She had a nice, friendly reserve about her, and a quick wit, and a lot of style."

A few weeks after their first meeting at Pinewood Studios, Exton ran into Chris again at a luncheon. This time he asked her out. Their first date took place on October 16, 1977, a date which thereafter was referred to as "our anniversary" during their decade together. Appropriately, given Chris' stage background, they went to a serious play—Julie Harris in *The Belle of Amherst*. Afterward they had dinner at an

Young Chris, at age eleven, as Captain Big Jim Warington in *Little Mary Sunshine* at the Princeton Day School. Chris said he escaped into acting because of a traumatic childhood. (PRINCETON DAY SCHOOL YEARBOOK)

Acting, dancing, and singing at fourteen in a rehearsal for *Finian's Rainbow*, at Princeton University's McCarter Theater. Chris credits actors like John Lithgow with "practically adopting me." (PRINCETON UNIVERSITY LIBRARIES)

LEFT: Filming *Superman* in 1977, Chris poses on the Brooklyn waterfront against the New York skyline. Chris was chosen over 200 actors for the role and would reprise the part three more times, forever linking him with the comic-book hero. RIGHT: Chris hangs some 24 stories over Manhattan during the filming of *Superman*. A self-described risk taker, he did all of his own stunts for the movie. (AP/WIDE WORLD)

The Canadian actress Margot Kidder, Lois Lane to Chris's Clark Kent, and Chris at a gala premiere of *Superman* in 1978. (AP/WIDE WORLD)

With Jane Seymour on the set of the lushly romantic *Somewhere in Time* in 1979. The actress would name her son after Chris when she gave birth in November 1995. (AP/WIDE WORLD)

LEFT: Backstage with Swoosie Kurtz after their opening night performance of *Fifth of July* at New York's New Apollo Theater in 1980. Kurtz later won a Tony award; Chris played a gay paraplegic Vietnam veteran. RIGHT: Chris and girlfriend Gae Exton at the New York premiere of *Superman II*. They met in 1977 when Chris accidentally stepped on her toe while wearing his Superman costume. (AP/WIDE WORLD)

With comedian Robin Williams in 1981. They first became pals when they shared an apartment while studying together at Juilliard. Williams was one of the first to visit Chris after his tragic accident. (AP/WIDE WORLD)

Chris with Exton and their children, Alexandra and Matthew, then two and six, returning to London after a ski trip in America in 1985. His next role would be in *Anna Karenina*. (GLOBE PHOTOS)

Italian restaurant where they evidently found enough to talk about—they were still at their table when the place closed. Because of her recent separation from David Iveson—and the criminal charges then against him—Exton was wary of any romantic entanglements.

"Gae was fragile as an eggshell when we met," Chris told *People*.

"I didn't want him to kiss me," remembered Exton. "I was scared of my physical attraction to him. The first night he took me out, I jumped out of the taxi, shouted 'Bye!' and ran away. The first kiss didn't take place until the third date."

"She was shocked that I wasn't going to muscle past the door into her bed. I think the fact that we tiptoed into the relationship helped," Chris said.

Exton moved into Chris' rented London apartment on Knightsbridge Mews in February 1978. Chris said the relationship worked because she *wasn't* an actress.

"My two or three serious relationships before had all been with actresses. Competition killed them all. This time I got it right. I had found the first woman I could safely let go with."

Any reluctance to marry soon could easily be blamed on his traumatic childhood. Chris denied that to *Cosmopolitan*.

"It's true that I was the product of a certain polarity in a divorcing family, but I refuse to trace my attitude back to my parents. That's a sixty-five-dollar-an-hour [psychotherapist] question."

After keeping the romance secret for more than a year, Chris unveiled his relationship with Exton in dramatic fashion. He had already been linked in gossip columns with actresses like Farrah Fawcett, Goldie Hawn, Suzanne Somers, and his *Superman* co-star Valerie Perrine. Putting those rumors to rest, he showed up with Exton at the royal family's *Superman*

premiere benefit with Exton by his side. In grand
style the two went public and confirmed their love
affair to reporters just after being introduced to
Queen Elizabeth II on December 13, 1978.

"I'm going to have to be a public person, but I
was keen on Gae not becoming a household name,
because then we could lose what we have," he said
at the time.

If the Salkinds could get the queen to show for their
London premiere, then they would settle for no less
than President Jimmy Carter on the other side of
the Atlantic. An entire early December weekend in
Washington, filled with cocktail parties and dinners,
was organized that built to a grand finale—the
screening of the film inside the Eisenhower Theater
at the Kennedy Center. Ticket prices began at $500,
and a complete package of dinners and parties
topped out at $1,000 per person, benefiting the Spe-
cial Olympics.

The Salkinds and Pierre Spengler had already been
running trailers to audience cheers in the movie
houses since summer. In *Life* a two-page full-color
photograph of Chris from the waist up at the critical
moment of transition—opening his shirt to reveal the
crest with the S inside—was the only thing on the
page save "The Movie" in the upper left-hand corner
and "Opening for Christmas" on the far right. Two-
page ads, known as "double trucks," were running
in most New York and Los Angeles papers. The tag
line, "You'll believe a man can fly," had been added.
The budget for advertising was nearly $10 million,
huge for the time, but according to Sid Ganis, the
Warner ad chief, "not superhuman, not outrageous."

Warner wanted to make both a national splash
and a lobbying effort with politicians in the nation's
capital, and they certainly had the opportunity to

accomplish the latter. The gala evening found Jimmy and Rosalynn Carter sharing their presidential box with Teddy Kennedy. John Glenn, Eunice and Sargent Shriver, Arnold Schwarzenegger (described by the *New York Times* as "the body builder who dates Maria Shriver"), and D.C. mayor Marion Barry were among those milling around at the reception prior to the movie. The eclectic group of movers and shakers also found Barbara Walters with "her date," Alan Greenspan, Phyllis George, Roger Mudd and Baltimore Colts quarterback Bert Jones. It was the kind of evening where those present would exclaim the next day at lunch to a friend, "Everyone, absolutely everyone, was there."

"Politics and show business," Ted Ashley, the chairman of Warner's film division, mused before the premiere, "it's a great combination. And look, let's face it. Where else is the president going to show up at a movie?"

Henry Kissinger had a line ready for the reporters: "I want to thank Warner Brothers for making a movie about my life," he joked.

Gene Hackman staked out a quiet corner at the reception in the Kennedy Center's atrium and defended his $1 million salary by saying, "I didn't ask for that much money. They volunteered it."

He was with his two teenage children and appeared unflustered by the questions until a reporter began: "Don't you think the fact that Superman does not deal with the black question—"

Hackman interrupted the questioner before he could finish: "That's the most idiotic question I've ever heard, and you are an ass," he shouted before storming away.

When Chris and Gae Exton arrived at the premiere, he was cornered by Ethel Kennedy. She introduced him to her two teenage sons, Chris and Max, and asked him, "Do you know what my two sons want more than anything in the world?" She then answered her own question by saying, "That cardboard replica of you." (Warner Brothers had put an eight-foot color cutout poster of Chris as Superman between the elevators.)

"Sold American," Chris cried out to Kennedy, telling her she could take it home after the screening.

Exton seemed amused by the attention Chris was getting. A woman asked her how it felt to be the girlfriend of America's newest sex symbol.

"I never think of him that way," Exton answered. "I can't see that all this will change him at all. Hopefully. But those could be famous last words."

Chris and Margot Kidder were described by one newspaper as "lovely, gracious people who seem, incredibly, still unaffected by the vast hoopla surrounding this extraordinarily expensive film, variously price-tagged at $35 to $40 million, and the fame it will bring them."

Kidder had expressed a desire to meet the president's brother, Billy Carter. But Carter's loose-cannon sibling was a no-show, much to the relief of many. She had splurged on a white chiffon dress for the premiere and shown up with a gardenia in her hair and *Saturday Night Live* bad boy writer Michael O'Donoghue on her arm.

When asked how they had met, the iconoclastic O'Donoghue said loudly, "I picked her up in the streets. She belonged to any man for the price of a drink!" As Kidder giggled, he added, "Besides, if she chose me over Superman, imagine how good I am in bed."

"Am I afraid of typecasting?" Kidder said, repeating a reporter's question. "Are you kidding? I'm finally financially secure. I'm as happy as a clam."

Chris was asked how it felt to be a movie star. He threw back his head and laughed. "I don't know.

This is only the third day I've been one. Come back in a year and I'll tell you."

Chris said the Warner studio was giving him "a blank check to do whatever I want. . . . I'm extremely ambitious and I work hard enough to make it pay off. It takes twenty years to make an actor and I'm halfway there. But who knows? Maybe someday I'll wind up in a home for old Supermen and playing shuffleboard."

He described the flying sequences as "a sexual dream, a fantasy we've all had."

Richard Donner was still nervous, saying, "I made the film and I'm my biggest fan. I love it. The real test will come with the kids who pay four dollars a ticket. They're the ones I made it for."

What the crowd saw that night was a biography of Superman for the first half: his leaving Krypton, being adopted by Ma and Pa Kent, then leaving his small-town roots and moving to Metropolis to fight for "truth, justice, and the American way" by fighting cartoonish criminals, the most prominent being Gene Hackman's Lex Luthor character.

The black-tie crowd seemed not to have attended many action movies. They clapped sedately instead of cheering when Chris as Superman held the San Andreas fault together and were too quick to laugh, drowning out Chris' topper "I never drink when I fly," of a Lois Lane line.

Because of the crowd's reaction Donner said he wanted to recut the film again. If the movie flopped, he said, "I'm going to Mexico, dig a hole, and jump in."

The next evening a similar extravaganza was held in New York. Chris attended that one as well. The second premiere attracted luminaries who ranged from Gilda Radner and Dick Cavett to New York governor Hugh Carey. Mario Puzo showed up wearing a gold-embossed Superman shirt, twirling around several times for photographers.

There were still four days to sweat before the opening.

If reviews could be deposited in a bank, *Superman* could have dropped in a billion dollars in goodwill the day it opened. For Chris the news was even better.

"This superproduction turns out to be prodigiously inventive and enjoyable, doubly blessed by sophisticated illusionists behind the camera and a brilliant new stellar personality in front of the camera—Christopher Reeve, a young actor at once handsome and astute enough to rationalize the preposterous fancy of a comic book hero in the flesh," wrote Gary Arnold in the *Washington Post*.

There was more, much more. In a four-thousand-word review of the film, Arnold also added: "Reeve's charm and assurance save the show from the potentially unfortunate consequences of epic pretensions. I can't think of another newcomer who ever shouldered a heavier burden of illusion, publicity, and commercial expectations. Reeve is such a skillful and discreetly ingratiating actor that he transforms the burden into a cheerful light workout, finessing his incredible identities as deftly as Superman might divert a runaway locomotive.

"Clark is wittily differentiated from Superman. Reeve varies his appearance, voice, and behavior just enough to make the masquerade credible. He has fun playing the roles straight, allowing the humor to emerge from the fundamental improbability of his character. His winning grin may establish a conspiratorial link with the audience, but it never violates the integrity of his character.

"Ultimately Reeve seems to resolve all the traits and conflicts that originate in Superman's impressional youth from the baby transported across countless solar systems, from an advanced but doomed civilization to the small-town teenager struggling to reconcile his otherworldly prowess with a homely American upbringing.

"This could be the start of an extraordinary career. It's not often that such an attractive appearance, good humor, and resourceful technique fuse in the presence of a single young actor."

Chris would have no excuse to mope on a beach this time around. *Newsweek* would cheer: "Christopher Reeve's entire performance is a delight. Ridiculously good-looking, with a face as sharp and strong as an ax blade, his bumbling, fumbling Clark Kent and omnipotent Superman are simply two styles of gallantry and innocence. And Margot Kidder is adorable . . . funny, raunchy and tender."

Newsweek said Harold Pinter would admire [Kidder's] impeccably timed pauses ("How big are you . . . tall are you . . . Do you . . . eat?).

Even Pauline Kael, who normally ignored commercial movies, would write in *The New Yorker*, "Christopher Reeve, the young actor chosen to play the lead in *Superman*, is the best reason to see the movie. He has an open-faced, deadpan style that's just right for a windup hero. Reeve plays innocent but not dumb, and the combination of his Pop jawline and physique with his unassuming manner makes him immediately likeable. In this role, Reeve comes close to being a living equivalent of comic-strip art."

Chris had tried to keep a low profile through the months leading up to the opening. Except for the obligatory premiere appearances and the press interviews, he holed up in New York, disappearing once for more than a week to captain a fifty-foot Swan sloop from Essex, Connecticut, to Bermuda for a Canadian businessman. After flying home, he would compare the straightforwardness of the elements he faced at sea to the movie business.

"If you're out five hundred miles off the coast of South Carolina and you see a force-ten gale coming, you know what you must do to survive it. Show business is devious, people maneuver, people play games. But on sea or in the air, it's clean, it's direct, and it's simple."

On the evening of December 15, as hundreds of critics began cheering his name and with *Superman* opening across America, lines of moviegoers snaking down the block and around corners, Chris tried to keep his soul. At Cooper Union Forum in New York City he hosted a concert of Vivaldi, Mozart, and Liszt. The music was performed by a group of heretofore unknown professional musicians. According to Kenneth Simsarian, organizer of the concert, "Chris did it because he once had dreams of being a concert pianist and certainly knows what it means to be an unknown."

The dollar figures being racked up by *Superman* at the box office meant that Chris could probably choose to read the phone book for his next film and get at least a million dollars for his presence. The first week ticket totals of more than $12 million were, at the time, the highest figure ever garnered by a motion picture in the week before Christmas. It would go on to break industry attendance records for any holiday period up to that date and would soon leap into an elite league of films—one of the top five grossing films ever and the biggest gross numbers ever for Warner Brothers (surpassing *The Exorcist*), eventually taking in more than $300 million worldwide.

There was but one sour note. Marlon Brando had filed suit against the Salkinds and Warner for $50 million. To get the film made, Alexander Salkind had made a major mistake, doling out percentage points that, in the end, exceeded more than a hundred percent, much as Zero Mostel had done when getting investors for his Broadway musical in the film *The Producers*. A Warner Brothers source told the author that Brando had been promised 11.3 percent of the profits against salary, Mario Puzo, 6 percent, and Richard Donner, 5 percent. But Warner's contract had the movie studio entitled to get 100 percent. The filmmakers evidently never believed the movie would show real profits, given its huge cost and had paid themselves handsomely "up front." The case would be settled three years later with Brando alone winding up with a reported $12 million.

The actor, whose previous roles had elevated him to mythic proportions, also received the worst notices of any major star in the movie. One critic accused him of "issuing pronouncements instead of speaking lines."

Brando aside, the rest of the cast was lauded. Vincent Canby wrote in the *New York Times* that "the brightest moments are those very broad ones supplied by Mr. Hackman, Mr. Beatty, and Miss Perrine, whose bosom submits to her bodice only with a fight."

The film's catch lines swept the nation, particularly in single bars. Superman's lines in his flight tour of Metropolis: ("I've got you, Miss Lane." She: "You've got me? Who's got you?") spoken over John Williams' elegant score were repeated with varying degrees of double entendre.

Chris began to get movie scripts—stacks of them, hundreds of them. He also began to get fan letters by the tens of thousands, many of them from women that were pornographic in content.

"Can Superman really screw when flying?" one letter read. Others asked him to fly into their bedroom and perform unusual sex acts with them. Chris told one writer, "I have a little file, and I keep the juicy ones." *Penthouse's Forum* magazine published a doctored photo of him flying, with a near naked woman inserted in place of Lois Lane that Chris called "a cheap shot."

He was not yet guarded in his comments. There were no attempts at mystery by the young star—and there would rarely be any. Chris Reeve has throughout his career always been more accessible than most major stars in Hollywood. When asked by *Playboy* in 1980 if he did drugs, Chris would say, "I occasionally smoke grass. I try to stay away from the snow. I think snow storms are bad for your health. But none of these things are essential or important in my life. It's strictly take it or leave it."

In another interview with the BBC, Chris would admit to first having sex at sixteen but saying he had "been dating since eleven." And he would candidly tell columnist Arthur Bell of the *Village Voice* that he had received an early morning obscene phone call from a male admirer who "invited me to perform certain sexual services." Calling Chris "the sweetie pie who plays the kid from Krypton" as well as "the 6'4", 225 pound sweetie pie [Bell liked the endearment] with blue eyes, black hair, a jutting jaw, artistic looking hands" as well as "fabulous lips" the seemingly starstruck interviewer wrote that Chris had complained to him that he now had "to sneak into Burger King through the back door."

Superman was nominated for three Academy awards—original score, sound, and visual effects. It would win for the latter. At the British Academy Awards, held a week before the U.S. ceremonies, Chris was given the Most Promising Newcomer award, a category not on the American Academy's list. At the same time he was also named one of the "top ten young men of the year" by the U.S. Junior Chamber of Commerce. Appropriately, it would be for "helping young boys deal with the trauma of a broken home."

After the Hollywood Oscar ceremonies, Chris went backstage and formed a semicircle with John Wayne and Cary Grant. Chris had never met Wayne and reached out to shake his hand. The two eyed each other, both noticing they were nearly the same height. Then after the introductions were made, Wayne turned to Cary Grant and said, "This is our new man."

Grant did not disagree. Chris thought it such a compliment he told the anecdote for months.

With the all-out raves for his performance in *Superman* (Chris said "I've got a lot of glue and tape, and I'm saving those reviews. I'm not ashamed to admit it") and the box office records it was setting, it's understandable that Chris felt that any movie he chose for his next role would be a hit just because of his presence in it. After thumbing through a stack of scripts and getting call after call from studio chiefs, he turned down several starring parts that, in retrospect, would have added to his bankability as a major film star.

He told his agent to "throw out the garbage . . . feel free to build a bonfire—a lot of the offers are so way out, they're just weird."

Chris knew whom he wanted to work with—"the Varsity: Alan Pakula, Sidney Pollack, Lumet, Michael Apted, Ritchie—that gang—Arthur Hiller, Colin Higgins. I want to work with the pros, the top team of experienced people—David Lean, George Cukor. I like the old masters."

One role he refused was the lead in *American Gigolo*. John Travolta had bowed out because he was committed to *Urban Cowboy*. (Chris had already refused that part.) A million-dollar offer was made, but Chris demurred. Later he would say he "found the idea of a man servicing older women for money quite distasteful." The role eventually went to Richard Gere and helped to make him a star.

Another film part, the lead in *Body Heat*, went to another friend from Juilliard, William Hurt. "I didn't think I'd be convincing as a seedy lawyer," Chris would say later. His agent was said to be "horrified" over the money his client was passing up. But Chris seemed to want to play a different type of leading man.

"They've had an awful lot of brooding leading men—complex, secretive characters played by guys like DeNiro, Hoffman, Pacino. I suppose I can offer a simpler alternative," Chris told the *Detroit News*.

Chris was reported to be making a film called *Dink Stover at Yale*. When that fell through, the papers wrote that he was about to sign for the remake of *Mutiny on the Bounty* in the Fletcher Christian role (Katharine Hepburn called the film's producers and lobbied for Chris to get the part). The movie, re-named *Bounty*, after being delayed four years, earned good critical notices for Mel Gibson.

"It was tempting," Chris said years later. "It had a fine Robert Bolt screenplay, Anthony Hopkins, and eighteen weeks in Tahiti, but . . . it wasn't for me. I need to get excited and I just couldn't feel it."

The script he did choose, the time-travel romance *Somewhere in Time* for Universal, was one which his agent and managers all urged him to turn down. Its tiny budget of $4 million (it eventually went a bit higher to $6 million) concerned his agent almost as much as the $400,000 fee his client was getting—less than half as much as he would have received for *American Gigolo*. (The crew was told it had to accept a 20 percent pay cut in order to work on the film.) Chris called it "my way to escape the cape" project. There was one good sign: The role had been coveted by Dustin Hoffman.

"My team to a man told me not to take the part," he told the *New York Times* as he arrived at the film's central shooting location, Mackinac Island, off Michigan's upper peninsula. "They said I should only do a movie directed by Michael Cimino (then the director of the moment, praised for his Academy Award–winning *The Deer Hunter*). It should be opposite Jane Fonda (she had just won an Oscar for *Coming Home*) or Barbra Streisand. But I like the character—a man who's incomplete. He has all the material things he needs, all the comforts, but he's missing a passionate commitment to something other than himself, and goes in search of it."

Rather than Jane Fonda, the costar playing his love interest, Elise McKenna, would be Jane Seymour. The British actress had first made a strong impression as the enigmatic Solitaire in the James Bond film *Live and Let Die* some six years earlier. She had also been featured in the three-hour premiere of a short-lived science fiction TV series, *Battlestar Galactica*. But she was far better known outside the United States. She was not a movie star of any great magnitude.

"I understand the risk I'm taking—or at least I think I do," Chris told Wayne Warga. "I'd rather head for deep water. Doing something very romantic is tricky—but then so is getting someone to fly. I welcome the challenge. In this film, it's an intense part where you have to bring out your emotional life, which is why I became an actor in the first place."

Mackinac Island presented several problems for Chris. The old resort, dominated by the Grand Hotel, bans cars but has a large population of horses—Percherons, saddle-breds, hackneys, and Kentucky high-steppers—to transport tourists around the island in carriages. That was also how the film crew had to travel. Chris, allergic to the four-legged beasts, avoided them by pedaling a green Schwinn bicycle to the locations.

"It's not exactly a small problem," Chris complained. "There are six hundred of them [the horses] on the island."

He sometimes forgot to take his allergy pills and would spend time before a scene dabbing his watery eyes with a tissue. When Chris arrived on the island, the hotel's publicist had rushed over with a horse-drawn carriage but was shooed away by producer Stephen Deutsch, who believed it could cause such an allergic reaction that the shooting schedule could be delayed.

Another problem was the horse manure itself, which vied with the island's famous lilacs for domination of the olfactory senses. A crew of four was employed by the hotel to scoop it all up. They collected between fifteen and twenty cartloads a day. Still another hindrance was the mosquitoes. An assistant on the film's set was assigned to spray the outdoor locales thoroughly before each take.

Seymour joked throughout the film about Chris' clumsiness. At one point he stepped on a pair of custom-made $400 shoes Seymour wore that had been replicated for the film's era. For the rest of the film's shooting, she teased Chris by calling him "Superfoot."

The film had such a low budget that the filmmakers rented a single hotel room for the three stars of the film to share as a dressing room (Christopher Plummer was the third principal). At one point, three of the period costumes were laid out on the bed in the room. A maid came along to turn the covers of the bed down, and seeing the three different sets of clothing, left three chocolates on the pillow.

Tourists jammed the island during the shooting, all trying to get a glimpse of Chris. "Eat the fudge, then see Chris Reeve," was how Chris spoke about the daily disruptions. Finally, he promised to tour the state ("Traverse City, Grand Rapids, Detroit") after the movie was over and sign autographs. That never took place, but he did show up at a girl's college the day after shooting ceased, dancing with coed after coed.

Somewhere in Time was an adaptation of Richard Matheson's 1975 novel *Bid Time Return*. The story takes place largely in 1912, with Chris' character of Richard Collier falling in love with the photograph of a dead actress (Seymour) and then traveling back in time to woo and win her love. John Barry did the score, relying heavily on Rachmaninoff's *Theme of Paganini* to create a lush soundtrack and composed a title song hoping to hit the pop charts. Jeannot Szwarc, a French director who had been credited with saving *Jaws II*, seemed an unlikely choice for director, but he understood the challenge.

"The old obstacles between lovers—marital vows, honor, duty—do not work anymore," he would say. "*Brief Encounter* was the last film that really worked with the obstacles of characters respecting marital vows. And if the girl is physically handicapped or dying as she is in so many 'love stories' it's a cheat. . . . We have a strong and original obstacle between our lovers. They are separated by time."

Szwarc had been offered a big-budget science fiction film at a higher fee by a studio. Like Chris, he had turned down more money to make what he believed was going to be a timeless romantic statement.

Chris had told Gene Siskel when he was beginning to film *Somewhere in Time*, "I'm sure there will be cynics in the audience who say, 'Oh, come on, this is ridiculous.' But those are the same people who think that Heidi is a little pain in the ass who is forever yodeling, and that the kids in *The Sound of Music* should have been drowned at the beginning of the picture."

Certainly there were many cynics among the nation's film critics when the film opened in October 1980. Gary Arnold, who had lauded Chris without reservation for *Superman*, now said, "Perhaps it's preferable that a young star as attractive as Christopher Reeve should blunder into a minor embarrassment like *Somewhere in Time*. The next time an equally swoony opportunity arises, he may be immune to the temptation."

Those were some of the nicer comments. "Reeve can't prevent his character . . . from degenerating into a lovelorn laughingstock," Arnold wrote. He called it "embedded in clichés," dismissing it as a "harmless laugher." He blamed the film's failure on Jeannot Szwarc, who he said "appears to go out of his way to make Reeve squirm."

Gene Siskel, who had pegged Chris as the next great American actor in earlier interviews, now seemed embarrassed by Chris' effort.

"He plays his character as earnestly as he played Superman, but the effect is all wrong," he wrote in the *Chicago Tribune*. "Reeve looks too bulky, too big, too cartoonish for the role. Then again, he is asked to do some outlandish things—stare into a tape recorder, sweat raindrops, and look searchingly into space."

"Christopher Reeve has become a sluggish, cardboard cut-out character," said Peter Brock in the *San Francisco Chronicle*. He called *Somewhere in Time* "a pretty postcard—but no genuine human greeting has been written."

Vincent Canby wrote, "Unfortunately, his unshadowed good looks, granite profile, bright naivete and eagerness to please—the qualities that made him such an ideal Superman—look absurd here."

One critic took the opportunity to essay a very personal attack on Chris, even making fun of his walk, which was indeed unusual as a result of the Osgood Schlatter's disease he had suffered as a child, and saying his voice sounded like someone "who had inhaled a helium balloon."

Variety, the show business trade paper, was one of the few to like it, saying Chris was "a fine actor with both star power and versatility . . . a first-rate and exciting romantic lead, able to handle both comedy and drama with equal skill." That essay was undoubtedly the only review Chris showed to his mother.

Though the box office receipts were negligible, *Somewhere in Time* would be reborn years later as a cult film. Today a *Somewhere in Time* fan club exists, with more than seven thousand members worldwide. Groups of college coeds frequently rent the video for its unabashed romanticism. While undoubtedly pleasing Chris and Jeannot Szwarc, this late blooming of the film couldn't have been foreseen back in 1979.

Gae Exton didn't go with Chris to Michigan for the filming of the romantic fiasco. She had a career, and that was fine with her lover.

"I can't do with pretty girls who are just 'good company,'" Chris told one interviewer at the time. "The woman who is doing nothing with her life is not for me.

"She is the only person I want to share my life with," he later added in an interview with Rona Barrett. "Gae's got brains to match her looks, and she doesn't give a flying leap about being the girlfriend of Superman. If I were to tell her, 'I'm really tired of making movies, I want to be a bricklayer,' she'd say, 'Terrific.'"

Exton became pregnant in March 1979. The child was unplanned, and she would say later, "It was the nicest mistake we ever made." As it is with most pregnant women, her condition was impossible to hide. The press soon began to refer to its upcoming birth as "the Superbaby." Chris and Exton seemed to feel no need for marital union.

"Having been married once, I'm in no hurry to do it again, she told *Us* magazine. Chris and I have an excellent relationship the way it is, and we don't want to change it. We're a couple in everybody's eyes—I think most people forget we're not married."

Chris and Exton believed their firstborn would be a girl. They began referring to the expected child as "Kate," telling friends they were sure it was a girl— she was prenamed after Katharine Hepburn. Their prediction would turn out to be embarrassingly wrong.

Matthew was born—blond and blue-eyed just like his father—at London's Welbeck Hospital on December 20, 1979. He weighed seven pounds, five ounces. Chris, who professed to be squeamish at the sight of blood, had planned not to be present ("I thought I'd phone in from my club"), but changed his mind at the last minute.

"There was a great satisfaction when Matthew came forth and I was the first person he saw," Chris said later. "He was placed on Gae's stomach and opened one eye and took a look at me. The first human he saw was me! That was the kind of thrill that is really indescribable, and I think I would really have missed something if I hadn't been there. It strengthens the bond between the three of you tremendously."

Chris was saddened by one event that often results from fame. He tried to telephone his father to let him know his son's name. He couldn't reach him for several days, and by the time he did his father had already learned the name from a television news report.

"Dad passed it over, but I knew there was a certain hurt there," Chris told reporter Fred Robbins.

Though Chris was present for the birth, and ordered two cases of champagne for Exton's room to share with visitors, it didn't stop him from flying immediately to Switzerland after Matthew's birth to ski. He said it was his only time off from filming *Superman II*, and he needed the vacation. Exton didn't seem to mind.

"He works so hard, and besides, afterbirth blues were setting in and I didn't want him to see me weepy," she loyally told *People*.

Chris was furious about one report on the birth of Matthew. A magazine had called his son "illegitimate."

"He's not illegitimate," Chris fumed to one writer. "His name is Reeve. He calls me Daddy. I was in the delivery room when he was born. I'm with him twenty-four hours a day when I'm not working."

Exton didn't seem to be bothered by the label. She would express the desire to have a second child, but this time with the benefit of marriage.

"One illegitimate child is fine," she said, "but two is, well, tacky."

Chris saw it differently. He had an extended metaphor for marriage which he didn't hesitate to give: "A wife is an oxygen tank strapped on your back. A lover is the beautiful tropical fish. You can't do without the oxygen tank, but you went down underwater to find something else, that beautiful purple fish. A wife should hold that same fascination as the tropical fish. She should not be something that supports your life, but *is* your life. But I don't see that happening in many marriages."

The press didn't care what Chris said. Several reports had the two marrying in April 1980, "just after completing *Superman II*." They said that Exton was "finally free" because her divorce from David Iveson was final. The gossip columnists wrote that the ceremonies would be performed by one Franklin

Reeve, "Christopher's father, who has a justice of the peace license." The ceremonies would take place they claimed, at Franklin's home, "in Higganum, Connecticut." And, promised Jack Martin, in his *New York Post* column, "Robin Williams will be best man!"

6

*"Imagine, Superman changing
diapers!"*

—MODERN SCREEN

As Chris settled into domestic life with Exton and
Matthew, he lived much more stylishly than he had
in his West Eighty-third Street days. The two had a
duplex co-op penthouse apartment, still on the West
Side, but on West Seventy-eighth Street, just around
the corner from the American Museum of Natural
History. It wasn't *Architectural Digest* beautiful, but it
had a working fireplace, a library, skylights, and ten-
foot windows. Sailing and Broadway play posters
filled the walls. Surprisingly, there were no memen-
tos from *Superman* visible anywhere. Chris had a
cedar fence built around the perimeter of the penthouse's garden for Matthew's safety. A Scottish au
pair lived in. In London's Chelsea district on Knightsbridge Mews they rented a five-story town house
with rear garden from the actor Denholm Elliott. A
small house in the Hollywood hills, with the obligatory swimming pool and Mercedes, completed the
new lifestyle.

At the nearby Van Nuys Airport, where he kept his
planes—there were now three—Chris had a fledgling

charter service called Reeve Air (Slogan: "Reeve Air gets you there"). Chris and two pilot friends would chauffeur corporate executives around the country in one of his planes whenever they found time. It didn't hurt business when the passengers went home and told their spouses that they had just been piloted by Christopher Reeve.

"When they come out to the airport and see that Superman is the pilot, I can't get them to buckle their seat belts," Chris complained laughingly to a reporter.

Exton proclaimed Chris to be a super dad. "He really loves the baby. He can get a meal together for him and help him eat. He dresses him and takes him to the park. He even changes diapers—but he doesn't like it too much."

The magazine *Modern Screen* seemed stunned by this revelation, "Imagine, *Superman* changing *diapers!*" it italicized.

Exton gushed to the fan magazine that soon they would "get married, buy a house, some horses, and some dogs, and have more children. Then, of course, we'll live happily ever after."

Chris told a different story to another interviewer: "Both Gae and I have been burned to some extent by marriage. My parents divorced when I was three. Gae had a rotten first marriage and resolved never to marry again. It's no big deal."

He seemed to shrug off his future, concluding, "By the time he [Matthew] goes to school, I'll probably be washed up anyway."

Committed to making his unconventional family life work, a direction which often affects children from broken homes, Chris then said, "Matthew is one of the nicest presents that's ever happened in my life. Going home every day is like Christmas; there's this kid who thinks you're wonderful and you don't have to tell him any different. I don't look at it as a responsibility, but as a joy to be involved in while introducing this new person to the world.

"Every day you see new things through his eyes, the simplicity, like how a blanket can be fascinating for three hours! And the rest of us need airplanes, telephones, Jacuzzis, and all this junk we need to keep ourselves alive."

Chris also believed Matthew had to be given the opportunity to be his own person. "It's important for a father to forget a kid isn't just the chance for an improved version of yourself. Robin Williams tells me that all the time.

"[Matthew] is one side of my life that balances out the other, which is looking for adventure. I've had a long time being single, messing around, having good fun, and getting into trouble, and now to have some security as well is a very nice counterbalance."

That Chris was still very much in love with Exton and committed to his view of what a normal family life should be was evident. That he was still afraid of a legal commitment because of the terrible childhood he'd experienced was a fear he would admit to several times. And Matthew couldn't change that fear.

Instead of marriage, he expressed his love for his son by guesting on the new TV series *The Muppet Show*, spoofing his superhero character, or appearing as Prince Charming (opposite Bernadette Peters) on Shelley Duvall's cable show, *Faerie Tale Theatre*. Matthew was more impressed by those efforts than if Superman himself had flown through the window of their Central Park apartment.

Nuclear family aside, Chris still found time to behave a bit wildly at times—particularly when Robin Williams was around. The two did a silent cameo together on an April 1981 *Saturday Night Live*, then turned up on the cover of an invitation for a New York nightclub's BLT party two weeks later. The initials stood for "Black Tie, Lingerie, and Toga." Chris and Robin wore tuxedos and roller skates; the women with them wore garter belts and merry widows. They were seen around New York so much at night that the *New York Daily News* called it "The Chris and Robin Show."

The Salkinds doubled Chris' salary to $500,000 for *Superman II.* They had no choice. His contract had been allowed to lapse, which gave Chris' agents more clout in the negotiations. The Salkinds at first tried to take him to court, saying that Chris "has failed and refused to accept payments which were and are being tendered to him in connection with the completion of *Superman II.*" But Chris' lawyers were quick to point out that the original contract was for both movies being shot simultaneously. It wasn't Chris' fault, they argued, that the Salkinds had run out of both money and time and failed to complete the two films. While Chris was in Japan, promoting the first *Superman*, the father-and-son movie moguls capitulated.

The half-million dollars were still just fifty percent of Gene Hackman's salary, and though it was Chris who had dominated the first film and would be depended upon to do the same for the second, it would be Hackman who got top billing. Brando ("will not be missed," *Variety* would snipe) and Donner were both out. Their lawsuits against the Salkinds were still pending. The legal wrangling at times halted production. Margot Kidder's part was cut. She got sixth billing because she was a bad politician. She had unwisely chewed out both of the Salkinds, accusing them of both "cheating" her out of $40,000 and "blatant dishonesty."

"I love Lois Lane," Kidder bravely told a reporter. "I could play her till I die, but I'm not going to die if I don't play her."

Much of the footage that had been shot by Donner

(the film had been nearly fifty percent complete) was scrapped, and Richard Lester, who had been omnipresent during the latter part of the first film's shooting, took over for the seven-month schedule.

"We missed Dick Donner very much, all of us," Chris told the *Los Angeles Times* after shooting was completed. "Throughout the film we tried to preserve his style and intentions. It was very much as if he were the architect who'd done the blueprint and we were just the contractors."

Chris said that Lester had "done a great job of preserving Donner's tone. Even so, he doesn't want his name on the film. And I understand that. After all, he was just carrying out someone else's blueprint. I hope if Donner sees the film and likes it, he'll have his name on it. There's got to be somebody's name there, or otherwise they'll think it was directed by one of Pinewood Studio's cleaning ladies."

Lester's name appeared prominently as director in the credits when *Superman II* opened in America in June 1981. Donner, who had the right to "A Richard Donner Film" under the title, had his name totally removed from the credits.

One of Lester's directorial flourishes was transforming villainess Sarah Douglas' character. In the first film she had been an asexual robotic space alien. Now she became a kinky provocateur wearing a costume of leather and organza with black boots that stopped at mid-knee.

"Someone asked me how I got so evil," Douglas would say, "Well, they got me up too early in the morning, put a short wig on over my hair, and put white makeup and black lipstick. It took two hours, and after all that you *feel* evil."

The filmmakers also devised a new way to film the flying scenes. Instead of using cranes with wires attached to a harness, the special effect wizard Zoran Perisic (who had gotten the technical achievement

Oscar for the first *Superman*) devised a new system in which the actors were placed on their stomachs in plastic body molds which were attached to a forty-foot-high pole. The pole carried the actors over a series of runners that gave the flying sequence a "smoother look" according to the film's technical department.

Terrence Stamp, who played the evil General Zod in the first and second outings, took his part in *Superman II* very seriously. He told a writer that he had studied films of Hitler, copying *Der Fuehrer's* expressions of bored invincibility for the scene where he took over the White House.

On a per-day basis, even more money was spent on *Superman II* than the first time around, considering that about half of the footage had been shot and paid for in 1977 (Donner had shot 1,400,000 feet of film—the average film shoots just under 400,000). Shooting locales included Norway, Niagara Falls, Paris (where Chris' character foiled the attempted nuclear bombing of the Eiffel Tower), and St. Lucia, in the West Indies.

"They didn't stint on money for this picture," Chris said when promoting the movie. "We flew with a big unit to the island of St. Lucia for just one scene. It was for a shot of Superman landing in a rain forest to pick a flower to take to Lois. Terribly romantic and a great scene for the picture, but I hate to think what it cost."

In Norway, Chris got in hot water. The Norwegian government was up in arms.

"We were doing this scene where I'm walking back and forth in solitude among the vast Arctic wastes," he told writer Clifford Terry. "We're about ten minutes from the North Pole—way the hell up there, five and a half hours north of Oslo by car. We're staying at this old hotel and having a gay time getting drunk every night and playing billiards and having these incredible meals—wonderful time—and I'm doing this shot. I'm standing out in the middle of the road and there's nothing but mountains and snow and polar bears, and this Norwegian reporter shows up, having tracked the company all the way from Oslo to get a quote from Superman."

Chris said when the reporter asked him how he liked working in Norway, he answered that "he loved being in the middle of nowhere." The "middle of nowhere" quote seemed to incense the Norwegians, and Chris was forced to do a mea culpa to their tourist board.

"What Christopher Reeve was really saying was that after the hustle and bustle of the big city, how refreshing it is to come to your country, with its peaceful, tranquil solitude," Chris said he told the Norwegians.

Again Chris was game to do virtually any stunt the filmmakers asked of him. One dangerous sequence required him to hang over the rapids leading to Niagara Falls, his body rigid, for a flying shot. When the scene was threatened by the flashbulbs of camera-carrying tourists, Chris had the crew ask them to stop. When they wouldn't, he struck a deal with them. He told the gawkers he'd sign autographs and pose for pictures until everyone was satisfied if only they would let him finish the scene. The flashes stopped. Chris signed for two hours.

Chris now said he was even amenable to a third fly-by.

"No question. I never forget how much I owe Superman. If it hadn't been for him, I wouldn't be talking to you. I'd probably be out there parking cars."

After filming the second *Superman* epic, Chris again turned down a $1 million-plus movie offer to spend July and August doing serious theater at the Williamstown Theater Festival in the northwest corner of Massachusetts. It was the first time he'd been back since 1968.

Williamstown would become an annual summer ritual. Telling the press he needed "breathing space," he played consecutive major roles in three classics: *The Cherry Orchard*, *The Front Page*, and *The Heiress*. The million-dollar movie part he could have had was exchanged for a salary of $225 per week.

Without taking a break from the stage and refusing several more lucrative film roles, Chris then agreed to star on Broadway in Lanford Wilson's Chekhovian drama, *The Fifth of July*. The salary was better than at Williamstown—$5,000 a week or 7.5 percent of ticket sales, whichever was greater. The part he chose to play—an embittered homosexual and paraplegic Vietnam veteran, Kenneth Talley—was far from the Broadway roles typically chosen to showcase movie stars, which Chris, like it or not, had become. The theater piece was a sequel to the play *Talley's Folly*, which had won the Pulitzer Prize.

The role was as challenging as contemporary theater gets. Chris' part required him to portray an unlikeable character who was undergoing internal turmoil. As Kenneth Talley, Chris had to decide whether or not he should sell his family's failing farm and thus admit another defeat but different from the kind he had experienced in Vietnam.

"The media thinks *Superman* was the focal point of my life," he told writer Victoria Breen. "It's not. When the playwright who'd won the Pulitzer Prize in 1980 [Lanford Wilson] called and asked if I'd like the lead in his next play, I just said, 'Oh, my God! Yes!' I didn't care if the part was a Martian, a taxi driver, or a Fig Newton! I didn't think, 'I'm going to play a gay cripple just to blow people's minds.' I don't care about my public image or planning some crafty campaign strategy. I just wanted to know, 'Is this a good play where the audience will have an emotional and funny experience?' "

When a reporter asked him if playing a gay man onstage might alienate some of the millions of fans who'd flocked to his straight-arrow *Superman* roles, Chris was quick to answer.

"You'd have to be a real bigot to think that what goes on that stage is distasteful. I think the relationship between Kenneth and Jed (played by Jeff Daniels) is about the most beautiful homosexual relationship ever written for the theater."

Surprisingly, gay men would protest Chris playing the part, feeling that it should have gone to a gay actor. This led to *After Dark* magazine's sly comment that perhaps it should also "be played by a crippled Vietnam veteran" too. Chris later said he chose the role partly for its sexuality.

"It was difficult for people who identified me with *Superman* to come to the theater and see me sitting on stage, and in the first scene my boyfriend comes in and kisses me on the lips," he told Andy Warhol's *Interview* after the run. "Audiences used to gasp. They couldn't deal with it. But they stayed through the course of the play and its humanity and the emotion got to them and they came backstage afterward totally blown away."

Chris grew a beard for the part. Inevitably, he was greeted on the streets of New York with, "Hey, Superbeard!" By now he was being stopped by fans and asked for autographs. He would sometimes attempt to finesse the obligation when he took Matthew to Central Park to play. He now tried to remember to carry his son on his *right* arm, so it wouldn't be free for signing. He was a reluctant movie star, always stressing his acting credentials.

"Today you can't be a star without being an actor. This is not the era of Tab Hunter," he told the *Washington Post*.

"There is a whole category of leading men—Ryan O'Neal, Lee Majors—who don't care anything about the process of acting. It's not that I'm so good, but I've always wanted to be a real actor. I've had a lot of training, and I want to use it."

To show he was "a real actor" Chris made sure there was no mention of *Superman* in the *Fifth of July* theater playbill.

Chris said some of the "real" actors he admired were, "Katharine Hepburn—my guardian angel— and Albert Finney, Nicol Williamson, and Richard Chamberlain . . . all of them mix stage and film work. I think that's the right thing to do."

Chris took the role of Kenneth Talley in *The Fifth of July* not because his name would be above the title (the first time in his life he had been given that honor in any stage production), but because he wanted to have the chance to experience the kind of normal life he had missed as a child. For the first time he was part of a natural family unit—mother, father, child. Acting in a Broadway play was a job—certainly a demanding job, but one which offered regular hours. Every evening after the show, he tried to get home (via the Eighth Avenue subway) in time for Johnny Carson's monologue. Exton would often greet him with her specialty, steaming, soothing clam chowder, which he sipped in front of a roaring fire. Late at night, he read the authors his father had most recently suggested, including John McPhee (he had taught Franklin at Princeton). He did the normal things that any father did—roll a ball to Matthew and wait for it to come back. Most mornings he would play the piano for more than an hour, learning more about his favorite composers, Ravel and Debussy, and at times practicing *Clair de Lune* over and over. His search for a regular life had ended for the moment. For Chris, life was as normal and as satisfying as it would ever be.

Chris was proud of his ability as a pianist. When he appeared on Merv Griffin's television show in early 1981, he played an original piano composition he had just written, called *Ode to the Sailplane*. He soon joined an irregular high-stakes poker group, playing badly but having fun at neighbor Carly Simon's place. One could say that except for the legal documents which sanctified marriage, Chris had the family and routine he had been seeking.

All the same, Chris had rushed into *Fifth of July*. He had only a seventeen-day rehearsal period and no out-of-town tryouts before audiences began streaming in for the previews. He admitted to being "wooden" on its opening night, November 5, 1980.

"The critics were right. . . . I'm growing into the role, but now I'm into it," he told Rex Reed shortly after it opened.

Chris had researched his part by taking up residence in a Veterans Administration hospital in order to experience the daily routines of paraplegics. He also befriended Mike Sulsona, who had lost both his legs in Vietnam. The veteran showed Chris how to use artificial legs and walk with arm braces.

"He taught me the meaning of optimism," Chris later said of Sulsona. "He's lost his legs, but he's become a painter, sculptor, playwright, he's married and has a three-month-old baby. He's become somebody."

Chris admitted that his name had been put above the title of the play to sell tickets. Warner—the same Warner that had bankrolled *Superman*—was the chief backer of the drama, and it wanted a principal who would assure success. William Hurt—Chris' Juilliard pal—had played the part in its original incarnation, but was still largely unknown at that time.

Chris was the first to credit cast members like Jeff Daniels, Swoosie Kurtz, and Amy Wright with having "flashier parts" than he did. He told Reed it was "the thing I'm proudest of in my career so far. I keep throwing the passes, and the other characters keep making the touchdowns."

In rehearsal, Lanford Wilson had written one line which read, "Superfaggot strikes again." Chris had it deleted as soon as he read it.

The young actor told one writer he'd take any role if it was a good one, no matter what the character's sexual orientation, declaring, "I'd play a drag queen if it was a great part."

His notices in *Fifth of July* were mixed, depending largely on whether the critic who reviewed it saw it opening night or a few days later.

Howard Kissel of the garment industry trade paper, *Women's Wear Daily*, wrote that Chris "gives a sensitive performance, punctuated by a scathing wit. Reeve makes a deeply believable part of the character rather than just a way of getting laughs." Jack Kroll in *Newsweek* noted that "the love of Ken and Jed [is] the most natural, touching—and funniest—homosexual relationship yet seen in a Broadway play. . . . Christopher Reeve, whose charming performance in the movie *Superman* was underrated, is a young but long-committed stage actor, and he's effective and winning."

But the *New York Times*' Frank Rich, then the most powerful critic on Broadway, would write, "Mr. Mason [director Marshall W. Mason] has made some serious casting errors starting with Christopher Reeve in the pivotal role originated by William Hurt." He would go on to say, "Mr. Reeve works earnestly, and in the later scenes, he lets us see some of Kenny's pain. But by then it's too late. His placid face never suggests someone who has lost his legs in the hell of Southeast Asia, and his voice lacks presence and maturity."

Rich's remarks hurt Chris. He was quick to defend himself in an interview with columnist Earl Wilson.

"I became acquainted with a real Vietnam amputee whose philosophy is optimism," Chris told Wilson. "They don't want people thinking they're sad. I didn't think an audience wanted two hours of me being sad."

Many critics couldn't separate Chris' Superman image from the play and dwelled on it. *Time* made sure to mention that "through the marvel of commercial casting, cinema's Superman has become a homosexual cripple. Reeve gives his role the old college try—fervent amateurism." And Joel Siegel would note just a few hours after the drama's New Apollo Theater opening on WABC-TV, "Christopher Reeve may be Superman on the screen, but he was all Clark Kent tonight."

"You haven't made it until you've had a few bad reviews," Chris told a writer in response. "There's a little resentment by people who don't understand I've been in the theater a long time. I've been in eighty-five plays and only four movies, and they still ask, 'What's this Superman guy doing on Broadway?'"

Chris tried to take the constant attention by the media in stride. Sometimes he would escape the pressure by grabbing costar Jeff Daniels—the two speeding to Chris' Cherokee in New Jersey—and flying to Vermont for a day of skiing, then zooming back just in time to go onstage.

The Fifth of July would go on to be nominated for five Tony Awards (Kurtz would win for best actress) and would run—501 performances—longer than any other Lanford Wilson play. Chris left the play in June 1981 to rush back to Massachusetts, where he appeared in armor and helmet as Achilles in *The Greeks*, a five-hour classical drama at the Williamstown Theater Festival.

Chris was killed in the first act of *The Greeks* but had to wait around each evening for three more hours—usually lying down on the backstage grass and contemplating the rural beauty of the Berkshire Hills—just to take his bow. He explained how the two-stage Williamstown Theater (the largest one has 521 seats) held such an appeal for him in the *New York Times*, crediting much of it to its artistic director and founder, Yale professor Nikos Psacharopoulos.

"Nikos sent me the script, but I told him I'd do it without even reading it," Chris said of *The Greeks*. "I said, 'Nikos, tell me what to do and I'll do it.' This is the first classical part I've played since I was a drama student at Juilliard in 1974. You can't come on like a plumber. For me, Williamstown is like a continuing adult-education program."

He added, "Nikos hires names only if they fit the bill. Donny Osmond will not play Othello here."

Chris said he also liked the low-key life available to him in this corner of Massachusetts near the borders of both New York and Vermont. "I come here to escape. I wander around the town barefoot, and nobody bothers me. Those of us who are 'names' get enough attention elsewhere."

Escapes aside, any serious actor would have leaped at the chance to be in *The Greeks*. The spectacular staging of the production included sixty professional actors and a ten-piece orchestra, all appearing for a fraction of their normal fee. *The Greeks* cast that summer included some of the cream of the American stage: Celeste Holm, Edward Herrmann, Kate Burton, Blythe Danner (and her then very young daughter, Gwyneth Paltrow), Carrie Nye, and Donald Moffat.

"Chris only made movies to support his theater habit," an official of the Williamstown Theater Festival joked to the author. With the exception of 1982 and 1993, when movie schedules conflicted, Chris would perform at Williamstown every year between 1980 and 1994.

* * *

After *The Greeks'* short run he began shooting the film version of yet another theater hit, the mystery thriller *Deathtrap*. On Broadway he had been replaced as Kenneth Talley by *The Waltons'* Richard Thomas. Thomas would also re-create the role for a cable television movie of the play a few years later. Laraine Newman of *Saturday Night Live* fame replaced Swoosie Kurtz at about the same time.

Chris believed that *Superman II* was better than the first one. He was able to get an early print and screened it for the cast and crew of the *Fifth of July*. He told them he thought it had a "lighter tone, more action and humor . . . it's not so pretentious." The *Fifth of July* ensemble gave it a standing ovation.

The Salkinds, knowing the Superman fable was presold and already expecting great reviews, took an unprecedented motion picture gambit with the sequel. The film had actually performed in some international markets better than it had in the United States. Shrewdly, the entrepreneurial Salkinds had Warner Brothers distribute the film *backward*, opening the film outside America (the first showings were in Australia and Johannesburg, where it set South African box office records) in December 1980 before putting it into theaters in the United States midway through 1981.

Again, there were several benefit showings in the U.S. for Special Olympics. Warner Brothers repeated its lobbying triumph of the first film by getting the Reagan administration to allow a pre-screening brunch to be set up on the lawn of the vice president's house. George Bush took several opportunities to be photographed with the tall movie star who now personified the Man of Steel to the world.

Chris, who had arrived at the brunch with both Gae Exton and Matthew, was asked by a reporter covering the event if he was pleased with his acting in the movie.

"You can't really ask an actor if he likes his own work. If you say yes, you sound conceited. If you say no, you sound insincere. I think the audiences will like it."

Exton, in a ruffled minidress, carried seventeen-month-old Matthew on one arm. He was described in a newspaper the next day as "flaxen-haired and blue-eyed, with his name tag stuck on his back." A local scribe asked Exton if their son would be Superman when he grew up.

"No, he's going to be a lawyer," Exton said adamantly.

"He can be his daddy's lawyer," a friend of Exton's added.

"I tell you, with all of them taking percentages—lawyers, agents—" Exton said before thinking of what her remarks might mean and cutting herself off in mid-sentence.

The wait that the American Superman fans had endured seemed to be worth it if the critics were to be believed. In the *New York Times* Vincent Canby loved it. "It's that rare film phenomenon—a movie far better than the one that prompted it." David Denby in *New York* magazine called it the "best spectacle movie of the season" and wrote "just as before, Christopher Reeve's little smile and charming modesty makes the conceit work. By openly enjoying his role, by showing an actor's pleasure in the notion that putting on glasses makes one a eunuch and taking them off a stud, Reeve takes away the queasiness that we might feel; he turns the fantasy into a sophisticated joke. With his suits that fit awkwardly, his heavy shoulders drawn up in embarrassment, Reeve as Clark Kent is like an athlete at a press conference—abashed, out of it. Encased in those ridiculous blue-and-red tights, however, his bulk is no longer a burden; he's muscular, but lithe, clean but not square, and when he raises his arms and glides into flight . . . he's beautiful."

The *Los Angeles Times'* Sheila Benson called it "the most interesting *Superman* yet." The praise was not a left-handed compliment. "The film's fun comes from character, dialogue, and performance, not effects [though] there are, of course, enough effects to fill a dozen Saturday matinee serials."

Of Chris she said, "In his two roles, Reeve is even better than he was in the first film, boyish and mannish, torn between his love for Lois and his love and duty to mankind. (Has Reeve varied the Clark Kent role slightly? It feels that way.) His moment of revelation is directed like an old vaudeville turn, a change of character with the actor's back to you. When Clark Kent finally drops all pretenses and turns around to face Lois as Superman, with no intervening phone booth, the moment pays off perfectly. (A look around the audience at this moment found wish fulfillment reflected on more than one rapt, upturned face.)"

Warner Brothers mounted an unsuccessful campaign over the winter in an attempt to get Chris an Academy Award nomination. Taking out full-page ads in industry trade magazines, the ads quoted David Ansen of *Newsweek*: "Good as they all are, the comic-heroic mixture wouldn't jell without Christopher Reeve's sweet, courtly presence at its center. . . . Reeve's bashful gallantry is thoroughly winning."

After being passed over for the nomination, Chris was interviewed by Gene Siskel, who described him as "super mad," writing "he denies it, but don't believe him."

Siskel added that the Academy had also added insult to injury by not yet contacting Chris for membership in the Academy of Motion Picture Arts and Sciences.

"I wasn't expecting anything," Chris told Siskel

about not being nominated, "but it would be nice if performances could be judged on merit alone and without regard to the kind of film they're in, so that it would be acceptable if you give a good performance in what turns out to be a big box office film.

"Don't portray me as personally wounded, because I didn't expect to win anything. When Warner Brothers told me they were going to mount an Oscar campaign for me this year, I said, 'Save your bucks. Spend them on someone else. It's hopeless.' "

Superman II would eventually earn 80 percent of the amount taken in by the first movie. The first week's $24 million take was a record, surpassing *The Empire Strikes Back*. That figure is somewhat misleading, since it was up against both the huge numbers of the original and had to spend most of the summer fighting for the same audience with *Raiders of the Lost Ark*, the year's eventual box office winner.

There were other rewards. Chris' image now appeared on hundreds of products. Warner Brothers was trying to break *Star Wars*' merchandising record of $400 million in sales, and Chris now got a tiny royalty on each sale of a doll or calendar.

At the conclusion of the credits for *Superman II* the final line read "*Superman III* is coming soon." When the Salkinds were asked by the press how soon was soon, they shrugged their shoulders. In truth, they had no idea.

After leaving *The Fifth of July*, Chris' frequent separations from Gae Exton because of various stage plays and movie schedules shot in unusual locales, and their unusual situation—a child without marriage while proclaiming tranquil domesticity—inevitably led to press rumors that Chris was involved with other women. One of them he was reported to be seeing while filming *Superman II* was Koo Stark, the soft-core porn star who had become famous for dating Britain's Prince Andrew. "Chris and Koo are old pals," asserted the supermarket tabloid *The Star*, adding that Gae Exton was "more than a little miffed."

Chris claimed he and Exton had an understanding. "Sometimes in a year I might spend three months away. But there will be no bed checks, no calls at six A.M. to see who's there. Men just don't want to be nailed down. . . . A smart woman knows the more rope you play out, the more a man feels he doesn't have to be there—and the more likely he is to come back."

Chris said he "dated" women other than Exton when they were separated by continents. He claimed to always send her a telegram to warn her to ignore the reports that connected his name with other women in the gossip columns—there was no romance.

"Before I met Gae, there was a period of hyperactivity. I got around at lightning speed, put in a lot of miles. But when I met her, I made a choice and it worked. It continues to work well. When you have something good at home, you don't stray."

Despite his protestations, a celebrity columnist would write at the time, "Chris and Gae Exton are together, 'but just barely' say friends."

Determined not to be typecast as Superman and knowing there was already a third superhero effort on the drawing boards, Chris began playing another gay part, this time in a movie. In the $10.5 million budgeted *Deathtrap*, he would not only play Michael Caine's psychopathic lover but shock some *Superman* fans by kissing Caine—who spent much of the film clad in a $2,500 Sulka robe and a pair of $300 Sulka pajamas—full on the mouth. Chris' passionate manner with Caine was far more erotic than any scene he had ever shared with Margot Kidder.

"Michael and I had a real *La Cage aux Folles* routine going off-camera to get in the mood," he joked to *People*.

Deathtrap is a whodunit thriller about a playwright who kills his wife (played by Dyan Cannon in the movie) for her money so he can be free to live with his male lover in style. Interestingly, in its original stage version, one of the chief investors had been Claus von Bulow, who would soon be accused and tried for the crime of putting his wife in a long-running coma for her fortune.

Always the assiduous researcher, Chris spent several days with criminal psychologists at the Bellevue Medical Center in New York City.

Later in life, Chris would sometimes refer to the parts in *Somewhere in Time*, *Fifth of July*, *Deathtrap*, and the film that followed it, *Monsignor*, as "my weird period." His calculated attempt to escape the image of the superhero, while certainly laudatory for a serious actor, in retrospect would fail. Though he would play against type in role after role, there would inevitably be comparisons with the superhero he had created. In the end, the attempts cost him great sums of money that could have been earned from a series of sure-fire larger-than-life movie roles. In fact, other than *Superman*, Chris has never played that type of action hero on a motion picture screen, usually opting for films that are adapted from stage plays, films that are period pieces—with the requisite costumes which are anathema to modern audiences, films that are adapted from classic literature, or films that mocked his image.

"I wouldn't take a part unless it was weird," Chris told writer Judith Michaelson. "I had a little weirdness period. Not only am I not a romantic here, but if you give me a script, I've got to be either psychotic, homosexual, or in some other strange way corrupt."

Chris said it was his "pompous, self-important

way" of telling the public "screw you, I'll tell you who I am, so don't you tell me."

While Christopher Reeve would repeatedly claim to interviewers that money or the idolatry that mass audiences impose on a major star were neither important nor desired, there must have been times when he regretted that posture. In the years ahead, as his stature at the box office began to fade, there would be times when a screen role he really wanted was passed on to a brighter star strictly for those commercial reasons. The defeats would be hard to swallow.

Chris was an actor of the first rank until the late eighties. In the early 1980s, he could have had nearly any role he asked for, and the role of Clifford Anderson in *Deathtrap* was a great part. It was also the sort of role from which a "movie star"—the type who reads the gross box office receipts in *Variety* each weekend—would walk quickly away.

There were indeed good reviews for *Deathtrap*, and Chris would get to work for Sidney Lumet, a director he had always admired. The twenty-five-year film veteran treated the shooting schedule like a stage play, scheduling daily rehearsals, an exercise Chris was used to but which Caine despised. On the first day on the set Lumet told him the reason he had gotten the part because "anyone who can make me believe they're Superman can be in my movie."

The ticket sales on its mid-March 1982 opening weekend were considered okay. *Deathtrap*'s $2.2 million first weekend ticket sales in 341 theaters were considered decent, considering the film's content. A murder mystery containing a subtle gay theme and set almost entirely inside a single room on a Long Island gentleman's windmill farmhouse was not something to draw in Hollywood's idea of its core audience. "Core" to tinseltown was two teenagers on a Friday night date in Kansas. Its final ticket sales barely nudged over $20 million, respectable for the genre but barely profitable for the Warner Brothers studio.

On the night of its opening, Chris took Franklin to a private midnight screening of the film at New York's Criterion theater. Franklin, who rarely attended movies, rubbed shoulders with Chris' peers, which included the likes of Lauren Bacall, Lena Horne, and Cher. The next day the *New York Post* ran a picture of the two of them together, calling Franklin a "Superdad" and commenting, "Doesn't he look too young to be the father of Superman?"

Chris' notices were as good as anything he'd ever received in theatrical films, including the *Superman* movies.

David Sterritt in the *Christian Science Monitor* said Chris was "just right," and David Ansen would write in *Newsweek* that Chris had shown "new facets of his talent" that "shows he need not be harnessed to Superman forever."

Gene Siskel paid him the most generous compliment of all when he compared Caine with Chris: "These two actors tread a fine line between being theatrical and simply being a pair of hambones. If I had to choose one performance over the other, I would choose Reeve's, simply because he is so good at getting intensely angry without seeming silly."

"This role calls for a schizophrenic personality of a radical different sort, and it must have appealed to Reeve as a means of shocking viewers out of the tendency to identify him with the Clark Kent–Superman role," wrote Gary Arnold. "He ingratiates himself in a fresh way by impersonating a charming menace, extending his range to the amoral, treacherous aspects of human nature."

Chris told writer Lewis Archibald that the reviews weren't important—what he really missed were the friendships he had formed on the set. He had been saddened when *Deathtrap* wrapped; he said he was having a hard time adjusting.

"You know, one thing about movies, and maybe why you learn to concentrate on the present, is that in the movie business people come and go out of your life so quickly.

"You make a movie, you have an intense involvement with somebody, and they're gone," Chris said wistfully. "Six weeks and bye-bye. It's a brief period of real intensity. Because you're digging into important stuff and then—gone.

"You can always get them on the phone and you can always write them a letter and you're always saying you'll stay in touch and you mean it, and yet the relationship often has to change and becomes reduced to something else. It's like people who have survived an accident or a hazardous trip. Somehow daily life is less interesting, and the relationship tends to pale a bit. It's never quite as much fun."

The ultimate success of *Deathtrap*, like most movies, would be judged by the cold and hard numbers added up in a theater's ticket window and reported to the studio executives who could make or break acting careers with the stroke of a pen. Unlike *Somewhere in Time*, there had at least been a profit, but the numbers were far less than satisfying. That Chris would have many more chances for a break-out film which could have erased the Superman image was undeniable. And for the big money, one could always look forward to *Superman III*.

Chris said he was grateful just to have the privilege to be able to choose from both movies and Broadway.

"I really thought I'd act in regional theaters for the rest of my life," he told writer Diana Maychick at the time. "I never expected stardom. So I'm not complaining."

7

"He's young and just developing."

—FRANK YABLANS

By the time Chris got the *Monsignor* part, starring as a corrupt priest who falls in love with a postulant Carmelite nun (Genevieve Bujold), and funding the Vatican with cash from the Mafia, he was weary of all of the prying into his personal life. The constant speculation in the press about whether he would or wouldn't marry Gae Exton had begun to bother him. He fretted about it in 1981 to *Parade* magazine:

"We live in a culture where heroes are set up and then torn down again so the public doesn't have to feel inferior. Well, I'm not feeding the system anymore.

"I've been terribly vulnerable—talking about my child, about my relationship with Gae, why we're not married. . . . I've worn my heart on my sleeve. Well, I'm through with that. I don't want to share intimate details. There's nothing in it for me. I'm keeping my personal life closed and my wittily self-deprecating anecdotes for my family and friends. It's not for public consumption anymore."

Chris also said he would begin ignoring the press critiques of his movies.

"I gave that up some time ago, after I read the bad reviews for *Somewhere in Time*," he said. "*Superman II* got good reviews, but you can't believe one set of notices and ignore the next. So now I don't read any of them."

But Chris' public acceptance has always come from the frank and open relationship he's had with the public who buys the theater tickets. The *Parade* interviewer undoubtedly caught him on an off day. He has continued to speak candidly since then—certainly more than most film stars—and about issues other than his acting. It has always been impossible for him to be other than forthcoming. One could say it's part of his charm.

Chris celebrated the beginning of the sixty-seven-day shoot in Rome for *Monsignor* by flying across the Atlantic solo in his Baron and nearly killing himself. He tried not to tell anyone about the trip.

"I didn't want the studio getting in a flap or Frank Yablans (one of *Monsignor*'s producers) to freak out."

Michael Caine was one of those who spilled the beans. He told the *Globe* tabloid before Chris left America, "I think Chris is either very brave or nuts to try this. A lot of things can go wrong up there."

Apparently a lot did. Chris, who was quoted as calling it "no big deal," had several near disasters.

Chris said after the trip that a ground station in Greenland had given him wrong information on the flight over, which if true meant he was due to run out of gas and crash into the ocean before setting his plane down halfway across in Reykjavik, Iceland.

"I was one worried fellow for a half hour. Then I decided they had to be wrong. And they were—I landed in Reykjavik five minutes ahead of schedule," he told the *Los Angeles Times*' Roderick Mann.

Modest about the feat, Chris said it was "hardly in the Lindbergh class," yet he confessed to moments of doubt as he flew over the Atlantic in his little plane, asking himself, "What do I think I'm doing?"

Variety agreed with Chris. The trade paper reported that he had gotten lost between Iceland and Britain. Instead of flying into Glasgow, Scotland, he had flown too far south and had to land at Luton Airport, near London. *Variety* said that Chris was angry at himself for making the mistake.

"Reeve gets a bit fed up with air traffic controllers asking him if he's using a 'plane,' " an airport spokesman was quoted as saying. "It's just as well we didn't ask him this time."

By now many of Chris' contracts had a clause that forbade him to fly during the shooting of a film.

"They're quite right," Chris said of the contractual insertions, "for me, flying is the ultimate thrill."

Monsignor was yet another unlikeable part. And Twentieth Century Fox nearly made it more so with a blasphemous promotion. The studio was going to promote it as "the Man of Steel becomes the man of God" until Chris complained that it was demeaning to both productions.

Producer Frank Yablans who, with David Niven, Jr., owned the rights to the film's story, were enthusiastic about Chris' participation, believing that their choice for the lead role was capable of the film's demands.

"*Superman* was as much a mistake for Chris as the nude calendar was for Marilyn Monroe. Chris has never shown the depth of his abilities. He's young and just developing," Yablans told the press.

"Chris is totally believable in the role," enthused David Niven, Jr. "There's no way to connect him with the actor who plays Superman."

Chris boned up for the part by attending a Catholic retreat run by the Paulist fathers in Oak Ridge, New Jersey. "At first I felt very out of place among all these people who had made a real strong choice about their commitment," he told the *New York Post*. "But look, I've been a professional actor since I was fifteen. Each day is a passport to a new world, so every day requires a different commitment."

When asked what his own religion was, Chris called himself "a lapsed Episcopalian."

Chris' resentment of the press may have had its genesis with the media coverage of an alleged love affair he supposedly had with the Teutonic screen goddess of the sixties, Ursula Andress, while filming *Monsignor* in Rome.

The supermarket tabloid *National Enquirer* called it "a scorching romance," saying "they've been spotted holding hands, kissing, and cuddling in public.

"This romance with Christopher has knocked years off her age," an "inside source" told the tab about the forty-five-year-old actress. "She's like a young and radiant woman again.

"They both have told me how much in love with each other they are. Ursula is old enough to be Chris' mother, but he has really flipped over her."

The actress had recently had a son by actor Harry Hamlin, naming the "love child" Dimitri, but the two had just "separated"—not that they had ever married. Chris would later defend himself by saying they had just been comparing child-raising techniques and looking at each other's baby pictures.

"She has spent long evenings with him at a villa he's rented outside of Rome," it was breathlessly reported, "I've seen them kissing in the moonlight."

A tabloid also quoted a waiter at Rome's Rainieri restaurant, who confided: "They were like young lovers. She would lean across the table and whisper in his ear, and they would hold hands. He kissed her tenderly on the cheek several times."

Columnist Liz Smith wrote that Chris and Exton "were having their problems" but took a different tack. She blamed it on Chris' "partying with Robin Williams and the boys."

In *Monsignor*, Chris would perhaps receive the worst criticism by film pundits of his career. The movie, its director, Frank Perry, Genevieve Bujold ("a career-ending role," one critic panned), and all who were involved with the picture were given a lambasting by the entertainment press. It didn't help that, despite a big studio push, the film did paltry business, earning just $3.3 million on its first weekend in late October 1982. Catholics saw it as a slam against their church and hated it. Their whispers, along with the devastating reviews, led to a dramatic drop in business the week after its opening. The final ticket sales were just over $12.5 million in the United States and Canada.

"Frank Perry's new one, *Monsignor*, is so delightfully bad that one seldom has the urge to leave the theater before the movie has exhausted its nearly endless supply of preposterous moments," penned Kenneth Chanko in *Films in Review*. He added: "Christopher Reeve takes to these roles like a duck to water—remember *Somewhere in Time*?" He ended his remarks by writing, "He beds a more-than-willing postulant without telling her what he does for a living, leading to the movie's penultimate howl: Sister discovers her lover's true identity during an elaborate ceremony—it's Super priest! I harbor an unusual, one might say, unorthodox prayer: Might we be 'blessed' with a sequel?"

"Only his best friend or his best accountant can explain why the talented Reeve signed on for this ecclesiastical geek of a movie, which wins the *Inchon* award as the most gangrenous Turkey of the Month," Jack Kroll chided in *Newsweek*.

Most of the critics had not yet been able to divorce Superman from any new character Chris was playing—even a priest. Typical were Sheila Benson's comments in the *Los Angeles Times*: "As guided by Frank Perry, Reeve is not only at sea in any of these emotions, his performance is somehow familiar. You could swear that his Superman suit is only a heartbeat away under his cassock and that when his postulant-lover, Genevieve Bujold, presses him to reveal his troubling secret, what he will blurt out is not, 'I'm a *priest*,' but 'I can fly!' "

So severe were the aftershocks of the *Monsignor* debacle that Bujold would only have one more major role, supporting Clint Eastwood in *Tightrope*, and Frank Perry wouldn't work for years.

Shortly before the first *Superman* movie became a monster hit, Chris had met Sean Connery at a London party and asked for his advice on sequels from a James Bond point of view. Connery's three rules:

1. "Be in Outer Mongolia when they try to find you for the sequels."
2. "If that doesn't work, I'll give you my lawyer, and he'll stick it to them."
3. "You better be good in the first one or you won't have that problem."

With two giant hits in *Superman I* and *II*, as well as near unanimous praise for his portrayal of the Man of Steel from the press, Chris certainly had a right to ask for another salary increase for the third time out wearing the cape (Rex Reed called it "a threequel"). This time he got $2 million—more than he'd been paid for the first two combined—and top billing. Still, it was merely half of what his new costar, comedian Richard Pryor, received. Coming off a string of blockbusters like *Stir Crazy* and *Which Way Is Up*, Pryor was at the top of his career. Though reported to be "steaming" and ready to walk off the *Superman III* set, Chris publicly claimed not to care.

"He's been around longer than I have, and he deserves his four million," Chris told a magazine. He added that top billing was more important.

But like Margot Kidder, Chris too now had harsh words for the Salkinds, saying they were "untrustworthy, devious, and unfortunate people." The Salkinds, feeling that Kidder was expendable and could be jettisoned from the movie, but that Chris' participation was absolutely crucial, said that his remarks were "out of character."

In fact, Alexander Salkind now claimed not to even know Kidder. "First of all, I don't know why she is saying all these things about us," he said in his thick accent. "I mean, I never even met the lady. I don't want to meet actors. Her side of it is that we didn't want to pay her this money and because of that she got a lawyer and eventually got a million dollars."

Thus Kidder, deep in the Salkinds' doghouse, was relegated to two scenes and exactly eleven lines of dialogue in the third film, appearing in the first three minutes and just before the final credits. This time she was billed ninth. It was a token appearance.

Kidder was replaced as the female romantic lead by Annette O'Toole, who had impressed the producers in a kinky little film, *Cat People*. O'Toole's first day on the Pinewood Studios set found her disoriented by jet lag. She had rushed to London straight from a wrap of *48 Hours*, the Eddie Murphy–Nick Nolte blockbuster.

O'Toole, who told reporters that unlike Kidder, "I did read Superman comics when I was a kid," was disappointed that Lois Lane was given such a small part, feeling that a rivalry between her character, Lana Lang, and Kidder's Lane for Superman's attentions would have added spark to the production. It was soon determined that her scenes with Chris' character had no chemistry (O'Toole described her romance with Superman as "bittersweet, not hot and heavy"). The movie had lost its romantic fire.

Gone the third time too were Gene Hackman, Ned Beatty, and Valerie Perrine. In their place were Robert Vaughan as an evil businessman and the British jazz singer Annie Ross as his vamping sister coconspirator. Pamela Stephenson was the third villain, playing a Dolly Partonish cartoon of femininity. (She would go on to become a regular on *Saturday Night Live*.)

Richard Lester was back as director, but this time his vision was to attempt to use Pryor's comedic skills and make the movie into a frantic action comedy, as he'd done with *The Three Musketeers* and the first Beatles' film, *A Hard Day's Night*.

Lester began the movie with Pryor, as computer whiz Gus Gorman, performing a series of sight gags. Instead of the future of the world or thousands of lives being at stake, the central plot centered on Robert Vaughan's character trying to corner the commodities market by manipulating weather satellites. It was not the kind of problem with which most visceral action fans could identify and was seen by many to mock the legend that the first two films had preserved so well.

The Salkinds spent lavishly on the third film— some $35 million—believing they could do no wrong. The cast spent another five weeks in Alberta doing scenes depicting Clark Kent's attendance at his high school reunion in the Midwest, which in Lester's words, "looks more like Middle America than Middle America does—like Idaho with a tinge of Montana."

Despite all the expenditures, Rex Reed called the third epic "Supertrash," complaining that Chris had been made into a "big flying drone" which made him "mean, greedy, avaricious, and nasty." *Newsday* said the series showed "signs of mettle fatigue." *Time's* Richard Corliss was one of the few to like it and reserved a lot of praise for Chris.

"Superman is a role that offers as many pitfalls as opportunities: surrender to parody and the part becomes as two-dimensional as newsprint; emphasize the stalwart heroism and the audience falls asleep. Reeve brings both a light touch and sufficient muscle to Superman. And when he goes bad, he is a sketch of vice triumphant, swaggering toward the vixen Lorelei (Pamela Stephenson) for a sulfurous kiss. It is largely to Reeve's credit that this summer's moviegoers will look up at the screen and say, 'It's a hit . . . it's a delight . . . it's a super sequel.' "

Superman III opened in mid-June 1983 and grabbed more than $13 million its first weekend, displacing *Return of the Jedi* as the leader in receipts. But it left a bitter taste in the throat of its core audience, and the movie was quickly killed via bad word of mouth. The second weekend's receipts dropped off steeply, and it was gone in many theaters by mid-July. Still, the total return of $60 million, while far from the numbers turned in by *I* or *II*, was enough to keep the franchise alive.

Later, Chris would tell writer Deborah Caulfield that the third sequel had been motivated by "greed" on the part of the producers. "There are some things about commercial filmmaking that are in *really* bad taste. For a film to be commercial, it must earn money, and that results in strategic planning in certain degrees—the goal to earn even *more* money. When it comes to a showdown between quality and integrity and commercial expedience, guess who wins?" Chris rhetorically asked the reporter.

Chris also vowed never to make another *Superman* movie.

"Look I've flown, become evil, loved, stopped and turned the world backward. I've faced my peers, I've befriended children and small animals, and I've rescued cats from trees. What is there left for Superman to do that hasn't already been done?"

Chris had called the first *Superman* "a valentine to America in a more innocent age," but he said by the third film Richard Lester had "wanted his comic book to be no more than that, deliberately placing tongue in cheek."

Chris now felt his Superman years were behind him. He admitted to one interviewer that his original contract had called for him to do a series of seven films but that he had "found some good lawyers." He could still legally play no other type of superhero. The Salkinds had managed to insert a clause in his contract for *Superman III* which forbade him from playing "a character other than Superman who possesses more than mortal strength for seven years following the film's [*Superman III*] opening."

The Salkinds professed to be indifferent to their star's farewell. They had another kind of superhero waiting in the wings—*Supergirl*. Applying the same formula as *Superman*, they chose an unknown New Yorker, the doe-eyed Helen Slater, for the title role. She had a similar background as Chris—having graduated from New York's School of the Performing Arts, the institution that inspired *Fame*. They surrounded her with veteran film stars. This time the cast included Faye Dunaway, Peter O'Toole, Brenda Vaccaro, and Mia Farrow. Dunaway (the Salkinds' first choice was Dolly Parton) admitted she had the Hackman role.

"I loved that comic villainy . . . so I thought it would be fun to have a go myself," she said.

Slater worked out in the same gym and used the same weight-lifting program through which Chris had gone, hoping to expand her twenty-nine-inch bustline. The film was shot at Pinewood Studios on the same sets used by the *Superman* crew. The Salkinds were, if anything, certainly consistent.

There was one major difference—instead of a Donner or even a Lester, the luckless Frenchman Jeannot Szwarc of *Somewhere in Time* drew the director's chair.

The film drew only a yawn from American audiences. There would be no sequels for the "gal in the cape." The Salkinds, who'd cut costs on the *Supergirl* movie, were already optimistically trumpeting their next spectacular by the time it opened. It would be titled, *Santa Claus: The Movie!*

With the $2 million from the third outing Chris was certainly well off by most standards, but the gossip press made him out as somewhat of a miser. They pointed out that he "only" bought Exton a Volkswagen Rabbit as a way of celebrating his $2 million deal on *Superman III*.

"This is a guy who can afford a Rolls-Royce, but he just can't believe his success," a friend was quoted. Several reports said he didn't trust banks.

Chris reportedly had helped Gae Exton by partly bankrolling her new modeling agency. Exton's firm, Legends, soon had offices in both New York and London. Yet it was evident that Chris didn't feel comfortable with his wealth. When chauffeurs picked him up to take him to a photo shoot, Chris would often instruct the driver to park the limousine around the corner, not wanting friends to see him leaving in such style. Finally, an out-of-work actor friend told him to "just cut the crap. Instead of hiding it [the limousine], why don't you just enjoy it? Have fun for all of us."

Several newspapers in 1983 wrote that the reason Chris and Exton hadn't married was because she wouldn't agree to sign a prenuptial contract he had had his lawyers write up. The problem, the press said, was that Chris was willing to provide child support but not alimony, since Exton already ran her own business. Chris was reported to be about to "make a clean break" from the relationship.

"The love between them is gone," a scandal sheet speculated.

Chris appeared to have studied the problem. "I just read Henry Fonda's life. He married five times. His conflict seemed to be that of a decent man with an ancestral streak of integrity who came into conflict with a very passionate man with strong instincts. The result was a mask. He talked about the moment in each relationship when compromise began, and he simply had to get out," he told writer Joan Barthel.

"I'm talking about basic compromises, not about who smokes or who doesn't, or who likes to sleep with the air conditioner on. I'm talking about mammoth compromises—when you know you're dying inside, not fulfilled by the other person, neither giving or getting anything, when you're just taking up space. I've had relationships in the past when you really know it's over but you don't have the heart to say it. And that doesn't do anybody any good. When that happens, both people owe it to themselves to figure out a way in which they can be free again, with no harm done and no harm intended."

Whether "the love between them had gone" or not, the question soon became moot—Exton and Chris announced in mid-1983 that there was another baby on the way. His secretary, Natalie Singer, then told a newspaper, "There is no prenuptial agreement because they are not getting married. Everyone assumes that because Gae is having another child that they will wed, but they have no plans to marry."

Exton had sonograms taken of their second child. When they learned it was a girl, there was a friendly debate over the names Sarah and Alexandra. Alexandra won, but the decision was not announced until several weeks after she was born. She would be born in London—nearly four years to the date after Matthew's birth—and in the same hospital. Both Exton and Chris said the child was planned, with

Exton emphasizing, "Three or four years is good spacing."

Chris was in Yugoslavia while Exton went to the maternity ward, filming a movie he thought suited him tremendously. It was about flying, and he would get to play a pilot. When Exton was about to give birth to Alexandra, he rushed back to London. Whatever rifts had arisen over prenuptial questions, were, for the moment, healed.

The movie Chris had been making, *The Aviator*, had him playing a grizzled airmail pilot—complete with a jagged facial scar—who flies letters and packages in the late 1920s. He did the piloting of the antique aircraft for the movie himself, even though it cost the producer $7,500 in insurance each time he went aloft. Cameras were mounted on the wings for reaction shots in midflight as he flew through the Serbian mountain ranges.

For the first time in his film career, he was also allowed to direct—the scenes are those in which his character was attacked by wolves after he has crashed his plane into the side of a mountain. Chris did the shots himself, without benefit of a stunt double.

"It wasn't really dangerous," he said, a little nonchalantly, at the time. "They were trained wolves; you can't get scared of animals with names like Max and Ivan. All you do is hold a piece of chicken or meat in your hand, and on command they go for it."

Chris would later say he chose to do *The Aviator* because "it's deliberately romantic, old-fashioned family entertainment—the kind of film they don't make anymore. I have a weakness for films like this, where there are no intellectual demands of any kind. There's nothing wrong with just a good story, without any highbrow responsibility."

The Aviator should have been highly commercial, a star vehicle for Chris, given his flying credentials. It was based on a best-selling Ernest Gann novel. He was given a supporting cast that included Rosanna Arquette, Jack Warden, and Tyne Daley. George Miller, the Australian director of the *Man from Snowy River*, was behind the camera. Instead it turned out to be simply dull. Test screenings were so ill-received that when it came time to release it, MGM-UA gave it only a limited distribution in a handful of theaters, and that was only for contractual reasons. Chris would later tell friends that after seeing the finished product, he had personally asked that it never be released.

The movie industry newspaper *Variety* would describe its commercial outlook with three words: "Does not fly."

Chris confessed to reporter Jerry Parker in early 1984 that *Superman III* had not been up to the standards of the first two. He told the writer that was why he'd do no others.

"I decided back in 1981, when I read the script for *Superman III*. I said I'll do it [*Superman III*] because I'd said I'd do it, but it wasn't up to the mark. Something was missing. They left out the warmth and the humor."

He now desperately wanted to leave Superman far behind. Chris began looking for a serious role in a film which would not only show what he was capable of, but a movie that would turn out to be profitable at the box office. *Somewhere in Time, Monsignor*, and to a lesser extent, *Deathtrap*, hadn't done that. In his public pronouncements, though, Chris claimed the commercial prospects of a film no longer mattered to him.

"All the work I've done since the age of fifteen has always been regardless of my image. I just hope that it's a decent piece of work.

"Today's actor is willing to be a movie star if his luck decrees it, but he doesn't go out of his way in search of it. Starhood is not a really noble achievement: to get a good table in a restaurant or fly first-class is not something to brag about."

Chris said he had learned a lesson from *Monsignor*. He now called the finished product "perverse."

"I played a corrupt priest, not a real priest. What happened in that movie is they tried to homogenize him, they flattened him out. I don't want to get on *that* case, [but] it was a necessary failure because it brought me back to my senses and brought me back to me."

That Chris would finally achieve praise in a box office success was inevitable given his talent and persistence. That it would come from a nearly forgotten 1886 novel written by a nineteenth-century author was unexpected. Yet it would be Henry James, an Indian filmmaker from Bombay, and a northern Californian who would be responsible for Chris getting the best film role of his life.

8

"Superman can act!"

—CANNES FILM FESTIVAL

By 1984, Ismail Merchant, James Ivory, and writer Ruth Prawer Jhabvala had been making films together for two decades. Many of their motion pictures had been made for fewer dollars than the cost of Chris' forty Superman costumes—often under $100,000. They paid their screen talent next to nothing. Like Woody Allen, and the later films of Robert Altman, movie stars soon fought to be in their productions, knowing that they would be given a chance to show their abilities without several million dollars riding on their perceived power to draw an audience into a movie theater.

Merchant and Ivory had discovered actors Christopher Walken and Sam Waterston. Greta Scacchi, Sean Young, and Helena Bonham Carter had begun their careers with them. Stars like Paul Newman and his wife, Joanne Woodward, would work in their films for a tiny fraction of their normal fees. They were, if anything, an aspiration for those who considered themselves serious actors.

Chris had long been aware of the Merchant-Ivory-

Jhabvala team. He once compared the trio to "discovering a small vineyard in the Napa Valley, which never intends to mass-produce its wine, but people who know wine will always return there.

"I know their work. These people make handcrafted films," he said.

So Chris jumped at the chance to play the Mississippi lawyer Basil Ransom in their upcoming production of *The Bostonians*, Henry James' novel of nineteenth-century feminism and repressed lesbianism. He certainly didn't mind being the third part of a love triangle with the great British actress Vanessa Redgrave and newcomer Madeleine Potter. It came at a great monetary cost.

Though Chris tried not to reveal it to the press, it was *The Bounty* that he turned down in order to act in *The Bostonians*. He had traded a million dollars for a little more than ten percent of that in order to have the opportunity to show off his talent. Perhaps he felt if he told too many friends about his monetary sacrifice, he would be thought a fool. Chris' agent disapproved, and the resulting quarrel they had over the decision resulted in a dissolution of their relationship.

"I wanted to be an actor, not run around with a machine gun," Chris told *Entertainment Weekly* later.

Industry observers speculated at the time that California's James Ivory and India's Ismail Merchant added Chris to the cast in order to create a little box office sparkle. In fact, the opposite was true. Several financiers vetoed the "Reeve idea" and thought Chris wasn't marketable in a serious literate film—that the art crowd would guffaw at Superman playing in an adaptation of a Henry James novel. The filmmakers had to fight to keep him, though it meant a loss of at least one film studio's investment, shrinking the production's budget to $2.7 million.

Redgrave, in the key part of Olive Chancellor, is

arguably one of the acting talents of this century. But her extreme political views, including a pro-Palestinian stance, were well known by the mid-eighties. This had caused Hollywood to shy away from her. Certainly, the six-foot Redgrave was a good physical match for Chris and was always the first choice of the filmmakers. The actress, however, refused their initial overtures, and her part was given to Glenn Close.

With production about to begin, Close got what she thought was a better offer. The other film was *The Natural* with Robert Redford. Close then began to make demands on the film crew, asking to be allowed to alternate between the *The Natural* set in Buffalo, New York, and *The Bostonians* in Martha's Vineyard but with Redford's film receiving her priority. That wouldn't do for James Ivory, and he again went back to Redgrave, who this time accepted.

With the possible exception of the months he had spent acting in *The Fifth of July*, the 1983 summer that Chris spent filming *The Bostonians* had to have been the most satisfying period in his life. His brother, Benjamin, had a home on Martha's Vineyard (Chris would also invest on the island a few years later by buying property close to Jacqueline Kennedy Onassis' family compound), and he had sailed many times in Cape Cod waters with Franklin as a child. He would often go out on his sloop at dawn just before the day's filming began. Gae Exton was pregnant at the time, and the relationship looked as if it was saved. And yet he had now concluded that they would never wed.

When author Judith Michaelson asked him if there were any possibility of the two marrying that summer, Chris answered firmly, "No, there's no possibility." When pressed further, and asked if they would always be together, Chris said, "Hmmm, a very good possibility. You can write that on the subject 'he's a total pain in the ass.' "

The gossip columnists thought otherwise. They noticed that Chris had rented an apartment in the Hancock Park section of Los Angeles "in the same building where Robin Williams has taken a pad." They also wrote that Exton was spending more of her time in England than in America.

As was his custom, Chris prepped for his part of Basil Ransom as if he were a university academic about to write a dissertation. He read and then reread James' novel four times. He studied Leon Edel's biography of Henry James. And to get his southern accent just right, he recorded the speech patterns of a Yazoo City, Mississippi, lawyer, Haley Barbour. (The attorney now heads the Republican National Committee.)

"I found Basil a very appealing part," Chris told an interviewer. "He's part hero, part villain—there's a strong contemporary theme. And with Merchant Ivory's reputation for integrity, I knew they would be faithful to Henry James."

Chris grew friendly with Redgrave during the shooting of the film. He claimed not to have been bothered by her defense of the PLO or her membership in the Trotskyite Workers Revolutionary Party. The admiration was mutual and would soon bear fruit with Chris flying to London to appear opposite Redgrave in yet another Henry James play, *The Aspern Papers*.

"There's an image of her over here [in the States] of being completely humorless, which is not at all true. She's childlike, warm, vulnerable, sweet, a person of great humanity, and one of the most gifted actresses in the world. In England her politics are not held against her; they accept her as the artist she is," Chris said.

However, to stay in character—in the film they were both essentially vying for the same woman—

Chris and Redgrave distanced themselves during the daily shooting schedules.

When *The Bostonians* was screened at the Cannes Film Festival in May 1984, the repeated refrain among the audience of film industry executives was the whispered "Superman can act!" And for the first time in any film, Chris, with his Rhett Butler mustache and shoulder-length hair, resembled neither Clark Kent nor Superman.

"I think that Clark Gable, wherever he is, would have approved of the way Basil goes about handling his women," Chris told the *New York Daily News*. The attitude is, well, you can come with me now or you can come with me later, but there's no doubt about it, she's coming with me. If that's done in the right kind of underplayed, gentle, compassionate way, it can work well in a film."

It was still May when *The Bostonians* opened in New York at a single theater, Cinema I. The nearly unanimous press raves and a regularly sold-out house—it sold more than $80,000 worth of tickets the first week—quickly expanded the showings to thirty New York area theaters. This was considered astounding for an "art" film with a tiny budget, particularly when it was fighting for theaters with the likes of summer blockbusters such as *Gremlins* and *Ghostbusters*.

David Sterritt called it "the best movie I've seen all year," and wrote, "Christopher Reeve, trading his Superman cape for a nineteenth-century model, is the soft-spoken Basil down to his toes."

Commenting on Chris' character competing with Redgrave for the young woman played by Madeleine Potter, Sheila Benson said, "Reeve (in a beautifully drawn performance) is an overpoweringly romantic figure, and since he means such dire mischief, it is a terrible duel."

Redgrave, besides terrific reviews, would receive

her second Academy Award nomination (she had won best supporting actress for *Julia* in 1977).

As for Chris, Archer Winston's essay in the *New York Post* summed it up as well as anyone: "Mr. Reeve makes you forget his Superman achievements 'faster than a speeding bullet.' Here he convincingly acts with dignity and conventional clothing."

Chris took the praise with pleased but amused self-deprecation. "At least there's little chance of T-shirt or lunchbox tie-ins," he joked to *USA Today*.

In truth, there were T-shirts. For doing *The Bostonians* Chris got (besides the $120,000 for playing his role) a home-cooked Indian dinner prepared by Ismail Merchant once a week, and when the film ended, he received a T-shirt which read, "I did it for curry."

After filming, Chris would befriend James Ivory. He would often visit Ivory's Hudson River Valley home, and he became inspired to work as an activist cleaning up the river's waters. His friend Robert Kennedy, Jr., once called Chris "one of the five most knowledgeable people on the subject."

"What Jim does beautifully," Chris told author Robert Emmet Long, "is to collect people around him who are passionate in their work, and to use the best of what they can do, whether it's the cameraman, the actors, or the costume designers. He absorbs it all, and when he's got all their inputs, he just stands back and uses the best of it. The actors need somebody with a rational and dispassionate intelligence to say, 'Thank you so much for all these things you're bringing me; now here are the ones I want to use.' He's a terrific judge of what's good and what isn't. Sometimes he doesn't know exactly how something should be done better, or what's wrong with it. But he can certainly say, 'No, not that. Let's try something else.' You end up really wanting to please."

* * *

Christopher Reeve, raised in genteel Princeton, New Jersey, an insular bastion of determined good manners, has long been considered an Anglophile by his friends. British expressions like *jolly*, *bloody*, or *keen* often pepper his conversation, and he has always been comfortable living in London.

So when Vanessa Redgrave phoned, just before Christmas of 1983, attempting to induce him to appear with her on the London stage in a revival of *The Aspern Papers*, yet another adaptation of a Henry James novel, Chris jumped at the opportunity. It meant passing up film roles that would have paid him a sum many more times that, as well as appearing in the play dressed almost identically as he had been in *The Bostonians*, wearing the same mustache and a similar costume. But James had now become a talisman of sorts, and the part also meant spring in London. It was certainly the city that his lover, Gae Exton, preferred. He flew there in early January 1984 for two months of rehearsals which included a short preview run at the Princess Grace Theater in Monaco.

The actress's father, Sir Michael Redgrave, had produced, directed, and starred in the premiere of the play in 1959, some twenty-five years earlier. The elder Redgrave was dying—a result of his long battle with Parkinson's disease—and his daughter wanted to revive it as a tribute to him.

Yet Redgrave insisted on giving it a face-lift, updating it for the eighties. She had it shortened from three acts to two, rewriting Chris' part to "fit a younger man." Her father had been fifteen years older than Chris when he inaugurated the role.

The third star of the drama, the venerable Dame Wendy Hiller, still going strong at seventy-one, put Chris in heady acting company. Hiller played her part from a wheelchair.

Director Frith Banbury thought Chris had a lot of

courage to step into a role created by Redgrave's distinguished actor-father.

"It seems that anyone who has the guts to come to London to play this difficult part is to be admired and congratulated," Banbury told *The Times* of London.

Chris' difficulty, Banbury said, was that Henry James always had "about four meanings of feelings to express behind some simple line. But he is also very rewarding to play."

Chris had every right to believe that Henry James was good luck for him after *The Aspern Papers* premiered at the Theatre Royal on March 8, 1984. In his favorite magazine, the theater critic for *The New Statesman* noted that he had been "prepared for the presence, but not for the depth and detail of Christopher Reeve's protagonist, Henry Jarvis. Standing and sitting with the deliberate formality of a Victorian portrait, his size will always make him something of a Superman, but in this case, his charisma is charged with a ruthlessness that is both repellent and fascinating."

The London *Observer* would echo *The New Statesman*'s sentiments: "Connoisseurs of star entrances should repair at once for the Theatre Royal, Haymarket. . . . Christopher Reeve, playing the ruthless American scholar in Michael Redgrave's dramatization of *The Aspern Papers* by Henry James, arrives with a predatory pounce upwards into the Venetian *sala* of Miss Bordereau and her niece. Don't ask me how anyone can pounce *upwards*—all that training on *The Daily Planet* must have helped (no more Superman jokes)—but pounce upwards is exactly what Mr. Reeve does, as if Henry Jarvis were so eager to get at the papers of Jeffrey Aspern that he forgets himself at the last moment and positively runs up the final steps to take the unwitting defenders by surprise.

"It is, physically and psychologically, a marvelous moment and compels in an audience anxious to clap whatever they can, a chilled and electrifying silence. The barbarians are no longer at the gates. Mr. Reeve remains watchable throughout."

Remarks like these and the *Daily Telegraph*'s seemingly astonished "He can act!" had given Chris a one-two punch of Jamesian satisfaction. He now said his acting career offered a myriad of opportunities. He talked about doing two movies each year in "two brackets." One would be serious, he said, one comic; one would be filmed during the spring, the other in the fall. A newspaper said he was plotting his career as "methodically as a computer programmer." Summers would still be spent doing stage work, Chris said, mostly at the Williamstown Theater Festival, where he had first acted more than fifteen years ago.

"If you look at all these things lined up on a table, it's a smorgasbord—a little of that on the plate would be nice, and some of *that*, which is why it amazes me when people ask, 'Do you feel you were typecast by *Superman*?' How can you even ask that question when you see I've been brought so many gifts by that role?"

Both Chris and Redgrave very much wanted to do a movie version of the play in Venice in the coming spring. But in spite of a screenplay by Harold Pinter and a directing commitment by John Schlesinger, the project was rejected by American film financiers.

Following his triumph in London, Chris was good to his word and again summered in Massachusetts, taking risky roles at his beloved Williamstown Theater during its festival. After portraying Ned Seton, the alcoholic, possibly gay, brother in Philip Barry's opulent *Holiday*, he performed in A. R. Gurney's new play, *Richard Corey*, based on a poem by Edwin Arlington Robinson. Reviews were strong for the show, in which Chris was called upon to play an admired figure who ends his life by putting a bullet through his head.

"The audiences were devastated," Chris told *Newsday* of his very un-Superman-like act. When he was asked to take it to Broadway via the Kennedy Center in Washington, he demurred.

"I'm sure it would go, but I'm not sure it would be satisfying to me. It was such a perfect little production at Williamstown. There was a time when I was struggling to show everybody my range, but now I'm past all that. I don't need to come and show off on Broadway."

He began taking another, smaller risk as well. On many nights after his performances in Williamstown he began showing up at a local cabaret, surprising the locals by singing ballads until closing. The former boy soprano had more than a creditable voice, and that, combined with his assured stage presence, drew rapt attention from those present.

Chris told a writer that summer how much he loved the art of acting. All those rumors about how actors had to undergo pain and suffering was nonsense, he said.

"I think that if you find it terribly difficult to perform, that's a problem that has to be solved, and then you go back to performing. But acting should be joyous. Acting should be fun. I always say to myself when I'm performing, 'Am I having as much fun now as when I'm out on my boat?'

"The answer is generally yes, because it's an uplifting thing, and you don't need to sweat and panic and freak out. Because you're releasing something. Hopefully, you're releasing the most beautiful and honest part of you. How can that be painful?"

In September 1984, just after being turned down for *Children of a Lesser God* (the producers thought he was too identified with his superhero roles) Chris flew to Budapest, Hungary, to begin filming his first TV movie. It was an adaptation of Tolstoy's *Anna Karenina*. His costar was Jacqueline Bisset. The Russian classic marked his third major vehicle in a row in which he found himself in a nineteenth-century costume, wearing a mustache.

"Have mustache, will travel," Chris joked to the *New York Times*, noting also that three of his last vehicles had also been set in the same decade.

Being in a Tolstoy epic undoubtedly pleased Franklin—an authority on its language and literature—however truncated a three-hour made-for-TV movie on CBS would shrink the book's contents. But it couldn't have made Gae Exton happy. When he had been asked by interviewer Arthur Stein, three years earlier, if Exton had pronounced any actress taboo (as his leading lady), Chris answered, "We have a joke about Jackie Bisset, who I think is one of the most smashing women of all time. I just know her on a casual, social basis, but Gae says that if I ever do a film with Jackie, then she'll be on the next train!"

9

*"Chris was supposed to kiss . . . my
cleavage."*

—JACQUELINE BISSET

When Chris arrived in Hungary to film *Anna Karenina* for CBS television, he was pleasantly surprised
to learn that the Superman series had never been
shown there. Incongruous as it seems, *Deathtrap* had.

"The people in the street, when they do recognize
me, think of me as a gay psychotic playwright," Chris
winked to *TV Guide.*

This was Chris' first TV movie, and its producers
were determined to make an epic of Cecil B. DeMille
proportions. Working with a $5 million budget, the
British film crew thought they could make the movie
look like more than $10 million using hundreds of
low-cost Hungarian extras. They began by hiring 350
extras for a ballroom dance scene and 360 for an
important horse-race sequence.

Anna Karenina was a worn vehicle. A 1935 filming
of the novel, with Greta Garbo and Fredric March,
was considered a classic, despite its flat black-and-
white look. There had also been a 1948 version with
Vivien Leigh, and an exhaustive ten-hour joint BBC-
PBS treatment. Even so, Chris seemed anxious to

play the role of the military officer, Count Vronsky, despite the well-trod ground beneath him.

"You can get 450 extras at a train station for the cost of 50 in Los Angeles or New York," Chris enthused to the *Washington Post*.

The film had the blessing of the Hungarian film board, whose chief was believed to be a Russian KGB agent. He used his connections to help *Anna Karenina*'s costume department bring in thousands of uniforms and vintage gowns from Moscow, adding to the authenticity of the production.

The country was primitive by U.S. standards. Bathroom facilities were limited. The crew lived on salted pork, with vegetables in short supply. This caused water retention among the actors, and as a result, Bisset's face swelled, her cheeks puffing out and reddening in the dank, cold Hungarian weather. Chris learned to drink his coffee laced with mare's milk. It was not a pleasant time. Even Hollywood couldn't export its living standards to the eastern European nation.

Chris was the only American among the British and Hungarian actors and crew. His role as Count Vronsky was also decidedly less important than Bisset's. He was asked by *USA Today* why he'd accepted such a secondary role.

"I don't play Stratego [a popular board game of the day] with my career as much as I should. I just think, 'Will I enjoy playing this part?' Friends told me, 'The first time you go on a prime-time vehicle, it should be yours.' That didn't concern me. I just thought: 'What a beautiful story. I'd like to be part of it.'

"*Anna Karenina* is the book you should have read at some point in your life," he lectured a reporter. "It's a page-turner, compelling reading. I remember reading it in college as a chore, and I couldn't put it down. I finished it in a weekend. It's possibly one of the best novels ever written."

Chris told the *Chicago Tribune* the book was "a study of marriage a hundred years ago. Just from a feminist point of view, it will make interesting viewing to see where we've come. It's a dilemma of marriage founded on something other than romantic and sexual excitement. It's a social marriage, a marriage of convenience [he was talking about Anna's marriage to Karenin, played by Paul Schofield], and suddenly 'the other'—the real reason people get married—which is sexual love and romantic fulfillment—is offered up to her as a possibility.

"Our primary function is to entertain and make an intelligent story. But if it causes twenty people to want to run and pick up the novel and study it, I think it would be great. For an education, you take a course. You go to school. That can never be the function of something like *Anna Karenina*. We're not trying to beat you over the head with literature. The primary function is to tell a good story, but why is it a classic? It's because something about the story transcends its time. You don't have to play down to the lowest common denominator. You don't have to play it down to the eleven-year-old mind. So much of television plays it down and, not being snobbish about it, how nice it is to have something that doesn't."

As usual, Chris prepared for the Count Vronsky role by assiduously reading not just *Anna Karenina* but the complete works of Tolstoy. This would lead to a disagreement between Chris and his long-time "crush," Bisset, on how to approach their parts.

"I felt she didn't want to explore the characters, to dig into the script," Chris would say. "Her way of working is to get it together on her own, which can be disconcerting to actors who are used to a different method. But if she finds it easier that way, we adjust—after all, she's the lead, and this is the part that demands the most of her as an actress."

Chris was quick to mitigate his remarks by complimenting his costar, even if it sounded left-handed. "She's always on time and word perfect. She's a top-drawer professional."

From her trailer, Bisset gave equally faint praise. "Chris rehearses differently. . . . You don't get much from me at rehearsal. I resent being overfocused. I just don't work like that. I wanted to be as instinctive as Anna is, not to plan anything. Chris needs to talk about things a great deal. His working process is more tortured than mine. He needs to know a zillion details before he focuses. Ironically, in the past I've been guilty of driving directors crazy with a million details, but on this project I'm entirely different."

The two had no complaints about their love scenes together, instead seeming annoyed only with the CBS censors. Bisset had become a star partly because of appearing in a transparent wet T-shirt in the 1977 watery thriller *The Deep*. Though she had a reputation for on-screen passion, she claimed to be grateful she wouldn't have to appear without clothes for this film.

"One of the great pluses of television is that you aren't required to do nude scenes. In one scene Chris was supposed to kiss the top of my cleavage, but the TV censors said it wouldn't wash. Now he kisses me on the neck instead."

Chris seemed a little disappointed. "No kissing below the neck. This put the kibosh on one of the scenes we were in the middle of. . . . I was just about to make my move, and got pulled back."

The new TV actor said that on second thought, intimate love scenes were probably a mistake anyway. "It's a distortion to make a classic novel play like *Dallas*. That's putting twentieth-century audience needs on top of the reality of the piece. In our piece the implications are made, but we don't cut to a bedroom to interest the audience."

If Gae Exton was at all concerned about Chris'

attraction to Jackie Bisset, she was undoubtedly mollified when she learned Bisset was in the middle of a tempestuous love affair with the Russian ballet defector Alexander Godunov. Though Bisset would sizzle on screen with Chris, her off-screen time was spent on phone calls to the dancer, famous for his flowing blond locks. She would run off at every chance for a clandestine weekend meeting just to see him. Godunov had just played Count Vronsky himself in a ballet adaptation of the Tolstoy classic. He gave Bisset advice.

"Here I was, British, playing a Russian lady from a Tolstoy book. We discussed it a little bit, and all he said was that I had the right temperament for the part," Bisset told *TV Guide*.

With a literate script by James Goldman, the screenwriter who had authored *The Lion in Winter*, the finished product was perhaps a little too high-brow for a network audience used to sitcoms and cop shows. A frequent complaint among the nation's TV critics was that Chris had been miscast and Tolstoy's novel had been condensed to "bare bones."

"The fault is not Miss Bisset's alone," wrote John O'Connor in the *New York Times*. "She is sabotaged by the casting. While Count Vronsky, the dashing lover, for whom she gives up everything, is played by Christopher Reeve, Karenin, her aging and neglectful husband, is portrayed by Paul Scofield. There is simply no contest.

"All done up in splendid military costumes, Mr. Reeve is indeed handsome, but rather distressingly lifeless. He seems to be devoting most of his energy to maintaining a reasonably accurate British accent. He ends up being the nineteenth-century equivalent of a big lug."

O'Connor's cruel analysis aside, there were many kind words as well for Chris. The *Christian Science Monitor* said that even though Chris played "the role of a lover a bit like Clark Kentovich at the beginning, he finally manages to integrate his own cool persona into a fairy believable Count Vronsky." He also called Bisset's Anna "a penetrating characterization."

"Reeve's Vronsky has the perfect pitch of the love-lorn naif—youthfulness, extravagance, and crass opportunism," wrote Monica Collins in *USA Today*.

Up against formulaic network fare on the night it aired—*Who's The Boss?* and *The A-Team*—it might have been at least optimistically calculated that *Anna Karenina*'s alternative charms might draw a large audience. It did not, proving once more that historic costume dramas set on foreign soil rarely fare well with a mass audience.

Chris told one reporter after *Anna Karenina*, "Since I've been in the nineteenth century for a year . . . the next two or three things [I do] will all be contemporary."

Being on television in a drama, no matter how well-done or literate, would only dim Chris' appeal in the eyes of the movie studio moguls. Film company executives were still of an opinion that truly big stars don't offer themselves up to the public in films which could be seen first for free in the home. In the future when Chris went up for a part, he would no longer be near the top of a studio's list. Playing parts simply because they interested him had enabled him to hold his head high, but had come at a monetary cost.

A part he wanted badly, *The Running Man*, would go to the ascending Arnold Schwarzenegger. That hurt. Chris needed a movie part that year which paid at least a million dollars. He needed money badly. Several years of a high-maintenance lifestyle that now included three homes, several planes—he owned a Piper Cheyenne II and an ASW 20 sailplane among others, as well as a forty-foot yacht, would eventually force him, however uncomplaining, into doing everything from commercials to audio books that ranged from *The Great Gatsby* to yoga meditation tapes just in order to keep his standard of living intact.

But nothing could keep him from going back to Williamstown for at least part of each summer, working for the price—as one writer would put it—"of a family dinner at the Russian Tearoom." The summer of 1985 marked the seventeenth year since he had apprenticed there in 1968. That July he starred with Karen Allen and Maria Tucci in the George Kaufman–Edna Ferber comedy *The Royal Family*. He sweated through the play each night—the part called for him to wear a fur coat in several scenes. After Williamstown he headed off to Martha's Vineyard for a brief family vacation. Looking to take his career in another path, he sent up a trial balloon in the press about attempting yet another dramatic challenge—directing.

"I'd love to take a good five-character play with a lot of emotional detail and work on that. I think I have the eye for it, and I feel I could really bridge the gap between the actor and the audience," he told a writer that summer.

By the end of 1985, Chris and Exton had begun to go their separate ways. They were now living together about half of the year. Exton was concentrating her career both in model management and as a casting director back in London. It wasn't going well. The British unions wanted to force her to work full-time on her casting work as their regulations required, and Exton wanted to work less than that. She began to drop jobs in order to be with the children.

Chris did the opposite. Appearing to be a workaholic, he started taking minor assignments, like narrating *Dinosaur!* on CBS television.

Matthew was now in a private school during the fall and winter, which further prevented Exton's ocean hopping. The two shared time together mostly during major holiday periods.

"I'm a romantic, a dreamer," Chris would once confess in a moment of candor. "Gae is fundamentally a practical person. She's organized, focused in terms of common sense, always looking for the logic in things. I'm sometimes instinctive, impulsive. But Gae has the ability to ground me, to make me see things more realistically. She's a consistent person, whereas I tend to be moody. I blow hot and cold. I'm also transparent. I can't fake anything, whereas Gae can sometimes hold back emotions. For an actor, I'm a lousy actor."

After being passed over for *The Running Man*, Chris took the part of Count Almaviva in Circle in the Square's eccentric production of *The Marriage of Figaro* in New York, which put some of the characters on roller skates, and with cars and bicycles appearing on stage at odd times. Chris did part of the show with a Cary Grant accent. ("His efforts at clowning sink with the finality of pure lead" wrote the tough-on-Chris Frank Rich.)

"I don't like to leave the children behind [in London]," Chris told the *New York Daily News*. "But Gae and I are not the kind of parents who push children away to a baby-sitter."

Still, Chris said he couldn't pass up the role. "It's a totally different kind of theater than I'm used to—that's why I wanted to be a part of it.

"My own hope for my life is that I never chicken out. I'd like to keep feeling reckless about things and having that roller-coaster ride of up/down, success/failure—anything but play it safe."

Shortly after making that statement, Chris chose to be a guest at a high school located on Edwards Air Force Base in California. He chose the appearance so he could ride in a jet fighter trainer. ("I was at 45,000 feet, doing inverted loops, flying supersonic!")

It was impossible for Chris Reeve to ever play it safe.

His friend Sean Connery had once said, "Never say never again." After a twelve-year absence from the part that had made him famous, he succumbed to the promise of a large paycheck and the producers gave his final James Bond movie that title. Connery was candid. He had done the role for the money, he admitted, and now it was Chris' turn to do the same.

The rights to do future *Superman* films had been sold. The Salkinds—who had used up most of their goodwill with the cast and crew during the three productions—had auctioned the rights. They went to Menahem Golan and Yoram Globus, two Israeli cousins who had formed a successful directing-producing team that did low-cost movies. They were known in the movie industry as the "the two crown princes of schlock." They owned an independent film studio and a chain of theaters in England called the Cannon Group, which—though it sometimes seemed to be on the verge of bankruptcy—had managed to create a string of profitable action films starring the likes of Chuck Norris and Charles Bronson. Golan and Globus were particularly adept in taking a movie in preproduction and selling off distribution rights country by country while a movie was still in production. They would recover their filming costs sometimes long before the movie had been edited.

Golan and Globus soon found out that in order to presell a fourth *Superman* movie and get the fees they wanted, they had to guarantee that Chris and other key members of the original cast were going to be in the film. Chris needed money and would have quickly signed on with the two, but his agent Jim Wiatt took him aside.

Wiatt was said to have given him this advice: "The world wants to see you play this part [Superman], and I can get you $3 million to do it. But as a condition of the deal, I'll get Cannon to make another picture of your choice, and I'll get you another million. That's $4 million for one picture you want to see and one the world wants to see."

Chris and his agent met with Golan in December 1985 and presented a list of demands:

1. Absolute control over the contents of the *Superman IV* script
2. At least part of the directing responsibilities
3. Another picture to be made first. Chris could choose the script as part of the deal
4. Oh, yes—a fee of $4 million—for both films

After a few negotiations Chris got Golan and Globus to give him the contract he wanted. After all, he *was* the Superman the world wanted to see, and thus they couldn't do it without him.

The movie he chose to make, the gritty contemporary drama *Street Smart*, was an unusual selection given the many-costumed epics that he had chosen in the past. The script was about a failing New York journalist, Jonathan Fisher, who is driven to fabricate a magazine story about a pimp and his prostitutes.

"The central character is not likeable and definitely not a hero," Chris told the *Los Angeles Daily News*. "But he's like many people in their mid-thirties, facing a dilemma of personal ethics versus ambition. He's sort of lost, just getting along, but he wants to be famous. When he gets the opportunity, he takes it."

Chris said he knew he was taking risks, but that was part of the challenge of making a movie like *Street Smart*.

"I'm interested to see if the audience will accept me as a weasel in the film. I don't think I begin to redeem myself until the last ten minutes of it.

"Life is not about good guys and bad guys. It's about people trying to survive, it's about personal ethics versus the pressure to succeed. I felt it would be interesting to play a man who is really quite lost, very weak, dishonest, and stupid in many ways."

Chris couldn't read Tolstoy or Henry James to prepare for this role. Instead he accompanied New York City vice cops on their rounds for weeks, making friends with pimps and prostitutes. Chris told the *New York Daily News* that his eyes had been opened.

"The stereotype of what a hooker is has changed for me dramatically. New York is broken up into territories that are just as clear as in a wolf colony. Wolves pee in the snow to mark out their territory, and figuratively speaking, the same has been done in New York. For example, over on Eleventh Avenue near the Hudson River, you get black and Hispanic girls who are working for forty bucks a trick in the back of the car, or a quick one out on one of the piers.

"You move over toward Midtown, and you get the girls working the fancy hotels who will get into kinky things with businessmen, twosomes or threesomes, stage an orgy for the stockbrokers who want a dirty weekend."

Chris added, "Mayor Koch has helped to move the action out of Times Square and into the Thirties. There is some very attractive talent down there. Some women—if you didn't know they were working the street and had five guys already that night—I or any red-blooded guy might try to pick up. I talked with a girl named Candy who is eighteen years old, has been hooking since she was fourteen, comes from New Hampshire, and is drop-dead gorgeous. She's pulling in eight hundred bucks a night, five nights a week. She just totally doesn't look the type at all."

Chris admitted that there had been some interesting offers made to him while doing his research.

"A lot of the girls recognized me from films and

were excited not only to talk to me but to proposition me. At a discount. I also had some freebie offers, which is saying a lot, and some interesting combination offers."

Street Smart was shot in both Harlem and Canada, with the streets of Montreal there duplicating New York City because of its tight $3 million budget. Jerry Schatzberg, a specialist in contemporary melodrama—who had been responsible for *The Seduction of Joe Tynan* and *The Panic in Needle Park*—was brought in to direct.

Midway through the shooting Chris had to undergo an emergency appendectomy. He checked into a New York hospital on Tuesday, had the operation done with a local anesthetic, and was back on the set Thursday.

"Jerry [Schatzberg] said, 'You don't have to be here, nobody will think badly of you,'" Chris told the *New York Post* (Headline: STITCH IN TIME SAVES STEEL MAN!), "but I stayed, and we worked from nine P.M. to four A.M."

A week later Chris did a fight scene. Schatzberg worked it out so he wouldn't be punched in the abdomen during the battle.

Chris, Schatzberg, and the man who had written the script, David Freeman—it was autobiographical, based on experiences he had working at *New York* magazine—went over each scene together. Chris not only critiqued it but corrected Freeman's spelling as they went along. Input from Golan and Globus was also forthcoming. Not shy to offer advice, the two relied on their action-movie instincts, asking Chris to provide gun battles in the ghetto. Chris refused. There was one shootout in the final scene, but that had already been in the script. Golan and Globus' wish for continuous violence was vetoed.

The cast included Morgan Freeman, who would earn his first Academy Award nomination for his part as the pimp, Fast Black. Kathy Baker—who replaced Dianne Wiest—played the Times Square hooker, and Mimi Rogers was Chris' character's live-in girlfriend.

Freeman dominated the movie whenever he was on camera and got raves from the press. Chris, as the movie's centerpiece, got only a small share of the praise. Sheila Benson called it a "solidly fine performance. You could see why the role of Jonathan Fisher might have appealed to an actor who will have spent four films in Superman's clear-cut world of good and bad—this boyishly appealing, upwardly mobile ex-Harvard journalist is actually the film's ethical bad apple."

But critics still sought to take shortcuts in their essays by linking Chris to Superman. The first sentence in *Newsday*'s unfavorable review began, "It's a bird, it's a plane, it's newsman!" It closed the review with a prophetic, "Maybe it's up, up, and away time again."

Street Smart never got mass distribution. Its hard R rating and inner-city focus was unpalatable to small-town movie houses. While certainly a well-made contemporary film, it was not a vehicle that would jump-start Chris' now flagging film career.

After the filming Chris mused about the vagaries of being a movie star to *New York Native*: "[The toughest part] is the struggle between the actual creative work, and promotion, and the fact that there's a relationship between them that's difficult to understand. There's corruption on almost every level. You have to try to hang on to the original reasons why you became an actor in the face of manipulation from all sides. To hang onto the vision of what you actually have to say—what your actual worth is—in spite of all kinds of hype. Hype on one side and getting dumped on the other side. You're sort of buffeted by people who have an incomplete picture of who you are and therefore have all kinds of misinformation.

You should strive not to be swayed by that, to maintain a sense of purpose in spite of all the madness that's all over the place. It's a battle I think I'm winning, but it's certainly a struggle."

When Chris finished the shooting of Street Smart, he flew directly from Canada to Vermont. His father had a small summer place in the state, and Chris often skied in the Vermont mountains, favoring its famous Stowe resort. Chris had decided to campaign on behalf of U.S. Senator Patrick Leahy's reelection campaign, his first involvement in politics. Leahy, a liberal Democrat, was a proponent of various environmental clean-up laws. The senator wanted to use Chris' name as a way to increase donations and raise his own profile. Headlines in the Burlington, Vermont, Free Press that read, LEAHY CAMPAIGN ENLISTS HELP OF THE MAN OF STEEL were already infusing the Leahy campaign with enthusiasm.

After piloting his own plane into the airport of the state's largest city, he appeared at a well-publicized rally. The excited mob included several hundred people, mostly young women.

"I feel the time has come for us to realize there are no Supermen. But we have the next best thing—Pat Leahy in the U.S. Senate!" Chris said in his speech exhorting the crowd to go to the polls. He went on to praise Leahy for voting against aid to the Nicaraguan Contras as well as his work for arms control. Then he signed autographs.

A letter the next week in the Burlington Free Press compared Chris with President Reagan. It said that since Leahy's Republican opponent, Richard Snelling, had chosen to side with Reagan, it was evident that Leahy had chosen the better actor.

Leahy was reelected handily two months later.

Chris had his own ideas about the shape he wanted Superman IV to take. He had just narrated a PBS television show on world peace, and he thought his idea—that of Superman ridding the world of nuclear weapons—was a theme which would have universal appeal. To make the movie seem even more important, he had the film's title lengthened to *Superman IV: The Quest for Peace.*

"We're going for something emotional," Chris told the Associated Press. "Ultimately we would all like to see a world without nuclear weapons. The question is, why can't somebody just take them away?"

In the interview Chris began to express his own concern for the world's problems. "We're living in a global village now, and there has to be a new heightened awareness of our interactions as people on this planet. I, Christopher, see the world as Smallville [Superman's boyhood hometown], in a way. I hope for a new age in the next century where we begin to take responsibility for this planet as a whole rather than our particular little horizon right in front of us."

Chris hadn't made a Superman film in nearly four years. He could no longer risk lifting several hundred pounds of barbell weights, because he'd developed a herniated disk midway down his back. Still, wanting to look as fit as possible, ("Don't want my belly hanging over the yellow belt") he began doing sit-ups at the rate of between three and four hundred each day.

There would be no Pinewood this time. Instead, Cannon had a smaller studio, Elstree, in Hertfordshire, England. Chris did manage to get together most of the nucleus that had made the first two films a delight—Gene Hackman, Margot Kidder, Jackie Cooper, and Susannah York (York was not on screen but was heard as the voice of his mother). Cannon's choice for director, Sidney J. Furie, had decent credentials, having directed *The Ipcress File* and scores of action films. And Chris, working with two screenwriters, Lawrence Kohner and Mark Rosenthal, personally devised some new twists in a plot that had gotten tired. He began by giving his character two girlfriends. Mariel Hemingway was given a part as the daughter of the *Daily Planet*'s new owner, who has turned the paper into a racy tabloid. As Lacy Warfield, she lusted only after Clark Kent while Kidder's Lois Lane was restricted to a romantic liaison with his alter ego, Superman.

(Hemingway's big speech: "Are there any more like you back home? Strong, gentle, tall men with bright blue eyes—and *square*? Men who like to dance slow, the old-fashioned way?")

The plot had Chris' superhero character throwing a pile of nuclear weapons into the sun and then addressing the United Nations on world peace. His nemesis, Lex Luthor, felt that was bad for criminal commerce. And so on—the plot was simplistic but workable. Unfortunately, the Cannon Group literally ran out of money midway through the filming of the movie and actually released an unfinished product.

Changes were made to cut costs. One of Chris' big scenes, which had Superman landing in the middle of Forty-second Street in New York City to the huzzahs of thousands of people, was scrapped. Instead it was filmed on an artificial-looking sound stage in England.

Actor Jon Cryer, who played Lex Luthor/Gene Hackman's punk surfer nephew, referred to Chris' character as the "Dude of Steel," throughout the movie. He would tell an interviewer a year after the film was released that Chris had taken him aside just before the movie was scheduled to be released into movie theaters, telling him it was going to be "terrible."

"The movie was his [Chris'] idea and the idea was great, and the shooting was great, and Gene Hackman was doing wonderful improvisational stuff—I loved working with him—and then Cannon ran out of money five months ahead of time and released an unfinished movie," Cryer said.

"No, I am not kidding! Rent it. You will see. You can see the wires. They did not finish it. And they used the same flying shot like four times. That was the problem with it, and that's why Chris leveled with me and said, 'It's a mess.' And I said, 'Oh, great.'"

Cryer's complaints were also directed at the operators of the crane that controlled his flying sequence. "What happens is, they put a truss around you that is excruciating. You have to shove that whole area down there because you catch one hair and whoo, boy! It has these little sort of swivel pins on the side that they put a cable through, and it goes up to a huge crane, like they use for construction. And—you dangle. You dangle by your genitals, pretty much."

Chris soldiered through the shooting of *Superman IV* during the winter of 1986–87 knowing full well the film would not only be a failure, but could hurt his career. But he couldn't walk away from the film. Several hundred people had jobs in the movie. Their livelihoods depended on him. And there would have been legal action taken too if he had simply left the set. His live-in relationship with Exton had also officially ended that winter; they would admit to the split in mid-1987.

Perhaps sensing that he would see Matthew and Alexandra less in the future, he got them parts in the fourth *Superman* outing. They were cast as children trapped in a house with a tornado outside, and the threatening scenario could have served as a dramatic metaphor for the direction his personal and professional life seemed to be taking—total disarray.

"I trust the communication between Gae and me will be good enough so that we can work out whatever's best for the kids," he told *McCall's* in mid-1987, airing the separation for the first time and carefully choosing his words. "For now, they understand they have two homes, and they'll be fully loved and accepted in each."

However gently Chris tried to treat the breakup, the tabloid press smelled a scandal. That summer its headlines reported that Chris had met and was dating one Dana Morosini, "an actress." The stories noted that it was Dana who had looked after Matthew and Alexandra while Chris was acting nights at the Williamstown Theater Festival. This led to a screaming headline in the *Globe* which read SUPERMAN DUMPS HIS KIDS' MOM FOR BABY-SITTER! Calling Dana "a temptress," the story reported that Exton was "devastated" because "she had believed Chris would return to her."

"Gae and the children will never want for material things," the tabloid paper breathlessly reported, quoting a friend of Exton's. "But sadly, they will never know the happiness of a complete family. Chris loves the children, but he prefers being a bachelor father. The split has been especially hard on his son, Matthew, who can't understand why Daddy is living with the girl who used to be his baby-sitter."

The *Globe* ended with the source saying, "Gae can never forgive Chris for betraying her and their children. Nor can she forget that she was good enough to bear his children, but not good enough to be his wife."

A second tabloid story explained: "Geography also drove a wedge between them. She is English and wants to live in London. Chris wants to divide his time between London, New York, and a home on Martha's Vineyard.

"Gae has a very successful modeling business in London and wants to devote full-time to it. Following Chris around the globe, she can't possibly keep up with her business affairs. Fortunately, the breakup has been quite amicable, and they'll remain close.

"There's no big problem about money. Chris has already agreed to give Gae a substantial part of his *Superman* fortune. She and the children will be looked after for the rest of their lives thanks to the *Superman* movies."

The tabloid also quoted a friend of Chris' as saying, "Chris' lack of success in other roles has frustrated him," and that Gae was "tired of reading about his exploits in the gossip columns."

Chris' name *was* linked in London celebrity columns with Mariel Hemingway during the *Superman IV* shooting. A photo in one newspaper showed them dancing, their eyes locked on each other's face. Another gossip columnist had Chris seeing—incongruously—Whoopi Goldberg. And an Australian paper quoted Gae's father, Clive, as being particularly upset by the breakup and ready to be physically violent with Chris.

"If I came face to face with him now, I'd box him one," an angry Clive Exton was quoted as having said.

"I don't know about Superman—Super Rat would be nearer the truth. He's always had a roving eye for women and has had thousands of women throwing themselves at his feet."

A paper also quoted a woman whose children went to class with Matthew and Alexandra at the "exclusive Hill House school" as saying that Chris would often stay at hotels or apartments when he was in London.

"He went off to live in luxury, and she stayed home with the children. And I know that happened more than once.

"Her life revolves around the children. She doesn't seem to have many close friends visit, and she doesn't go out much at night. I think the children are well provided for, but they're not spoiled. She sends them to school on the bus each day, and even when it's raining hard, she's often standing outside waiting for the bus [when they return]."

The tabloid *Star* quoted Exton as saying that earlier she had wanted two more children, but decided "if we weren't happy, we'd do something about it.

"I don't need security. I'm quite independent and quite able to look after myself. I don't rely on Chris . . . I can always go out and find a job. I hate all this talk of me thrusting legal papers at Chris to sign. It sounds so sordid."

The *Star* also interviewed *Superman IV* production assistant Frances Ward-Smith, who said Exton had never visited the set of the movie.

"The children were there quite often, and they obviously loved Chris. He picked them up and swung them around and played hide-and-seek with them.

"They weren't overawed by it all. They'd obviously seen it all before. They were brought in and taken away by a chauffeur-driven limousine."

The nine-year relationship with Exton was over. *Superman IV* was about to flop, and further problems were ahead. Chris had hit a low in both his career and personal life.

10

"Superman, take Pinochet away!"

—CHILEAN CITIZENS

Dana Charles Morosini was born in New Jersey on March 17, 1961. The middle name, Charles, is her father's. Her first years were spent in the close-in, middle-class New York City suburb of Teaneck. She enjoyed the same kind of privileged (though much more stable) childhood as Chris. Her father is a doctor of internal medicine with a cardiac subspecialty; her mother, Helen, a publishing executive.

Her parents soon moved to nearby Scarsdale in Westchester County, New York—a much wealthier commuter community. Dana would graduate from Westchester County's Edgemont High School, where she acted and sang in several of its plays. A former teacher, Richard Glass, called her "a leader." A very popular student, Dana was voted "most admired" in her senior year by her classmates. In Edgemont High's 1979 school yearbook, she expressed her love of horses.

After graduation, Dana continued to pursue an acting career, studying with Chris' old mentor, Nikos Psacharopoulos, and eventually earning a master's of fine arts from California's Institute of the Arts in Valencia, near Los Angeles. The school could be called the West Coast's version of Juilliard.

Dana then began seeking professional roles on the stage, getting small parts in off-Broadway plays and summer stock. She also appeared in television commercials, including one for Tide laundry detergent.

Chris met Dana on June 30, 1987, her first season as a professional at the Williamstown Theater Festival. In nearly the same romantic fashion as he had done with Exton, Chris declared the date of that first meeting, "our anniversary." Dana was singing at the 1896 House, a Williamstown restaurant which had a late-night cabaret. Chris was sitting at a table with a group of friends after rehearsing for the Williamstown Theater Festival's production of the classic sex farce *The Rover*, where he was playing Willmore, a philandering scoundrel.

It would have been impossible for Chris to miss the resemblance between Dana and Gae Exton. Her long brown hair and her expressively large brown eyes were almost a carbon of Chris' former companion, though her facial features were softer, as if a fine gauze had been placed over the camera's lens.

"She just knocked me out," Chris would later tell the *Berkshire Eagle*. "A lot of people saw that happen. So I offered her a ride to the Zoo (a local after-hours haunt), and she said to me, 'No, thanks.' "

"My friends were telling me, 'You're crazy. Give us your keys. He wants to give you a ride!' and I said, 'Well, I have a car, I can get there on my own,' " Dana recalled.

At the Zoo, they talked raptly for an hour, oblivious to the people around them. Then Dana quickly kissed Chris on the cheek and disappeared into the night.

A few days later, they met by chance. They talked again, hardly able to break away from each other.

After sending her flowers and notes, Chris took Dana on their first date in a pickup truck he owned—for a late-night summer swim under a full moon at the nearby Margaret Lindley Pond. Dana at first believed it was a skinny-dipping invitation. But she thought Chris gallant when he volunteered to retrieve her swimsuit at the Williams College dorm where she was staying. That night they shared their first real kiss.

"It was a very old-fashioned courtship," Dana remembered. "He'd come over to watch me rehearse. He'd pick wildflowers and have them carried over by an apprentice. Talk about your college romances."

They began living together that November. Friends recall Chris as "goofy in love," citing a story that two years later, while performing on stage, he unabashedly announced that it was "our anniversary" to the audience from a Williamstown stage.

"It was very corny, but I couldn't help it," Chris admitted to an interviewer.

In addition to the "our anniversary" date the two also decided on "our song"—the Cole Porter tune, "It's Delovely." They would perform it as a duet whenever asked.

Chris was so enamored with Dana that he stayed in Williamstown when *Superman IV* had its grand premiere in London a month later. Exton went to the event with Matthew and Alexandra as her "dates." He might also have feared being taken into custody by the British government. Chris had been notified that he owed the British more than $1 million in back taxes.

Yet again, perhaps he just didn't want to field questions on why he had become involved in such a financially shaky creative venture as *Superman IV*. The film would open by taking in a very mortal $8 million the first three days, and wind up with just $17 million overall, less than a third of the total take of the relatively sluggish *Superman III* and less than the first two weeks' receipts of the original.

Chris expected the reviews by the media to be savage. They were.

"Willing suspension of disbelief is one thing, but when Superman wobbles and changes color as he flies through the air, when whole sets quake each time a window is broken, and when the scariest thing about Superman's evil opponent, Nuclear Man, is his copper spandex bodysuit, then the reality of *Superman on a Shoestring* replaces the comic book fantasy you thought you'd paid to see," essayed Juliann Garey in the *Village Voice*.

"Of the *Superman* series, this is supposed to be the socially relevant one," wrote Jamie Bernard in the *New York Post*. "The story idea, about ending the arms race, was supplied by a clearly bored Chris Reeve, who had only agreed to reprise the role for making *Street Smart*, which bombed anyway."

Michael Scheinfeld wrote, "When the Salkinds sold the *Superman* sequel rights to Cannon, the schlockmeister duo of Golan and Globus had a great opportunity to put something decent together and make a lot of money. But they threw it away with a shoddy production that makes Sam Katzman's *Superman* serial of the forties look like a paragon of invention. Christopher Reeve has been making the rounds lately, trumpeting this new film as a return to dignity and prestige. He was reportedly lured back with a huge salary, as well as receiving co-story and a second-unit directing credit; he should be thoroughly ashamed. If this is his noble escapism with a message, he had better stick to acting."

Chris, who had written much of the script, expressing what he had sincerely believed was a noble idea, would be given another headache as a result of *Superman IV*. A parapsychologist, Barry Taff, and a pediatrician, Kenneth Stoller, filed a civil lawsuit against Chris, Warner Brothers, and Cannon for $45 million, claiming that Chris had stolen the theme of *Superman IV* from them.

The two maintained they had mailed a summary of their plot to Chris in 1985 that was similar to what had wound up on theater screens. In their script, Superman saved the earth from nuclear destruction and then disarmed the superpower nations. They also claimed to have sent copies to his secretary and Warner Brothers.

According to Chris, their script was received but set aside like dozens of others, and he would testify he had never read it. But Taff and Stoller got Chris' home phone number and began a series of repeated calls to him.

Chris' attorney, Louis Petrich, told the author that their pestering of Chris finally paid off, and he took the pair's call.

"Chris had never read the treatment," Petrich said, "but to be polite, he told Taff and Stoller that their ideas were interesting and during the conversation he thumbed through their script."

Petrich called the lawsuit "frivolous," and Chris countersued the two for $100,000 for defaming him. He became furious whenever it was brought up by interviewers.

"The suit is against myself and against Warner Brothers, claiming that I took somebody else's idea," he told Larry King. "I most emphatically did not, and I can't comment more than that. Unfortunately, the individuals, the plaintiffs, are trying to wage a smear campaign in the press. I simply won't respond to it."

Much was made of the suit by the media as it got closer to a court date, particularly after columnist Art Buchwald won a similar lawsuit against Paramount Studios. Buchwald claimed that the studio had usurped his twelve-page summary for what became the Eddie Murphy hit *Coming to America*.

"We never had any intention of settling," Petrich told the author. "We just weren't about to put up with the stuff they were claiming."

The lawsuit finally went to court in early 1990. At the pretrial hearing, the judge asked the parties if they would submit to a decision made through the American Arbitration Association. All parties agreed to the suggestion, and the matter was arbitrated there with the pediatrician and parapsychologist writing team losing decisively. But that wasn't the end of it. The two took it back to the courts, and when they were rejected, they appealed it all the way to the California Supreme Court, losing once more.

Though Chris had won the battle, the suit cost him both a lot of money and anxiety, as well as causing some damage to his reputation in spite of his ultimate victory. Financially, it couldn't have come at a worse time. With the cloud over him and after the debacle of *Superman IV*, the fiftieth anniversary of Superman in 1988 was hosted by Dana Carvey. Only clips from Chris' early days as the Man of Steel were shown.

Chris had made all four *Superman* films in England. By 1988, because he owed the British government so much money in taxes, he had begun to take jobs he would have normally disdained. Still the dreamer, Chris had also gone ahead and purchased a country property in April 1986—a 35.7 acre farm in the Berkshire Hills for $260,000. The country estate was located between the New York state line and the Williamstown Theatre on Treadwell Hollow Road.

The five-bedroom, six-and-a-half bath, two-story house was modern—rough cedar on the outside and a combination of light cherry and pine woods inside. There were two fireplaces. Chris began expenditures of more than $100,000 improving his acquisition.

"After all those years of going to Williamstown," he told writer Kathy Larkin, "I realized how much I loved the place. The house is facing the wrong way for the view, so I'm adding a wing and dabbling in landscaping—put an orchard here, move the pond there."

Chris said there would be room for many of his sports on the property. "I can park my glider, and there's a cross-country ski run, livestock, a trout stream, and a pond."

He also began purchasing thoroughbred horses, taking riding lessons and boarding them at nearby Bonnie Lea Farm and across the state line in Old Chatham, New York.

That same year Chris also contracted for a custom-built, forty-six-foot Cambria yacht at a cost of more than a half-million dollars. He named it *The Sea Angel*. The boat was designed to suit his large six-foot-four-inch frame.

"Reeve wanted a wide-open feeling, a two-person galley, a large main saloon, a traditional, but larger, forward V-berth stateroom, and less teak above deck for easier maintenance," David Walters, the builder, told *Sail* magazine.

He added that Chris told him he wanted a "clean, airy boat." The yacht specialist said he constructed the bunks to be seven feet in length so they would accommodate Chris' height. *The Sea Angel* was also built with an adjustable keel that could be made more lateral during rough weather.

The Rhode Island builder called it a "proper yacht" for Chris. He defined that as a boat which was "comfortable, seaworthy, easily handled, good-looking, strong, and have great performance."

Chris celebrated his new acquisition by sailing it from Sag Harbor on Long Island to Camden, Maine, a distance of nearly four hundred miles.

"I'm an action junkie," Chris admitted to *Us* magazine after purchasing *The Sea Angel*.

When asked to define the term, Chris explained, "It's just a flip term to describe the kind of person

LEFT: A 1987 studio photo for *Superman IV: The Quest for Peace.* (AP/WIDE WORLD) RIGHT: With Tony Todd in CBS's made-for-television movie *Black Fox* in 1995. The movie is part of a trilogy of westerns that Chris filmed before his fall. (MONTY BRINTON, CBS)

Chris at a news conference in Santiago, Chile, in 1987. With him is his friend Angelica Dorfman and a group of Latin American actor activists. His heroism that day saved 88 lives and his appearance there was also credited with helping to rid the country of dictator Augusto Pinochet. (AP/WIDE WORLD)

Leaping over an obstacle in Southhampton Massachusetts, on May 14, 1995. Chris said just before his tragic fall two weeks later that "horse jumping is the most dangerous thing I do." (AP/WIDE WORLD)

With his wife, Dana, at the American Paralysis Association gala in New York on November 9, 1995. Chris was recently elected to the board of the organization, which is leading the fight for a cure for spinal cord injuries. (AP/WIDE WORLD)

Matthew and Alexandra—all grown up and helping their dad—at the London launch of "Push 2000," a project of the International Spinal Research Trust. (GLOBE PHOTOS)

Alone on stage at the 68th Annual Academy Awards in Los Angeles on March 25, l996. Chris and millions of Americans believe the day will come when he will rise from his wheelchair and walk away. (AP/WIDE WORLD)

who would rather not lie on a beach sunbathing. I get pleasure out of sports that involve endurance, skill, and precision—skiing, tennis, windsurfing, flying, sailing, gliders. I don't dabble. I try to do these things at an advanced-intermediate level, and I just enjoy it.

In addition, Chris had purchased Exton a house in England as a sort of good-bye gift, further straining his financial resources. He was adjusting to both his new personal life with Dana and to a professional life as a lesser star, which ultimately meant lower fees from the movie studios.

"Gae and I are very good friends, and we have a comfortable relationship," he told an interviewer after the breakup. "We have no issues of contention that I'm aware of in terms of how to bring up the children. They are equally at home in both houses—in the house that I gave Gae to live in, in England, and in our house here [Williamstown]. Gae is still very close to my mother, very close to my brother's wife. So, it was a happy ending in the sense that no one is suffering any trauma out of this. That took work. After we separated, we spent a year very painstakingly laying the foundation for the children's future and for our future. I think no matter what happens between a couple, you've got to find a way to be kind, to acknowledge, 'Look, there are differences that make it obvious that we're not life partners. But that doesn't make me a bad person or you a bad person.'

"There was never an incident, never an act of cruelty or a betrayal between Gae and me. It was just a growing awareness that we were the wrong people for each other. It's not sugary and fake, but we're friends. That's really all there is to say. That is the whole truth."

To pay for his new house in Williamstown, Exton's house in London, the yacht, and his big British tax bill, Chris began to take a variety of jobs that would have been considered *verboten* a few years back. One lucrative offer he accepted was to be a spokesman for the women's lingerie brand, Maidenform. Chris, Omar Sharif, Corbin Bernsen, and Michael York were each hired to discuss—on camera—their reactions to their lovers' undergarments. Chris' copy had him coyly discussing a former girlfriend who dressed plainly on the outside, but was something other than that beneath her outergarments.

"Underneath all that she'd wear all these beautiful, satiny, lacy things," Chris mused. "Lucky me."

An official of the advertising agency said that Chris' appeal was to women between twenty-five and forty. Corbin Bernsen, she said, had a younger appeal.

Chris also began reading audio books for fees that would have seemed miniscule during the Superman years. He made a video for General Aviation's "Learn-to-Fly" program, becoming its spokesperson. Principled as always, he did draw the line at doing a Japanese cigarette commercial, even though it would have paid him several hundred thousand badly needed dollars.

On November 22, 1987, Chris was at his country house in Williamstown when he got a telephone call from the Chilean writer and political activist, Ariel Dorfman. Chris had never met Dorfman but had just read an opinion piece he had written about terrorist activities in Chile of the Pinochet regime on the editorial pages of the *New York Times*.

"Until now, death squads had always singled out individuals for their warnings," Dorfman had written. "A judge who was investigating a torture incident, a trade-union official who led a general strike, a bishop who had called for the resignation of General Pinochet. . . .

"But on November fourth, a new form of intimidation was inaugurated: twenty-five of Chile's most eminent actors, directors, and playwrights (some of whom are my closest friends) received letters giving each until the end of the month to leave the country or be executed.

"That same morning, seven alternative theater groups, comprising fifty-two actors collectively, got similar messages."

The orders that told them to leave or be executed, Dorfman wrote, was from a military death squad called Trizano, named for a notorious Chilean who had become famous for hunting down and then killing thousands of native Indians in the nineteenth century.

Trizano called the actors "figureheads of international Marxism."

Dorfman pleaded with Chris to fly to Chile, a dangerous destination at that time for any American, considering the reputed brutality of the Pinochet regime. But Dorfman didn't want Chris just to visit—he wanted him to lead a rally on behalf of the Chilean actors in an attempt to try to pressure the Pinochet government's thugs into backing down from executing the thespians.

Chris asked Dorfman if his life would be in danger. Dorfman admitted that it would be.

"I can't guarantee your life," Dorfman told Chris. "They might want to kill Superman to make a point."

Chris asked for an hour to make a decision. He called back in less than half that time, telling Dorfman, "I'm going."

Dorfman would have signed his own death warrant if he'd gone with Chris. As a constant thorn in the backside of the Pinochet regime, he had been promised by several of Pinochet's death squads that his "throat would be slit" within moments after entering the country.

Instead, it was Dorfman's wife, Angelica, who said

that Chris shouldn't go alone. She would go, she said, serving as his interpreter.

"It's not only dangerous. It's a jungle in Santiago. I'll go with him," she told her husband.

"What do you answer when someone says, 'We really think you could directly save the lives of people?'" Chris would say later. "Do you say, 'I have to go to the bank or I have some letters to write?'

"Like most Americans [I knew] that Allende, the democratically elected president, had been killed and that there was an election coming up in Chile that could be rigged."

Chris said that before being contacted by Dorfman he had been unaware of the relationship between politics and art in a dictatorship and how much freedom there was for the arts in a democracy. He said his eyes had been opened. His energies had largely been directed to the safe causes "like homelessness, hunger, Save the Children, and cancer."

Dorfman hadn't thought of Chris first. He wasn't sure even what Chris Reeve represented. He had wanted Meryl Streep to head the rally, but she was filming the movie A Cry in the Dark in Australia. He called a friend, the writer William Styron, for his suggestion. It was Styron who told him to get in touch with Chris. He did so by contacting Margot Kidder, who gave him Chris' phone numbers.

Before Chris left, the Chilean activist told him that he believed his presence might attract enough attention that would force Trizano into halting its plan to execute the actors. Their political theater had embarrassed and satirized the Pinochet dictatorship, thus the threats.

"Chris clearly was in his Superman persona," Dorfman told the author. "But Superman is bulletproof, Chris was not."

The Chilean told Chris that Trizano operated covertly, abducting Pinochet's opposition by night, with most of them never being heard of again. By shedding light on Trizano's threats toward the actors and exposing their plan, Dorfman and his friends believed that the terrorist organization would lose credibility. Alerting an international audience through a major actor, particularly one who was perceived as Superman, would, Dorfman believed, force the group "to crawl back under their rock."

On the morning of November 30, 1987, Chris arrived in Santiago, Chile. He was accompanied only by Dorfman's wife, Angelica, a German actor, two actors from Argentina, an actor from Spain, and a Uruguayan theater critic. Chris was the only one who had world recognition and voluntarily became the leader from the outset. A cartoon in a local paper greeted him, portraying him as Superman, flying Augusto Pinochet out of the country by carrying the dictator in his arms much as he had done on screen a decade before with Lois Lane.

Chris had twenty-four hours—midnight on that final day of November was the deadline—until the actors were scheduled to begin being killed by the death squad.

Before he had left America, he had helped coordinate a writing campaign to Pinochet. It caused telegrams and letters to begin streaming in from international stars that included the likes of Sir Laurence Olivier, Julie Christie, Glenda Jackson, John Gielgud, Ingmar Bergman, Alan Bates, and Vanessa Redgrave.

But the mission had now become doubly dangerous because Chris was legally on his own. His travel to Chile was without any endorsement or protection by the United States government. Instead, his trip was sponsored solely by Amnesty International and the Actors' Equity Association.

Chris arrived in Santiago sleepy and disoriented. He had been unable to sleep during the eleven-hour flight. During the one-hour stopover in Peru, he had insisted on investigating the airport's capabilities rather than resting.

"I don't sleep on planes," he explained later, "I'm a pilot."

Chris thought Santiago was a lot like Los Angeles.

"I thought, God, what a great town, it's just like L.A. The rich people live in the hills just like Beverly Hills, and the poor people live in the flats, like Watts," Chris recalled.

"[But] there is a complete stratification of the society. North Americans live with at least the illusion of social mobility. In Chile, you just cannot move out of your level of society."

When he saw young actors in Santiago walking the streets "with white T-shirts that had bull's-eye targets on them" and words that read in Spanish, "Shoot Me First," he was clearly moved. He visited the apartment of a Chilean actor, Julio Jung, and watched the actor take intimidating phone calls. When Jung answered the phone, the only sound on the other end was machine-gun fire.

That afternoon Trizano increased its pressure. It sent a message to the Chilean Actors' Union saying that the actors would now have to face the consequences for going public and for ignoring the initial threat which instructed them not to contact the media. The death squad then named twenty of the more prominent actors and said at least one of them would be dead the next day.

"If you don't believe us," the message concluded, "ask one of the following." A list of five names followed. They were the names of people who had been missing for several months.

The rally at which Chris was scheduled to speak was called Vida y Arte, meaning Life and Art. It was scheduled to begin at eight that evening, in the small Natanael stadium, which had a capacity of five thousand. The site was in one of the poorest and more dangerous areas of the city. Still, the lure of Superman had the stands filled to overflowing two hours before Chris arrived.

"Superman, Superman—take Pinochet away," the crowd chanted.

Perhaps because of cheers like that, the Santiago police canceled the rally at seven o'clock, with troops arriving, setting up machine gun nests and cordoning off the area. The organizers were now very afraid. They believed the police meant business. The police did indeed. They began tear-gassing those present—Chris included.

The organizers became so frightened for the lives of their leaders that they decided upon an alternate plan. The rally was moved to another location twenty-five blocks away—a midtown garage that Chris later said looked like a "rusty airplane hangar." The second venue was potentially even more dangerous because there was but one door to the windowless building that, as Chris remembered was, "about ten feet wide." Several thousand people squeezed into the building for the rescheduled rally.

Chris had seen plenty of protest rallies at Cornell. But in the United States, he would say later, "There is a basic assumption that nothing is really going to happen to you. You can go in and speak your piece.

"[But] in Santiago, there were people hanging from the rafters, [and] there was a great deal of discussion as to whether I should go in there. After all, this was in clear defiance of police orders. What had begun as a statement of goodwill could definitely be construed now as political."

As Chris began to walk into the crowded building, while the heat outside hovered around ninety degrees, several of the organizers burst into tears. They believed Chris was about to be killed.

"I said to Chris, 'You don't have to go in there,' "

Angelica Dorfman told the author. " 'I can't guarantee your safety anymore.' "

She said Chris thought for a moment and then said simply, "I'll go in."

"The actors just didn't think I would come out if I went in," Chris later recalled. The local actors' union surrounded him with six bodyguards, and Chris walked into the packed building and began fighting his way to the stage. Inside, the Chileans screamed and stomped their feet, trying to touch the figure they identified with Superman and tear off pieces of his clothing. Chris said that it was like no display of fan worship he had ever experienced.

"Superman, Superman," they screamed.

"It was unbelievable, the kind of reception I'd associate with the pope, or the Beatles at Shea Stadium," Chris remembered. Outside the building, a pitched battle was taking place, with the police trying to disperse the horde of people who hadn't been able to get in by dousing them with water cannons and firing more tear gas.

As he took his place on the stage, the crowd began to sing in unison. It was a song of the anti-Pinochet movement, "He Will Fall." At that point the lights were turned out. Surprisingly, in the blackness of the building, the crowd refused to panic. The supporters stood silently until the lights were restored, which took nearly a half hour.

When Chris got up to speak, he had with him a letter that had been signed by many of America's most prominent actors and actresses (a small sampling: Susan Sarandon, Gene Hackman, Cher, Martin Sheen, and Mia Farrow). There were no microphones, so Chris used his stage training, speaking strongly to the back of the room. He read the letter, speaking at times in Spanish but mostly in English. He had had only French and Latin in high school, but still he began with a game "*Nosotres, actores y artistas.*"

He told the crowd he would return to America to let his people know "what brave and beautiful people you are." As he spoke of his "amazing day," a singer began to strum a guitar and croon a revolutionary tune behind him. After the rally he told Angelica Dorfman he was "totally exhausted."

The next day, the Pinochet regime backed away from the death squad order.

"There's no doubt that Chris put his life in jeopardy that day," David Hinkley, a former California regional director of Amnesty International, told the author.

"He was the leader. Chris Reeve deserves the primary credit for saving eighty-eight lives. He also helped bring awareness of Amnesty International's work to the entertainment community."

"Chris is an example of how one can relate his art to his life," Ariel Dorfman said. "Chileans can never be thankful enough for his presence there that day."

Chris was modest about his heroism. He tried to play down his role to the *Los Angeles Times.* "This was not Superman to the rescue. It was me as a private citizen, and as an actor in a country where we take the freedom to perform for granted, helping fellow professionals in a country where they do not.

"If you know me as Superman, fine. But we have to remember that Superman is light entertainment. This was real life. This was not just an adventure story, this was not in the comic books."

Ariel Dorfman, though, would suggest that it was Chris' image as Superman that had made General Pinochet retreat because "he was palatable to all sides in Chile—the left, the center, and the right."

Chris later said he would do the same thing again, but "probably not in Chile, because it would look like an individual crusade.

"[In Chile], life and art go together. Here, art is a nice decoration for our life. Here, we can imagine change and we can see change. That can't happen in Chile. That's something they have to imagine in the theaters."

A year later the Pinochet government was voted out through a *plebiscito* (a yes or no vote of confidence)—one of the rare instances that a dictatorship has been ousted through the democratic process. Dorfman gave Chris part of the credit in helping bring about his country's return to democracy.

"It was very difficult to get rid of Pinochet," Dorfman told the author." And it's fair to say that Chris was at least partly responsible for his removal."

In 1988 Chris was the recipient of one of two awards given by the Walter Briehl Human Rights Foundation, an organization of psychotherapists who work with torture victims.

11

"You are a great guy."

—DONALD TRUMP

When Chris took the part of the preppy Blaine Bingham in what was the fourth film version of *The Front Page*, it was the first time since *Superman* that he had accepted the third billing in a motion picture. In the movie, retitled *Switching Channels*, he was billed after his friend Kathleen Turner (playing the role which Chris had once played on stage in Williamstown—it was a distaff remake) and the oleaginous Burt Reynolds. Coloring his hair blond for the part, he appeared to be trying to play his role in disguise. But any movie must have seemed better than suffering through the indignities of *Superman IV*.

"Blaine is such a weenie," Chris gamely told a gathering of reporters, "but I got a kick out of playing him because he's different."

The plot had Chris playing a foppish nerd who meets Kathleen Turner's news reporter character at a resort and proposes to her. Turner later decides she can't leave her news beat or her ex-husband boss, Reynolds.

One of the few genuinely funny moments in the

movie—and one that Chris wanted highlighted so that he could once again distance himself from his Superman image—is the scene in which he became trapped in an elevator on the twenty-seventh floor of an office building. Chris' Bingham falls to the floor kicking and screaming for help because he suffers from acrophobia. It caused the cognoscenti present in the theaters to utter knowing laughter.

"My agent flipped out with that scene," Chris said later. "She thought it would hurt my image—but it was a delightful diversion from *Superman*."

Director Ted Kotcheff called Chris' performance a "comedic masterpiece," but that was more likely a loyal exaggeration. The reviews for the strident movie were mixed, with Chris' performance rating only slightly better than the film.

Time wrote, "Christopher Reeve brings a nice macho wimpitude to the role of her new beau—he's Clark Kent with a preening ego."

And Sheila Benson observed, "Christopher Reeve has the most thankless role as Christy's [Turner] brand-new fiancé, Blaine Bingham . . . [who is] utterly expendable. The script makes him the billionaire owner of a chain of sporting-goods stores, and Reeve, checking his newly lightened hair in every stray mirror, makes the most of him."

Jeffrey Lyons inexplicably called it "Christopher Reeve's best role."

But just as typical were David Denby's harsh remarks in *New York* magazine: "Christopher Reeve, who plays the pathetic rich suitor—the Ralph Bellamy role—really is pathetic on-screen."

Hal Hinson in the *Washington Post* wrote that the idea wasn't "half bad. But to say that the job director Ted Kotcheff and his cast . . . have done with the idea of *Switching Channels* is half bad wouldn't be doing it justice—it's bad all the way. And then some."

Switching Channels, like so many of his attempts to

shed his Superman image, failed. Turner, Reynolds, and Chris were now perceived as fading stars by the public, and reviews were generally like Hinson's—bad or indifferent. After picking up $3 million its first weekend, the movie lost steam fast, dropping theaters and ending up with just over $10 million. It was considered "a bomb" financially.

The three principal actors couldn't even carry the movie. Many of the reviewers focused on a scene-stealing Henry Gibson and character actor Ned Beatty as a crusading district attorney, singling out the two for most of their positive remarks. For Beatty, it marked his fourth appearance acting in a motion picture with Chris.

"I really did that movie just to fool around," Chris said a year later. "I thought it could work, but it was played much too broadly. None of the characters was vulnerable enough to get much sympathy, and you ended up not caring about anybody."

He seemed almost sad when talking about how so many of his films had been unable to attract an audience.

"I've become philosophical about it. There have been so many highs and lows, and I don't always want to take the roller-coaster ride anymore."

Chris always seemed a little reluctant, even a little embarrassed to talk about *Switching Channels*. In press interviews just before its opening, he seemed to want to talk more about the play in which he was then co-starring—the alcoholic, womanizing John Buchanan, Jr.—opposite a pregnant Christine Lahti. The drama was a revival of Tennessee Williams' *Summer and Smoke* at Los Angeles' two-thousand-seat Ahmanson Theater. He had gotten decent notices.

"Reeve seems wooden at times but largely turns in a respectable performance and even shines in the scenes where he's particularly cadlike," wrote Susan Spillman in *USA Today*. "Though we've come to expect Man-of-Steel purity from the Juilliard-educated actor, Reeve watchers will recognize his bad-boy moments as reminiscent of the scoundrel he used to play so well on *Love of Life*."

Chris had played the part before to sold-out crowds but weak reviews in Williamstown in 1986 with Laila Robins and Stephanie Zimbalist. He explained why he was repeating the part to writer David Galligan:

"I wanted the challenge to play a part I'd already done once before, to see what more could be found and what the difference would be. I'd never repeated a role before, so that was an interesting idea."

Chris admitted to a group of reporters at the time of his *Switching Channels* press tour that the stage was still his first love. He told them why.

"Stage and screen acting offer completely different challenges," he said. "In movies you have to be completely unself-conscious and to have no awareness that the camera is on you. And movies are filmed in bits and pieces, out of sequence. On stage, you get the satisfaction of telling the story all at once. You get a chance to deepen your work by repetition—some actors are bored by repetition, I'm challenged by it—and you have a direct relationship with the audience. You must be aware of the audience. If not, your performance will die about five feet in front of the footlights. The stage, personally, gives me a lot more satisfaction. The theater is a much more demanding medium in which to work."

The reporters were told during the press junket that his fallback plan if he hadn't made it in the acting world was to "move to Alaska and become a bush pilot."

He was also willing to talk about his new lover for the first time.

"I met someone in Williamstown last summer, and we've been together since," he told Tom Breen of the

Washington Times. "Her name is Dana Morosini, and I'm very fond of her."

Chris was quick to add that marriage was "not part of the agenda," but said that anything was possible.

Even a *Superman V*?

"You know, I get a little annoyed when people say I've gotten too big for *Superman*, that I've forgotten that he made me a star. That's absolutely not true. I very much want to make a fifth *Superman*, but I want it to be a quality picture. I want quality as much as the public wants it."

"I'm looking for a big, big, big hit," Chris told the *Indianapolis Star* in late 1988. "That's a big change for me. I've always resisted blatantly commercial movies and just pursued whatever roles interested me, which has not always been a smart career move."

Sounding almost desperate, Chris concluded by telling his interviewer, "I'm always looking for scripts. The mailbox is open! Operators are standing by!"

It would be four years before Chris would appear on the big screen again. He was crushed after being turned down for the role of Sherman McCoy in Tom Wolfe's *Bonfire of the Vanities*. It went to Tom Hanks, and Chris was candid in expressing why he had become out of favor with the studio decision makers.

"I sat there and made an impassioned plea as to why it should be me," Chris told the *Boston Herald*. And they said, 'You'd be absolutely perfect. I think you'd be great casting for the role. And there's no way we're giving you this part.'

"What was not being said—the filling in the blanks said—'I'm not going to go with somebody who hasn't had a hit in two years.' That's the problem with this town [Hollywood]. It's just like stocks. Instead of being a sixty-dollar stock you're an eighteen-dollar stock."

Chris realized he had become the third or fourth choice of the big studios. He was frustrated, not sure how to rise again in the Hollywood studios' pecking order.

"There have been a couple of times when I expressed a very strong interest in a movie and the studio has said, 'No. Unless we get one of the top five people—Bill Murray, Kevin Kline, Alec Baldwin, Kevin Costner, and whoever—we won't make the movie.' I fall below that line. They'll even admit, after a reading, that 'you're really right for this, but based on your track record in the last couple of years . . .' These guys are just going by the ledger sheet, and because I haven't had a hit domestically in a few years, they can't justify doing a fifteen-million-dollar film with me. So there have been times when the movie hasn't been made, even though I'm standing there in the corner with my hand up saying, 'Me, me! I could do this!' "

Chris marked time by doing the made-for-TV two-part miniseries, *The Great Escape II: The Untold Story* for NBC. To his credit, he still couldn't just walk through the parts offered him. He researched his character, the Allied officer, John Dodge, as diligently as he had when doing *Superman*. Chris traveled to a library in Vermont that had a special collection of documents on the World War II hero's life, interviewed his son, Tony, in London, and his daughter, Phyllis, in Connecticut. In interviews, he sounded as if the hero's career was one he wanted to emulate.

"Dodge's life was one long adventure," he told one television writer. "He served in two world wars, climbed the Matterhorn, and swam the English Channel!"

Looking at photos of Dodge, he was struck by the strong likeness he had to the character he was called upon to play. "Surprisingly, I resemble him. He was tall, had the same hawk nose I have, and strong features. He also wore a mustache, which I wear in the film," he told TV writer Kay Gardella.

Chris said he had seen the original action classic, which had starred Steve McQueen and James Garner, when he was eleven. In order to prepare for the sequel, he said he rewatched the original "fifteen times. It's one of my favorites."

Essentially a four-hour standard action-adventure, the miniseries was at least noticed. "[*The Great Escape II*] is not as spectacular or star-studded [as the original, but] it is more than competent and quite exciting. Filmed in Yugoslavia, it has a nice look to it, a feeling of reality aided by attention to detail," wrote Michael Hill in the *Baltimore Sun*.

The two-parter did better commercially for Chris than *Anna Karenina* had. Its Sunday night first half broadcast finished a respectable twenty-seventh out of eighty-one shows rated during the first week of November 1988. The following night the ratings weakened slightly, as the film lost much of its male audience to *Monday Night Football*.

Although his appeal as an actor was slowly sliding downhill, some of his life's priorities—particularly Dana Morosini—were working out well for Chris. He elaborated on it to *Us*.

"See, what doesn't work for me in a relationship is where one person is out and does things and the other person stays home and cooks soup. One of the things that's so great about Dana is we sail together, we dive together, we ride together. She skis nearly as well as I do!

"I didn't put that right," he said, chuckling. "We're both really good skiers. She plays a good game of tennis. She's a great dancer. She laughs all the time. She thinks life is to be enjoyed. So I've got a partner."

When asked about the possibility of marriage, Chris still hedged, saying, "I think that I've had a hard time, since growing up I saw a lot of marriages that didn't work. The impression I got of marriage as a child was that marriage is not a stable institution. People make promises they don't mean and they don't keep."

He admitted, though, there was a chance of marriage with Dana Morosini. Was there any possibility of a wedding in the near future?

"A very strong possibility with Dana," Chris answered.

He also found time for noble causes. When Chris learned that an old Williamstown movie house, the Images Cinema, on one of the village's main streets had been purchased by a developer and was about to be torn down, he took charge to save it.

Joining an ad hoc committee of local residents, Chris went to the contractor and convinced him to keep the theater by scaling it down from its 400-seat size to 196 seats and use the rest for commercial space.

Chris then got together a group of actors who agreed to host a screening of their movies so that $50,000 could be raised to refurbish the old movie house. He got Merchant Ivory to give $500. He asked friends like Olympia Dukakis to appear for a showing of her film, *Moonstruck*; Paul Newman and Joanne Woodward to screen and discuss the film version of *The Glass Menagerie*, in which they'd starred together two years before; and Chris himself appeared to explain the making of *Street Smart* after it was shown. The townspeople packed into the little theater for the shows, paying a bargain ten dollars.

"We're all doing thirty minutes of questions and answers with the audience," Chris told the *New York Times*. He promised that local high rollers who gave $200 or more would get their names affixed to the back of a seat.

The plan was successful. The renovated movie house is still operating in Williamstown today.

Chris also used his name to help block the construction of a $350 million coal-fired electric power plant just over the state line in New York. He believed the project would rain down pollution onto the Berkshire Hills. He went to the state capital, lobbying against the project with New York governor Mario Cuomo.

John Seekwood, a member of the Sierra Club, later told the Williamstown *Advocate* that Chris "played a significant role in the apparent defeat of that project, as he has in other worthwhile causes. He was severely criticized in Albany for getting involved—but why shouldn't he?

"He didn't lend his name casually. He asked for factual information and got back to me with factual questions, sometimes playing the devil's advocate."

There weren't many major motion picture roles being offered to Chris by the end of the 1980s. And certainly none that he accepted. He seemed to have been forgotten by the major studios. Chris, who had been called a workaholic many times, took whatever came his way. Besides the British tax problem, a series of bad investments had shrunk his net worth to virtually nothing.

He did Fox Television's magazine show *The Reporters*, for which he served as a celebrity newsman for the hour program, reporting on the deforestation of the Amazon rain forest. He hosted television shows such as *The World's Greatest Stunts* and *The Valvoline National Driving Test* for CBS-TV. Once considered a superstar, he shared the spotlight on the Valvoline hour with Betty White and Meredith Baxter Birney.

When asked by the *New York Times* what his next films would be in 1989, Chris waffled, saying there were a number of maybes.

"They're in orbit," he told them. "It's that kind of year."

An actor's life is a life of rejection. Even the most successful stars are often turned down for roles by producers who feel they simply aren't right, or not skilled enough as an actor, or would otherwise strike a false chord in their production. And, of course, sometimes the rejection is strictly for commercial reasons. If another actor who can bring more bodies into the theater is available, then often the original choice is spurned.

Rejection was happening to Chris frequently now. Not on the stage as much, but certainly in major films. It was hard to take. And even when he chose to do serious theater work, there were often harsh, nearly personal attacks on him.

These thoughts may have been in the back of his mind as he prepared to take the role of Polixenes in Joseph Papp's production of Shakespeare's *The Winter's Tale* at New York's Public Theater in April 1989.

After telling the *New York Times* that *Superman* may have been "a main event for the public, but for me it was a detour," he went on to tell the newspaper that though most people thought of him as a movie star, the stage was still his first love.

"The theater is my home. I've done about one hundred fifty plays in twenty-one years. Many actors say their first love is theater, and you ask them when they were last in a play and they say, 'Ten or twelve years ago.' I do at least one, two, three plays a year."

After *The Winter's Tale* opened, John Simon, the influential *New York* magazine critic who has a reputation of writing his reviews with an acid-dipped pen, ganged up on Chris. "Polixenes [is] played by Christopher Reeve, the Superman whom trick photography projected into our skies and onto our screen and stage. He does not so much speak his lines as gargle

with them, in some sort of artfully snotty Ivy League
accent, while strutting or striding in his best Skull
and Bones [a secret Yale fraternity] manner. I kept
hoping he would transform himself at least into Clark
Kent, but no such luck."

Chris had told the *New York Times* before he had
taken the role that he sometimes got such "conde-
scending" remarks. But he said, "I try to be patient."
Surely, his patience must have been wearing thin
that spring.

There was other sadness as well. Early in the year
his friend and stage mentor Nikos Psacharopoulos,
the artistic director of the Williamstown Theater festival, had died, leaving a void in his life. Psacharopoulos was replaced by Peter Hunt and Austin
Pendleton. While Pendleton had once been Chris'
drama coach in New York, the theater would change
under their direction and, for Chris, would not seem
quite the same.

Still, Chris told a writer in 1990 that he considered
Williamstown his first home and that "I've worked
hard to become part of the community." He said he
no longer wanted to live where people were "ob-
sessed with status. In Williamstown, people care
about the community. You are judged individually
here."

He also said that he would never give up on New
York City. There would always be an apartment
there, he told the interviewer.

"I feel a commitment to New York, because everyone is so negative about it. Someone has to stick
around and work on it."

Chris had. He was then an active member of West-
pride, a civic group that was battling Donald Trump.
The millionaire was seeking to build a huge development on the west side of New York called Trump
City. Yet when asked to narrate a two-hour documentary (financed by Trump's arch enemy, developer

Leonard Stern) on the controversial Trump, and at a time he certainly could have used the fee, he refused, feeling he "would be perceived as biased." Trump quickly wrote a letter to Chris thanking him for his fairness:

> Your concern about the possible bias of a documentary on me sponsored by Leonard Stern, a man seemingly obsessed by Donald Trump, is laudable. I know that as a member of Westpride you have expressed concern about Trump City, my proposed development on the west side of Manhattan. I respect you for your opinions on that project, but I respect you even more for drawing the line at possibly irresponsible attempts to pass off as "documentary journalism" a seemingly never-ending personal vendetta against me by a man who does not feel good about himself. Leonard Stern seems to be having quite a few problems with life. Mutual aquaintances say you are a great guy—now I can see they are right.
> Sincerely,
> Donald Trump

Chris then met personally with the real estate and gambling tycoon at his offices in New York. The two reached a compromise, with Trump agreeing to build a project that more suited the sensibilities of the West Side activists.

Back in Williamstown that summer—twenty-one years had now passed since his first appearance there—Chris acted on stage playing a rare dual part. In the Civil War drama *John Brown's Body*, he portrayed both a Northerner and a Southerner, which required him to change his accent from scene to scene. If he was still smarting from John Simon's diatribe, Mel Gussow's remarks in the *New York Times* must have seemed a balm.

The critic wrote that the drama was "performed by a fine three-person cast" (Robert Lansing and Laurie Kennedy were the other two) and that "Mr. Reeve brings great conviction to his part." He also said that Chris had struck "one of the show's most plaintive chords" as he tried to track down the woman he had loved and was forced to leave to go off to war. Gussow summarized by saying that Williamstown's first effort of the 1989 season had begun "on a note of eloquence."

12

". . . a real turn on."

—DANA MOROSINI REEVE

"**R**eal life hit me in the face in the eighties," Chris confided to *TV Guide* in 1990. He was referring to the end of his relationship with Gae Exton and some of his bad movie reviews. But he was optimistic about the future.

"I have more to bring to the screen now. I'm sure I'm going to make my best movie in the future."

On the fate of the earth, a matter that now concerned him greatly, he told an interviewer for *Us* that he hoped the decade of the nineties "would become an activist decade like the sixties had been—the main focus is the globe. People are not going to stand dictatorships any longer. A certain level of personal freedom will be guaranteed around the world, and the global issue will not be freedom versus tyranny. The global issue will be the future of the planet as a place to live. What I get most involved in are things like toxic waste, recycling, water, deforestation, the greenhouse effect, and global warming. These are important issues to me, and if there's anything I can do to help along those lines, I'll do it."

Chris certainly did. He started 1990 by recording a series of public-service announcements for a proposed New York state law that would allow citizens to bring lawsuits against polluters.

"We urge everyone to write to Senator [Ralph] Marino and complain," Chris lobbied on the pages of *Newsday*. Marino was the chief legislator holding up the bill.

He was the off-camera voice and chief cheerleader for the Discovery Channel's documentary *Black Tide*, an account of the Exxon *Valdez* tanker ship's oil spill. *Variety* described Chris' narration as a "stirring commentary."

"The oil industry would like consumers to think that the *Valdez* was like the *Challenger* tragedy—a single error in an otherwise flawless track record," Chris lectured on the hour-long program. "But between November 1988 and January 1989, there were forty-three spills in the area." Chris concluded that the program he was hosting was "about moral and spiritual imperatives. If we can't wake up and make peace with nature and stop abusing this miraculous privilege called life, then we'll continue to inflict upon this Earth the tragedy of the Exxon *Valdez*."

A few weeks later Chris went to Washington and pressed legislators to pass the Clean Air Act. On the evening of April 3, 1990, appearing on *Larry King Live*, he kept a watchful eye on the U.S. Senate's vote on the bill, even though he was supposed to be on the King show promoting a movie he had made for Ted Turner's TNT cable channel, *The Rose and the Jackal*.

"I was the spokesman for Save the Children. I've done a lot of work for Child Hope, for asthma research, various green causes, but starting in 1986, I began to work in the political system more, and lately I've been getting very involved in a number of things, particularly the National Endowment for the Arts, the homeless, and dealing with the environment," he told the CNN broadcaster.

When King asked Chris if he didn't think he was taking a risk by being so outspoken, and that he might make people dislike him who ordinarily might attend his films, Chris gave this answer:

"Well, people who aren't going to like me aren't going to like me anyway. . . . Life is not a popularity contest. The better off you are and the older I get, the more confident I get in just sticking to what I believe in, making sure that I'm fair, rational, and informed, and then saying what's on my mind. And it's important also, as a star, not to be a rent-a-star—in other words, they just truck you out for any old thing, and you don't know what you're talking about.

"I think people suspect celebrities anyway as being self-promoting, and in the things that I do, whether it's campaigning for Patrick Leahy in Vermont, or whether it's working for the National Endowment for the Arts, I really do take the time to do my homework so that I'll have a certain credibility."

Earlier in the day, Chris had met with U.S. Senator Wyche Fowler, a Georgia Democrat, in a final push for the Clean Air Act. Fowler, a proponent of alternate fuels and alternate energy sources, told Chris that it would pass that evening.

Midway through Chris' discussion with Larry King, the broadcaster told him that the Clean Air Act had indeed passed by an 89 to 11 vote.

"That's very good news," Chris told King. "That's a much bigger margin than I thought would happen, so that's great."

As for *The Rose and the Jackal*, he had been cast in yet another costumed period piece, this time playing Allan Pinkerton, the founder of the Secret Service, in a Civil War setting. Not only was Chris in nineteenth-century dress, but this time he had been outfitted in a full beard and whiskers, affecting a Scottish accent.

The transformation hid his distinctive features and caused him to resemble a young Ulysses S. Grant.

He had simply fallen into the role, Chris told King. When asked if he had been chosen by the producers because he fit the part, Chris answered his interviewer, "I'm not even sure if they said this part fit me. It was 'We're going to shoot November 20 and we don't have anybody, let's call Reeve,' you know . . ."

Ted Turner, who likes movies set in the Civil War era (the Georgia tycoon had recently purchased MGM partly because it owned the classic *Gone With the Wind*), financed the film lavishly with a production budget estimated between $10 and $15 million. Chris' Pinkerton was the "Jackal" in the title, while actress Madolyn Smith Osborne played Rose O'Neal Greenhow, a spy who was both Chris' love interest and nemesis. Again there were mixed reviews.

"As written by Eric Edson, this is an engaging enough film, even if Pinkerton's outbursts of temper become almost laughable," wrote Kay Gardella in the *New York Daily News*. "Reeve lets out all stops, barreling through every scene like a bulldozer. What is achieved here is an exciting feeling of unrelenting tension between a man and a woman caught in a conflict of love and honor."

But a Norfolk, Virginia, newspaper would say, "Poor Chris Reeve is stuck with a pretty weird version of Pinkerton" and "becomes something of a peeping Pinkerton beneath her bedroom window." The critic, Mal Vincent, ended the review by saying, "Dixieland had best look away."

Chris returned to Princeton that May to attend the twentieth reunion of his Princeton Day School class. At the ceremonies, he was given the class Alumni Award for his "extensive involvement in human services." The school did not mention his acting achievements when presenting him with the award.

"He has given his time, his energy, and his mind

to human rights activities in places like Chile," Princeton Day School's headmaster, Duncan Alling, began. "He has gone into hospitals and spent time with young people and old people who are in great pain. He has worked for other types of volunteer and charity organizations—whether it's supporting them through his voice and his presence in terms of advertising or giving his own time to these people."

He then detailed Chris' Chilean heroism and went into literally dozens of charitable and social causes for which Chris had worked, ranging from Mothers Against Drunk Driving (MADD), the American Heart and Lung Association, the National Jewish Hospital for asthma research, and a Library of Congress program that urged children to read. He also named twenty others. It was a prodigious feat, but Chris told his former classmates he didn't really care whether or not people knew about his activism.

"If people are interested, they'll take the time to find out. If they're not interested, they won't," he told a reporter for the local *Princeton Packet*.

He said the day had made him "pleasantly embarrassed."

Chris' mother, Barbara, who was present for the award, said that she was "tremendously impressed . . . I'm very proud of all that he's done as well as the award itself."

The Alumni Day reunion took place inside the school's hockey rink with the ceiling containing balloons in the school's blue and white colors. Old photographs and pennants of his class filled the walls.

Chris told the crowd that he had just finished a national tour of A. R. Gurney's *Love Letters* with Julie Hagerty (the two had gotten raves), but was "beginning to branch out into producing and directing."

The school's headmaster noted that all Princeton

Day School students were required to perform at least ten hours of community service each year. He compared it to Chris' volunteerism.

"We think that volunteer work is a very important value to continue to promote," Alling told the audience as he awarded Chris a plaque. "It really is special to be able to give the Alumni Award to someone who has demonstrated extraordinary effort in this area."

The spring tour of *Love Letters* had been one of Chris' great triumphs. The two-character play with Hagerty had found drama critics receiving it in various degrees—all rapturous. Chris, who had certainly experienced his share of negative reviews, must have particularly savored Kevin Kelly's remarks in the *Boston Globe*.

"They're as good as it gets," the critic began, adding that he had seen it performed by five other two-person teams. "It's a wonderful performance. And so is Reeve's. He is handsome, charming, self-deflating, and so finely tuned to Andy's character that the final breakdown shouldn't come as a surprise but it does (at least it did for me). Reeve plays it straighter than, say Matthew Broderick, who, last week, gave the play youthful brio and made it funnier. Reeve doesn't get as many laughs, but he is closer, I think, to the essential pathos at the heart of Gurney's script. The emotion in Christopher Reeve reading the final apostrophic letter, the tears streaming down his face . . . well, there's nothing more I can tell you.

"*Love Letters* seems to me to get more remarkable each week. But right now I can't imagine it without Reeve and Hagerty."

After touring several cities for Heart Strings, an organization that matched national celebrities with local talent to raise money for AIDS patient care, Chris went back to Williamstown for yet another season of doing what he liked best—summer stock—

before an appreciative audience of serious theatergoers. This time, onstage with Blythe Danner in a reworking of the 1929 Broadway classic *Death Takes a Holiday*, Chris got some of the best notices he had yet received at the annual theater festival.

Typical was the *New York Times'* Mel Gussow, who wrote that "as the title character . . . Christopher Reeve has another role commensurate with his larger-than-life presence. Replacing his bright Superman cape with a cloak of spectral darkness, he is a not-so-grim reaper. More than anything, it is the actor's drollness that helps invigorate this creaky vehicle."

Chris and Dana moved in 1990 from his longtime duplex apartment on the fashionable West Side of New York to a less expensive neighborhood on East Twenty-second Street. The new eight-room apartment still wasn't cheap. The price was $900,000, though it had been on the market for $1.5 million. To keep his lifestyle afloat, Chris sold his largest plane for $300,000.

He had once been a major movie star. That status was in eclipse as the final decade of the century began, despite the bold statement of his best movie roles still "being in the future."

Chris appeared to be floundering, becoming mired in a series of quick, cheaply done made-for-TV movies that were, to put it kindly, forgettable. In 1991 he made a "now-you're-dead, now-you're-not" type of feature in Canada for the Lifetime cable network, *Death Dreams*, with Marg Helgenberger, who had just won the Emmy Award playing a prostitute on ABC-TV's *China Beach*. In the clichéd *Death Dreams*, his character's drowned stepdaughter talked to him from the grave. Leonard Maltin called it "hopelessly predictable and corny." Chris immediately made another such quickie, this time for the USA cable network called *Mortal Sins*, playing a priest again but with better results ("as smooth as pudding" and "first-class," *Variety* said of his performance). Instead of an attractive postulant nun from whom to take confession, as he had done in *Monsignor*, this time Chris had to listen to a serial killer blabbing to him about his most recent crime.

Another quick effort for CBS television had Chris making the segue from priest to pedophile in *Bump in the Night* with Meredith Baxter Birney. Chris's starring role required just seven days of filming. The finished film, Chris said, was "so chilling" that he would not allow Matthew (then eleven) and Alexandra (then seven) to view it.

During an interview with the *Washington Post*, Chris revealed that he himself had likely experienced a brush with a pedophile in his youth.

"When I was thirteen, I was involved in the theater and I was supposed to get some stills taken by a photographer. I came over to his house and he had a studio set up. But he asked me to take my shirt off and then I could imagine myself standing there in my underwear [next]. I went straight home and told my parents. Because nothing specifically had been done to me, there was no arrest that could be made."

Chris' part had him playing the molester of an eight-year-old boy, certainly nothing that might expand the membership roster of his fan club, but one which once again erased part of his superhero image. But he was worried about the perception of the children who were Superman fans.

"I seriously hope that parents will take control of the TV set on the Sunday night that this is on. There might be some kids out there who hear I'm in the movie. They've got to explain that just because he was Superman in one movie doesn't mean he's the same in this one and they should take the time to say an actor often pretends, that it's fun to pretend, that he doesn't really do these things . . . this is a movie for adults to watch, not for children."

Even though the part had just taken a week to film, Chris still researched his role. He spent several days looking at materials provided by the New York City vice police, particularly pamphlets printed by NAMBLA, the North American Man-Boy Love Association.

The pederast part was followed by what critic Tom Shales pronounced "a garbagey CBS movie," *Nightmare in the Daylight.* The plot this time had Chris playing a sleazy lawyer who mistakes actress Jaclyn Smith for his wife who supposedly had died several years earlier in an earthquake.

"Smith is beautiful as always, but she seems like she should be hosting a network morning show rather than acting like this," Shales wrote. "Reeve is embarrassing; another Superman bites the dust."

He acted in still another historical movie for Ted Turner's cable channel, TNT, an adaptation of Jack London's *The Sea Wolf*, with the leathery veteran action star Charles Bronson. Chris played an effete intellectual which contrasted with Bronson's more colorful villain, Wolf Larsen. Catherine Mary Stewart was the romantic interest.

There were narratives for PBS, noble efforts such as *The Road from Runnymede*, which celebrated the writing of the United States Constitution. He played a yuppie unable to deal with his father on a "Family Works" public television drama *The Last Ferry Home*, with a plot centered around saving the nation's small farms. Laudable as these were, few watched or cared.

He still found time for causes. When the National Endowment for the Arts needed his help, Chris was there. He took on conservative senator Jesse Helms, televangelist Pat Robertson, and their followers without fear of consequence. Both had wanted artists who received NEA funding to sign pledges not to create works that were offensive to their followers. The NEA won the yearlong skirmish with his help.

After the victory Chris wrote in *McCall's* magazine that "Fortunately . . . Congress decided that the NEA's critics should not be given official status as the moral guardians of America, and that politicians should not be empowered to decide what is art. Those decisions should be made, as they have been made for the last twenty-five years, by a panel of peers. And if an artist is found guilty of obscenity in court, he or she is asked to give the NEA back its money.

"That's fair enough. The courts have the authority to rule on obscenity as defined by community standards. Politicians should *never* have the authority."

"I urged Chris to run for Congress [upon the death of the Williamstown area representative, Silvio Conte] in Massachusetts," Jane Alexander, the former actress who heads the NEA, told the author. "He would have been ideal. He's an outstanding citizen who's passionate about what he believes and does his research before he speaks out on the issues."

In his personal life, Dana became pregnant during the fall of 1991. A few months later, just before Christmas, Chris, now thirty-nine, decided enough was enough and during a turkey meatball supper at the New York apartment asked her to marry him.

Chris told Britain's *Hello* magazine that he and Dana both blurted out, "Let's get married!" at the same time.

"Saying that was the sexiest thing," Chris told *People*. "We put down our forks and went straight to the bedroom. It was extremely erotic."

Dana agreed, "It was a real turn-on."

Escalating his memory of the conversation, Chris added, "It made me feel so horny!"

Chris began talking about the decision to himself, repeating the phrase "We're getting married" out loud for months, as if he couldn't believe the ceremony was imminent.

The two wrote their own wedding commitments to each other, setting a date of June 30 for the event—because it was the fifth date for "our anniversary." Events soon changed their plans. When they found out Dana was due to give birth before that day, they moved up the wedding arrangements so the nuptials would be certain to take place beforehand.

Chris and Dana exchanged their vows and simple gold bands before a Williamstown minister (who also conducted white-water trips as a side venture) on April 11, 1992. Franklin, Barbara, Matthew, and Alexandra were all present, as were Dana's parents, for the small wedding attended by forty-five other guests. The ceremony took place outside on a damp Saturday afternoon in a pastoral public setting, known as Field Farm, in South Williamstown.

"I love being married. I love it," Chris said to Dana every day during the first year they were married. "This is a good deal!"

There was no real honeymoon. Dana was in a play in New York, the Manhattan Theater Club's production of Donald Margulies' *Sight Unseen*, and Chris was promoting his first film of the nineties, a comedy for Disney's Touchstone division called *Noises Off*. Just three days before the wedding, he had promoted the movie in an interview with the *New York Daily News*, sounding a bit upset about the direction his career appeared to be headed.

"Look," Chris argued, talking about what had resulted from *Superman*, "a hit film creates opportunities. *Lethal Weapon* created *Hamlet* for Mel Gibson. If he had just walked in off the street and asked to play Hamlet, he would have been laughed at. A hit creates opportunities. You can make intelligent choices after that.

"I haven't made intelligent choices, though, I must admit."

Chris seemed to be speaking about the future as well.

"I'm trying to be careful about my choices. I take projects now on their merits rather than just career moves. If you do something because you like it, even though you don't make all that much money on it, and you find your lifestyle has to change because of it, well, maybe you should adjust your lifestyle. Otherwise you've just become a slave to it."

Chris had no illusions about his status in the movie industry. He told one interviewer: "[Robin Williams and I] followed parallel paths for a while. He was Popeye at the same time I was Superman. But now Robin is jet-propelled, and I'm paddling alongside in a canoe."

Dana gave birth to Will at the North Adams Regional Hospital, near Williamstown, during the first week of June. The name had many positive connotations. Besides being the same as the town and the theater festival where Chris had done some of his best work, it was also that of his great-great-grandfather who had come to America from Ireland in the 1860s. And it was also the name of the character Chris was about to play in a low-budget theatrical feature he was about to begin filming, *Morning Glory*.

Months before Will was born, they had joked about naming him Murray. If that had occurred, their son would have been named for the Murray Hill section of New York, where Dana's obstetrician had revealed Will's gender via a sonogram.

They also purchased another home that year, a secluded—the dirt road leading to it was unmarked—nineteenth-century farmhouse on seven acres. It was near Bedford Village in New York's Westchester County, for "about a million dollars," according to a local real estate expert.

"We love New York," Chris now said, "but we didn't want to raise our child in the city. It was time to move. We like our privacy."

The small estate was less than an hour from Manhattan. It was also close to Dana's parents' residence. They talked briefly about selling the Williamstown property.

"But we can't," Dana told the *Berkshire Eagle* in an interview. "I mean, this is where we began, where we got married, where our son was born . . . it's such a meaningful place to us."

"All my kids will be here this summer," Chris told columnist Jeannie Williams. "Matthew mostly likes tennis camp here. Alexandra and I ride together. And Will just likes all of it."

As for *Noises Off*, a movie version of a hit play, it was made on a tight budget—as it was mostly filmed on a single stage. The ensemble cast of good actors (many of whom were Chris' friends), had made their names on television, but their appeal to audiences had waned. Chris got seventh billing, but only because the credits were in alphabetical order. His name appeared after that of Carol Burnett, Michael Caine, Denholm Elliott, Julie Hagerty, Marilu Henner, and Mark Linn-Baker but before John Ritter and ingenue Nicollette Sheridan's (who, as the film's focus of titillation, spent most of her on-screen time dressed only in a bra, panties, and a garter belt). Chris' salary for the movie, $100,000, was the lowest amount he had ever received for starring on the big screen.

The slapstick, madcap comedy with lots of physical bits in its stagey scenes—Chris gamely hopping around with his trousers around his ankles and in one sequence dressing as an Arab sheik—worked well. But the movie, about a group of American actors doing a British play, whose accents volleyed back and forth faster than a ball across a ping-pong table, however erudite, was hard to follow. Box office returns were miserable in spite of good reviews.

Desson Howe in the *Washington Post* summarized the movie by writing that it "brings back the ageless joy of well-timed slapstick" but also aimed a vicious barb at Chris by calling him "the dullest actor of our time." Inexplicably, the usually grouchy Stanley Kauffmann of *The New Republic* found the opposite to be true.

"I can hardy believe this as I type it," Kauffmann wrote, "Christopher Reeves [sic], old cement-block Superman himself, is limber as the husband and is appealingly ridiculous backstage as the actor who plays the husband."

The summer that followed his marriage to Dana marked the last time Chris was to appear in a full-fledged play at the Williamstown Theater Festival. Director Michael Bloom's (he had also directed Dana in *Sight Unseen*) choice of the Hungarian playwright Ferenc Molnar's *The Guardsman* was typical of the type of theater and film vehicles with which Chris had now become associated, even more than *Superman*. The comedy had been written in 1909 and dusted off many times, including a 1931 movie starring Alfred Lunt and Lynn Fontaine (the legendary couple had originated it on Broadway). Chris' character of Nandor (the part Lunt had portrayed) was the jealous husband who tests his wife's fidelity, played by Ann Twomey. Given Williamstown's penchant for extravagant production values, the ten-character drama was a perfect way to end his run there, which had spanned nearly a quarter of a century.

Jeffrey Borak, the erudite critic of the local *Berkshire Eagle*, said Chris "gives an earnest, highly energetic performance, but it is a performance that is at odds with the measured style of the performance around him. His admirable spirit and energy are not enough to overcome a lack of style and focus."

* * *

Chris was nearing his fortieth birthday. Ilya Salkind, who had gotten back the rights from Golan and Globus, was making noises in the press about producing a *Superman V*, and one published report said Chris would "get $9 million" if he cared to put his tights and cape back on. Salkind talked out loud—perhaps to get Chris to lower his fee—wondering if perhaps Chris was "too old" to play the role. But Chris squelched Salkind's plans quickly by refusing even to consider donning the red-and-blue costume again. He said the Salkinds should have stopped after two *Superman* movies.

"After that I felt they started to go downhill. It's very hard to put quality on the screen. It costs a lot of money and you need first-rate people, and it was hard to keep that in place."

Chris said he felt the initial film, though, was "a part of American history."

He told writer Nancy Mills, "I don't want to even consider the number of sit-ups I'd have to do [in order to play Superman again]. I was perfect for the part at twenty-four, but I'm not the same person now. Why go back? If you're a slave to your bank account, you've lost something.

"In the late seventies and early eighties, when I was in a position to pick and choose, I don't think I was really ready for it. That can happen in this business, where the opportunity and your development don't go together, particularly if you have a big success early.

"One thing about acting that I like is that as you change, what's open to you changes. You get dealt new cards all the time."

Chris was about to be dealt "new cards." In the fall of 1992 he had gotten a phone call from his friend James Ivory.

"I've got a script for you," Ivory told him.

13

"A quite unlikely smash."

—VINCENT CANBY

"**F**or the past twelve years, those in the arts were forced to take up the battle lines and defend our existence. With the Clinton-Gore ticket, the life of the artist is not something to be ashamed of anymore."

Chris spoke those words at the Clinton presidential inaugural gala. He had gotten his political wishes in 1992. Working hard for the two candidates, he had been particularly attracted to the vice-presidential hopeful, Albert Gore, because of the Tennessee senator's vow to begin cleaning up the world's environment.

Campaigning side by side with Gore on a littered shoreline near Sandy Hook, New Jersey, during the fall, Chris had slammed the policies of the Bush-Quayle administration. "I've watched in despair as every environmental law is trashed by this administration and Quayle's Council on Competitiveness," he told reporters.

Gore joked about his supposed resemblance to Chris as they picked up cans and bottles with a horde of supporters on the beach, spreading his pro-environment message. He admitted to some facial similarities but noted, "They haven't seen me without my shirt on!"

Chris now had enough clout at the White House to get personal briefings from Clinton's deputy cabinet members. He took the opportunity, relishing the privileges of power.

Early in 1993, Chris made a little independent movie, *Morning Glory*, with Deborah Raffin. The distributor had neither the clout nor the funds for mass distribution, but believing it was a good product, opened it in a few major cities in the hope of getting good reviews. Positive criticism would enhance the price the filmmakers could then command from a pay cable channel, and give them quotes to put on the video rental packages.

Though the Depression-era drama wound up getting mostly negative notices (". . . gives simplicity a bad name," wrote Matthew Flamm in the *New York Post*), Chris got strong reviews, including this prophetic rave from *Newsday*'s Gene Seymour.

"Those who can't take Reeve seriously unless he's wearing a blue suit and a red cape will find themselves pleasantly surprised by the heft and subtlety he brings to his portrayal of Will. The strong-but-silent patina, harder to pull off than it looks, seems a perfect fit for Reeve, who hasn't had a break from the critics since the *Superman* features stopped coming. This movie isn't big enough to make Reeve a star again. But the impression he makes here is good enough to suggest that a reversal of perception—and fortune—won't be long in coming."

When Chris had seen James Ivory at the New York premiere of *Howard's End* in March 1992, he had almost begged for employment. After the film was shown at Lincoln Center he turned and asked, "Any part in your next movie, please."

Ivory hadn't forgotten. He soon called Chris with

the script of his new film, *The Remains of the Day*, saying, "You're Lewis."

The Merchant-Ivory-Jhabvala team had become more than just an art house power since *The Bostonians*. Years of critical acclaim, several Academy Awards, and a string of twenty-two mostly profitable motion pictures such as *A Room with a View* and *Howards End* had begun to attract mainstream audiences. Their films also began to open in suburban multiplexes in addition to the big city venues that had once been their only home. Jhabvala's stately stories were still being made for a fraction of a Hollywood studio's budget. A Merchant-Ivory movie that grossed $20 million—about the salary of a Tom Cruise or Julia Roberts—could nearly always be expected to offer good returns to the tiny studio's investors.

For *The Remains of the Day*, James Ivory offered Chris the part of a brash American congressman-millionaire who purchases an elegant British estate from its owner, a disgraced Nazi sympathizer. Chris didn't take time to contemplate his decision. He accepted immediately.

His part of Congressman Lewis was minor but essential, Chris was told. The dominant theme of repressed love that existed between two of the house's servants—the butler, played with great subtlety by Anthony Hopkins, and the executive housekeeper, Emma Thompson, whose assertive charm would prevent the film from becoming overly solemn—was the central story.

The script placed Chris in just ten scenes, but called for him to be an important figure in the opening sequences. Midway through the movie he was asked to deliver a pivotal speech against the Nazi government after a formal dinner, concluding that the British and French diplomats present were "decent and honorable and well-meaning gentlemen, but amateurs."

James Ivory generously allowed Chris to be given star billing in the film. His name appeared fourth in the credits, and before the picture's title, but after Hopkins, Thompson, and that of James Fox, who played the duped English lord who was sympathetic to the Nazi cause.

In an interview at the time of the movie's opening, Chris professed to be intimidated by working with actors of the stature accorded Hopkins and Thompson (both had just won Academy Awards).

"Jim's [James Ivory] had an amazing body of work, and I get very shy and insecure around great talent," he told a reporter. "I remember once trying to talk to Meryl Streep on an airplane. She came over to talk and knelt in the aisle. I was sitting there behind my dinner tray, and I turned beet red. I'd let some people know how in awe of her talent I was, and I was wondering whether anyone had ratted on me. I went to pieces. I started to sweat like I was eating curry."

Chris told *USA Today* that since he was now forty-one, it was "nice to be able to play characters with some mileage behind them. That's more rewarding."

The Remains of the Day opened on the first Friday in November 1993. Vincent Canby became an instant seer when he wrote in the *New York Times*: "Here is an exquisite work that could become a quite unlikely smash."

Smash it was. The movie was still drawing capacity audiences in hundreds of theaters six months later. It earned eight Oscar nominations, including all the big ones: best picture, best actor (Hopkins), best actress (Thompson—who was also nominated for best supporting actress for her part in *The Name of the Father*), best director (Ivory), and best screenplay adaptation (Jhabvala). Up against other serious motion pictures like *Schindler's List* and *The Piano*, it drew a blank at the Oscars, but female audiences adored the production, and ecstatic notices by some of the nation's best-known critics made it a "must-see" for discerning filmgoers.

On television, both Gene Siskel, Roger Ebert, and Gene Shalit as well pronounced it "magnificent" with the first two adding "Two thumbs up, way up!" In the *Washington Post* Rita Kemply said it was "a Merchant-Ivory masterpiece." That set the tone, but critic Michael Medved took the praise to new levels by ending his essay with "if you miss the chance of seeing it, you may not be guilty of wasting your entire life, like Stevens the butler, but you will have missed a glorious opportunity."

Mentions of Chris in the reviews were brief, as they usually focused only on the two main roles played by Hopkins and Thompson. (One British critic simply commented on his features, calling him "the spitting image of Al Gore.") When they singled Chris out, the notices were generally relegated to a phrase or two like "a well-utilized Christopher Reeve" in *USA Today* or "Christopher Reeve brings authority and Yankee energy to the one dissenting voice in the collaborationist circle" (*Variety*), or even more typically, ". . . heads a superb supporting cast," a line that appeared in several publications.

A year later Chris was asked by a reporter what had been the favorite movie experience of his career thus far. He named *The Remains of the Day*.

"I don't regard that as my movie—I was a visitor—but it's the best movie I've ever been in. Anthony Hopkins gave one of the best performances ever captured on film."

Any actor who is part of a wildly successful movie which earns eight Oscar nominations will see themselves advance in their industry. The halo effect from such a film is immediate and long-lasting. For Chris, *The Remains of the Day* meant a return to stardom. Perhaps it was not the same stature he had enjoyed a decade before, but certainly the part of Lewis had made his name rise again. He was now, if not at the top of the lists maintained by casting directors, at least again someone to consider.

He met with producers to discuss playing a "surprise" villain in a big budget movie, telling *Entertainment Weekly*, "the way to cast me is as someone you wouldn't suspect, who seems to be on the right side but is up to no good. I wouldn't want to do anything bland."

Chris continued as well his work for social and political causes. One issue about which he had begun to speak out strongly was the subject of censorship, an issue he had dealt with on behalf of the National Endowment for the Arts. Those who knew him probably weren't surprised to see Chris fly to Tucson, Arizona, just after *The Remains of the Day* opening in order to make a dramatic statement against the parents and faculty of a high school that had not only banned its students from performing a controversial play, but had fired the students' faculty adviser, who had suggested the production.

The drama was *The Shadow Box*, which had won both the Pulitzer prize and a Tony award in 1977. Its plot revolves around three terminally ill cancer patients and how they face death. The graphic language and intimations of a homosexual relationship shocked the faculty of the high school and some of the more conservative parents of the students.

"I thought it was a very powerful play that had scenes that the kids could get into," the fired teacher, Carole Marlowe of Flowing Wells High School, told the media. She had toned down the profanity but was still ordered to jettison the play after the principal began to get complaints. Marlowe was ordered to go through all of the nearly three hundred plays in the school's archives and black out every "objectionable" word. Then, after letting her class perform a scene during the school's Fine Arts Week, she was forced to resign, fired for insubordination. More than three hundred students had staged a walkout in protest.

Chris led some powerful acting names—Mercedes Ruehl, Blair Brown (his cochair at the politically active Creative Coalition), Harry Hamlin, Estelle Parsons, Robert Sean Leonard, Michael Tucker and his wife, Jill Eikenberry—into Tucson to perform the play in an impromptu reading at a packed 627-seat auditorium. The audience gave them a standing ovation at the conclusion.

Representing the actors on a nine-member panel that day, Chris was attacked by some of the audience but argued that parents who support school censorship were denying their children a valuable learning experience.

"What I hear this lady saying is that she is uncomfortable with things that don't resemble her or her way of life," Chris responded after being shouted at by one parent. "This country is founded on a completely different principle, which is tolerance and diversity."

The performance by Chris and his friends was later broadcast statewide on Arizona cable systems. The dismissed teacher was nominated by her peers for the state's Teacher of the Year award.

"Art needs to be protected," Marlowe said later, calling Chris and his friends' local demonstration "a healing experience."

After *The Remains of the Day*, there were movie offers again arriving by the dozen. Chris quickly chose three projects. First up would be an MGM big budget romance *Speechless*, where he was billed third behind Michael Keaton ("Batman and Superman in the same movie!" gushed one TV gossip) and Geena Davis. Next he signed with Universal to do a remake of the eerie classic *Village of the Damned* for the horror movie specialist, director John Carpenter. His costars were to be Kirstie Alley and *Crocodile Dundee*'s Linda

Kozlowski. He became the lead in yet a third film, a detective thriller with Joe Mantegna for the HBO channel called *Above Suspicion* (Dana was given a small part as a detective). That film, due out in the spring of 1995, called for him to play his role from a wheelchair.

Back in demand, Chris leased a four-bedroom house in the Hollywood Hills for $9,000 a month in which to live while the movies were shot and edited. It was a little flashy, with its city views, swimming pool, sunken living space, and billiard room, but one reborn could be expected to live like a movie star when in tinseltown.

After he had become settled in Los Angeles, he flew up to Anchorage, Alaska, to begin filming a special for PBS on gray whales. He wasn't just going to stand in front of the ocean and speak. He was chosen for his diving experience, and the part required him to go down deep into the ocean to observe one of the fifty-foot behemoths giving birth.

There was little time for sustained stage work in 1994. Chris still tried to keep his hand in, narrating part of a concert staging of Stephen Sondheim's forgotten musical, *Allegro*, at New York's City Center in March and that summer chaired Williamstown Theater Festival's Fortieth Anniversary gala, reading a scene from *John Brown's Body* and reprising *Love Letters* with Julie Hagerty, the two-character reading he had been so successful performing in 1990.

Chris would get good notices in *Speechless*, a movie based loosely on the real-life romance (denied by the scriptwriters) between Bill Clinton's campaign guru James Carville and George Bush's communications liaison, Mary Matalin. "The story's sidelines are especially enlivened by Christopher Reeve," wrote Janet Maslin in the *New York Times.* "Reeve, who plays Julia's [Geena Davis] other suitor, an egotistical television newsman in a shrapnel-torn vest, a reminder of the combat duty that won him the nickname of 'Baghdad Bob.' 'Well, at a certain point you don't worry about the Scuds anymore,' he remarks with a great show of casualness, 'you just do the job.' "

Essayed long-time perceptive Chris Reeve watcher Gary Arnold at the time: "Christopher Reeve's movie career has taken an eccentric turn for someone with an obvious star presence. He's a modest kick in *Speechless* . . . a superb member of the ensemble in both *Noises Off* and *Remains of the Day*. Mr. Reeve has quietly evolved into a versatile character actor before any sane spectator would have written him off as a leading man.

"It's only a matter of time before he's 'officially' rediscovered and celebrated, like John Travolta in *Pulp Fiction* this year. It should be fun for somebody to contrive the role that certifies his comeback."

The film opened just before Christmas of 1994. *Speechless* failed to ignite much response from audiences, though the domestic ticket sales—at just over $20 million—weren't embarrassing. Davis had produced the movie for her own production company with her new husband, Renny Harlin, and perhaps because of that, her romantic scenes with Keaton were lacking in any chemistry and passion, as if Harlin was looking over her shoulder. But since Chris wasn't called upon to carry the film, his new stature did not erode.

Before the movie opened, both Chris and Keaton told *Entertainment Weekly* that their "men-in-tights" days were definitely over.

"I pretty much had done with the character what I had wanted to do with the character in the first two *Batmans*," Keaton told the magazine. He had just been replaced in the third movie by Val Kilmer. (Keaton's successor was fired after a single outing to make room for *E.R.*'s George Clooney.)

"I was the custodian of the part in the late seventies

and early eighties," Chris said. "If they do it again [producer Jon Peters was now rumored to be considering a new version], there should be a new custodian for the part."

Four months later, Chris opened in *Village of the Damned*, using the publicity tour to comment on the state of America's children.

John Carpenter told reporters at one press conference that he had demanded Chris for "his quiet dignity and good acting" for the updated horror film, which has a small town fall under the spell of alien children.

"In the early 1960s the alien children were a metaphor for communism," Chris claimed, comparing the original film with the new one. He said that Carpenter's new vision was more personal.

"The emotional deadness [of the movie's children] is not all that different from what we see on the streets of America—kids who'll shoot someone for seven cents."

Chris also said he had faced a difficult time viewing the children as the villains of the piece.

"They were so sweet and adorable. They wanted to play Frisbee and sing songs, and I had to look upon them as an alien force."

Added to his usual no piloting of planes during the filming was a new clause: no horse jumping.

Damned, whose genre had begun to diminish due to a surplus of numbingly similar films, was largely ignored by the public, though again Chris was praised for his role as the town's doctor, Alan Chafee.

"Carpenter . . . shows no grasp of character development, plot line, or time passage," wrote critic Richard Harrington, who also didn't like the movie's "cheesy synthesizer score."

On another front, in the spring of 1995, Chris was a keynote speaker, representing the Creative

Coalition on the National Endowment for the Arts advocacy day, the organization's annual grassroots lobbying effort. It was a difficult time. Newt Gingrich's Contract with America plan had threatened to cut off the funding for arts programs, and Chris' speech was designed to rally the troops before heading off to Capitol Hill to buttonhole their congressmen and senators.

Chris said he had met with the Republicans in Congress and had been told by a legislator: "The National Endowment for the Arts is dead—it's going to be zeroed out, and there's no way you can organize a grassroots effort to save it; you don't have the support out there [because] people are tired of freebies for the lunatic fringe, and we're going to put a stop to it."

Professing to be taken aback by the congressman's aggressive stance, Chris said he was attempting a constructive dialogue with all of the members of Congress who opposed NEA funding.

"There is a crucial role for the government to play in developing the arts and culture in this country," Chris told the gathering. "I understand people who are troubled by some of the controversies. I agree absolutely that we have to take immediate, comprehensive measures to reduce the deficit. I'm as worried as anyone else about what kind of country we're going to leave our children."

Chris concluded by telling the crowd, "Our job is to convince them [legislators] that if they do [keep funding the NEA], they will have helped the United States take its place among other nations that do not fear the arts, but employ their governments to put them in service for the future."

In 1995, arts funding was cut forty percent by the Congress. The fact that it wasn't eliminated was considered "a moral victory" by the National Endowment for the Arts.

* * *

"I'm beginning to get the hang of it," Chris would tell friends in 1995 about the movie part of his acting career. He looked forward to doing yet another Merchant-Ivory film, *The Proprietor*, with the legendary French actress Jeanne Moreau (he had lost the title role in *Jefferson in Paris* to Nick Nolte). Working with Francis Ford Coppola in *Kidnapped* would be another plum.

Chris completed the filming of *Above Suspicion* in Los Angeles, and looked forward to the rest of his year. The summer season would be one of sailing, tennis, and of course, horse jumping. *Above Suspicion*, a tense thriller in which he played a young detective who becomes wheelchair bound and contemplates suicide, had many parallels with the fate which awaited him. Among them was his character's attractive wife, played by Kim Cattrall, and a young son. One scene in the movie had him turning to his younger brother and saying, "I'm paralyzed."

PART THREE

In the midst of winter, I finally learned that there was in me an invincible summer.

—ALBERT CAMUS

14

"I love your new tie!"

—ROBIN WILLIAMS

Christopher Reeve is not a superstitious man. He believes in making his own luck through hard work. Yet the history of actors who've played superheroes is fraught with disastrous fates. Some have called it a curse.

The original Superman, Bud Collyer, was heard on the radio for nearly a decade, beginning in 1940. Collyer used his real name, Clayton Heermance, for most of his run, which may have prevented him from being typecast. He went on to host TV game shows like *Beat the Clock* and *To Tell the Truth*.

A second portrayal was acted by Kirk Alyn, who played Superman in several fifteen-part serials between 1948 and 1950. Afterward he became despondent and complained of being typecast, with much justification.

"I couldn't get another job in Hollywood," Alyn would say. He had appeared in forty films before getting the Superman part but never got another after his stint as the Man of Steel. Alyn eventually moved to Texas, where he developed Alzheimer's disease.

Except for Christopher Reeve, George Reeves is the best-known Superman by virtue of the black-and-white television series in which he played the Man of Steel between 1951 and 1957. After the series ended, he was virtually unemployable, getting but one acting role, a guest shot on *I Love Lucy* playing (no surprise) Superman. Depressed, he died of a gunshot wound to the head in 1959 in what police termed a suicide, yet which his mother believed to be a murder. The cause of his death was never really solved to anyone's satisfaction.

The current television Superman, Dean Cain, had no previous show business experience unless one counts playing college football. Ironically, it was for Princeton, where he was almost as famous for dating classmate Brooke Shields than for his football heroism. Cain got the part only after dozens of actors refused to audition, believing the role to be jinxed.

Chris' Lois Lane, Margot Kidder, has seen her career and personal life spin out of control. There were few successful films after the Superman series. In the last decade she has had to file for bankruptcy, was paralyzed and in a wheelchair for several years, and had to help her only daughter battle bulemia. There were three failed marriages. On April 23, 1996, she was found by police, dazed and disoriented, barefoot, with superficial cuts and missing her dental bridge, in the backyard of a Glendale, California, residence. Kidder told police she was being followed by agents of her former husband, writer Tom McGuane. He in turn told police he had had no contact with her for nearly twenty years. Kidder was taken to the psychiatric hospital at UCLA for observation.

"I'm shocked and mystified. My heart goes out to her," Chris said shortly after learning of her collapse. "She was always there for me when I needed her."

Chris offered to help her financial situation by doing a series of readings of *Love Letters* with her, the two-character play in which he had triumphed with Julie Hagerty.

Two days later she was released into the custody of a family member. Destitute and broken, she was taken by the guardian, first to a private clinic and then back to her native Canada so that, according to one report, she could avail herself of the country's national medical care, a free program.

The two creators of Superman, Jerry Siegel and Joel Shuster, wound up as near paupers after selling the rights to their character in 1937 for $130 each. After Superman gained a renewed wave of popularity in the 1970s, their poverty was made public and Warner Brothers began paying them each a $20,000 per year stipend. Shuster died in 1992, and Siegel passed away in January 1996.

Other superheroes have had similar experiences.

Adam West, the popular Batman of the 1960s, later said that the TV series was "a hindrance to my career." Today he makes part of his diminished income from appearing at comic book conventions, where he signs autographs.

His TV partner, Burt Ward, who played his charge, Robin, said, "The stereotyping was just too great." He has disappeared from Hollywood.

The martial arts invincible hero, Bruce Lee, died on the set in 1973 at the age of thirty-two. Though drugs were rumored, his managers claimed that large doses of aspirin had made his brain swell, causing his death.

His son, Brandon, trying to fill his father's shoes, also died on a movie set twenty years later, when a prop gun that was supposed to shoot blanks was fired at him. It contained real bullets. The death was ruled an accident.

The Kessler Institute for Rehabilitation in West Orange, New Jersey, is about forty minutes from Manhattan. A campuslike complex of mostly two-story red brick buildings, it resembles a private college more than a hospital. Its setting is tranquil—woods and lawns surround it as well as a private golf course.

Kessler is used to celebrities. Dancer and actor Ben Vereen was a patient for several months in 1992 after being struck by a van attempting to cross a highway near his home in Malibu, California. The institution helped him to walk again by teaching him to use two canes. So grateful was Vereen that he returned several times to entertain recovering patients.

Shortly after Chris was wheeled into the Kessler Institute, Dana hung a poster in his room. It was a giant photograph of the space shuttle taking off from Cape Kennedy, Florida. Autographed by every astronaut, there was a message at the bottom which read: "We found that anything is possible."

Taking that slogan to heart, Chris told his new doctor, Marcalee Sipski, that he wanted to be "proactive" in his recovery efforts. He defined "proactive" as meaning "I believe I'm going to walk again."

The spinal cord specialist was pleased with Chris' spirit. She had seen too many patients arrive at Kessler in bleak, despondent moods which bordered on suicidal.

"One of the ways to be ready [to walk] is to keep the muscles in shape," Chris told *Today*'s Katie Couric in one of his first interviews after arriving at Kessler. "We do something called E-stim or electrical stimulation. It's something that literally allows you to sit on a bike and ride it—the aerobic workout is unbelievable."

Chris had noticed the dejection of the other patients. He was determined not to become that way himself.

"There are people who have no motivation to get

out of bed here. There are people who are sunk in despair, and I feel sorry for them."

Chris told Couric that the motivation he needed to recover was sitting at his right. Turning in that direction and looking at his wife, he said, "Without Dana, I couldn't do any of this. Without my kids, I couldn't do any of this. They're my reason to push and to keep going."

Chris' first week at the rehabilitation center was spent being evaluated by the Kessler staff. Sipski brought in her team of therapists—occupational, physical, vocational, speech, recreational, and respiratory—as well as a few medical specialists from nearby Saint Barnabas hospital. After days of quizzing, prodding, and poking their patient, they decided on a tough, intensive program.

Two days after Chris arrived at the rehabilitation center, he and Dana celebrated the day of their first meeting—"our anniversary"—in his room. She fed him the easy-to-chew hospital food and "toasted" their future with fruit juice. Chris would have liked to have had something more exotic. But foods with strong smells made him gag. When Dana had brought in several spicy Chinese dishes from a nearby carryout, the odor was so overpowering she had to eat it in the bathroom, carrying on a conversation with him through the open door. She later tried again with crab cakes, this time with more success.

"He believes that there is a purpose for everything, including his present battle," Craig Alexander, the director of psychology and neuropsychology at Kessler said two weeks after Chris had settled into the arduous routine. Alexander, who coincidentally was Sipski's boyfriend, said that Chris' recovery from his injury could be expected to take as long as two years, and that much of it would be accomplished after he left the institution.

Alexander announced that Chris was undergoing

four hours of therapy each day saying, "The immediate plan over the next couple of weeks will be to get Christopher into an electric wheelchair so that he is able to get around independently. The chair can be controlled by his mouth or his head."

"One goal is the weaning of [Chris] from his respirator," Sipski added. "Our medical staff has been heartened by his increase in vital capacity—the amount of air that he can blow out of his lungs. His speech has already improved a thousand percent, and he can now move his head from side to side, chew his food, and shrug his shoulders."

Alexander described Chris as "a passionate, intelligent, and confident man who strives to direct and control as much of his treatment as possible."

Chris' new routine started at seven in the morning. After being fed breakfast, usually by Dana, he'd begin his day of therapy. First his legs and arms were stretched to prevent the tendons and muscles from shrinking. Then a series of neck exercises began because, as Chris would explain it to friends, "Well, the way they put my head back on after the injury, it is not on the way it was before. It's a little bit farther forward."

He then would be placed on a device called a Regis Cycle, which would force his legs to move progressively faster, giving him an aerobic workout as well as preventing atrophy in the limbs. When he did that exercise, he wore a pair of custom-designed spandex shorts which had a dozen electrodes implanted inside. The electrodes stimulated his muscles by giving them minute shocks. These and other grueling variations went on for two to three hours, at which point Chris would be returned to his room for lunch with Dana that was usually followed by a quick nap.

His wife drove the eighty-five miles from their house in Bedford, New York, to Kessler in her black

Eagle Vision sedan each day—a round-trip of some three hours. Chris would later tell Larry King that Dana never missed a single day during the entire six months he spent at the Kessler Institute.

Dana was learning too. She was taught to do everything the nurses did. She learned how to turn Chris over every two hours while he slept and how to perform the more unpleasant tasks of changing his undergarments. Chris had no control over his bladder or bowel functions.

One of Chris' few pleasures that summer was being wheeled out onto the rehabilitation center's rear patio in the late afternoon, where he could face the fading sunshine and watch the birds flying from tree to tree. Even that seemingly benign pleasure was fraught with danger. Because he was paralyzed, his sweat glands couldn't function properly. On hot days the nurses would have to apply cold towels to his skin to keep him from overheating. His temperature would often rise above a point considered dangerous by the doctors.

The ventilator that breathed for him came with another smaller tube attached to it. From time to time it sprayed water into his mouth. That soothed the still-damaged tissues of his throat, which was still healing from his tracheotomy. The water also allowed him to swallow without gagging.

There were many complications in those early months at the rehabilitation center which quickly became crises. His temperature would sometimes inexplicably spiral upward without warning, and he would be rushed down the road to Saint Barnabas Hospital, where doctors would work frantically to stabilize him.

Another problem was bed sores, caused by his immobility. One would last for more than six months, progressing to where it opened, creating a hole and exposing the bone. The doctors considered performing a special operation before rejecting the solution as too dangerous.

"You become very knowledgeable about your body because you have lung problems, skin problems, bowel problems, bladder problems, all caused by the spinal cord. The brain can't get messages through to control these things," Chris would tell ABC's Barbara Walters.

"There's nothing easy," Dana added. "Everything is a struggle. . . . The thing that is hardest, I think, for me to think about is him playing the piano, because that's something not many people know that he knows how to do, and that's something that he and Will shared a lot."

On another occasion it was reported that Chris' heart had stopped when he took a new medication, Sygen. The new drug was a unique form of protein thought to aid the body in regenerating nerve cells. It was said that the Sygen drug had not merged well with the other drugs already present in Chris' body. He was again sped by ambulance to Saint Barnabas Hospital.

"It's possible that the Sygen caused him to go into anaphylactic shock, which can result in a patient going into cardiac arrest," neurosurgeon Karl Stechner commented.

Chris returned from Saint Barnabas the next morning. On his way to his room after the life-threatening experience, he was said to have joked to the nurses to begin keeping the Kryptonite out of his bed.

Another unusual therapy used by his doctors was hypnotism. The doctors believed that by planting happy thoughts and memories inside his mind, like the memory of "the birth of his children" or "his first Christmas gift," he would think positively.

There were psychology sessions as well, all designed to help Chris keep a positive mental attitude. And when his friends from the Creative Coalition—

actors like Alec Baldwin, Paul Newman, and Kim Bassinger—visited, it was Chris who usually had to buck *them* up after seeing their stricken faces.

Part of each day was spent helping him master his electronic wheelchair. The sophisticated device cost $40,000. He soon learned that a strong puff on the plastic straw would make the wheelchair turn right, and a soft one, left. A computer that understood verbal commands was provided. An attendant would strap on a headset, and Chris learned to E-mail and fax colleagues using the technology. He began to badger his agents on what potential future work he could expect and faxed Robin Williams jokes that he had thought up during the night.

Williams was a frequent visitor and, next to Dana and Chris' immediate family, the one on whom Chris could always count to be there for him. The comic would banter with him, at times treading a fine line, for instance once joking (about the respirator tube), "Oh, I love your new tie."

Chris would try to give back in kind, giggling and wondering out loud what would happen if he were to sneeze forcefully into his plastic straw—would his wheelchair then "pop a wheelie and fly out the window?"

When Chris began coughing because of the laughter, the respirator would fill with phlegm, and the attendants would have to hastily swab it out.

After a few weeks he began to learn to breathe without a respirator. It was like being thrown into twenty feet of water and being told to swim, even though one had never taken a swimming lesson.

"They come in and simply pull the plug and say, 'Breathe!' " Chris told Katie Couric. Later he began calling it the "breathe or die" technique of respirator therapy. It took months before he could go four or five minutes. By late fall, he could go ten. Chris likened it to climbing up a "big hill."

"It's harder work than walking up Mount Everest with a backpack," he told Larry King.

There were dark days, days he was so depressed that the most negative thoughts went through his mind. One tabloid reported that he had asked Dana to divorce him; another, that he had asked her to turn his respirator off and walk away after making a videotape telling his children how much he really loved them—Chris denied both emphatically.

"On behalf of all the fans, all of the people around the world who send me their love and support, I want them to know I never had any such thoughts or made any such statement," he said.

In truth, Chris couldn't think about leaving the world anymore. He had begun to believe that perhaps he'd been put on earth for a reason, that there was a purpose for his injury, and that was for him to use his name and his voice to find a cure for his plight as well as the other several hundred thousand people in the country like him.

"I think our Congress makes a huge mistake because they're running around trying to cut Medicaid, Medicare, and welfare, but the way you save money is you stop the disease. You don't try to deal with it on the other end. For example, $5 billion a year is spent on just keeping people with spinal cord injuries ticking," Chris said in 1995.

"Two hundred thousand people in the United States alone have the same problem as me, and a lot of them are very poor people. A lot of them are on welfare. A very small amount of money—say, as little as forty or fifty million dollars—if that would be spent on research, you could cure Parkinson's, Alzheimer's, multiple sclerosis, and spinal cord injury in the very near future. But I'll bet you, in my life, and maybe in the next ten, fifteen years, if the public will demand that the politicians spend that little bit of money, and make that investment, I'll be up and walking around again."

Chris currently believes that the key to his walking again lies with a new technique he calls "nerve cell transplants—where you take nerve cells from other parts of the body and inject them into the gap where there's broken nerves and trick the nerves into deciding to accept them and regrowing."

He believes that by "building a bridge" out of the body's own materials, is "far more promising than drugs." Other research partly confirms his theory.

Fred Gage, a doctor at the Salk Institute in La Jolla, California, is working with skin cells that he has genetically engineered to secrete growth factors and neurotransmitters. He reported in 1994 that the cells cause regeneration of sensory nerve cells in the spinal cord. Testing is continuing, but any treatment is years away.

One test, using newborn rats, found them overcoming hind leg paralysis after sections of their spinal cords were removed and replaced with transplants from fetal animals. In another experiment, several spinal nerves in the rats regrew after being treated with growth-stimulating biochemicals.

The spinal cord is a shimmering column of nerves that joins the brain to a human's nervous system. Delicate yet flexible, it is held in place by ligaments and roots inside the spinal column.

The medical profession believes that it's on the verge of knowing how to repair the nerves of the spinal column. "Why can't nerves heal like a bone fracture?" they ask. Nerves do regenerate. The problem that hasn't yet been solved is how to help them connect with one another correctly.

Yet, however encouraging this medical research, it should be stated that the capacity to regenerate nerves is easier in young rats. The young, more simplified body structure of infant rats has the ability to grow new nerves much faster and easier than that of the adult human body. Chris' answer, at the present rate of progress, may seem tantalizingly close, yet with the paucity of research money currently available, the solution is likely a cruel decade or more away.

By October, Sipski and Alexander were beginning to hint to Chris that his days at the Kessler Institute could be numbered. He was told that he would most likely be home before Christmas. Dana was busily transforming the Bedford house—widening doors and installing ramps. She couldn't find a place for an elevator without extensive construction, so Chris was denied access to the second level of the house.

He could begin to imagine a better future realistically now, even visualizing an end to his paralysis. The dark days were beginning to dwindle to brief black moments, and he took joy in small pleasures. There were times when Will asked for rides in the wheelchair around the hospital, clinging to him as they cruised through the corridors in the wheelchair as if it were a go-cart. And there were moments when Dana squeezed his knee or thigh, and his body surprised him by allowing him to feel her touch.

To display how far his recovery efforts had brought him, he made a decision to appear in public for the first time since his fall. The occasion was the Creative Coalition's annual Spotlight Award dinner on October 16, 1995.

And how could he not be there? One of the two recipients of the award was his friend Robin Williams. As he was also both cochair and cofounder of the group of celebrity activists, nothing could have kept him away that night from the $1,000 a plate dinner at New York's Hotel Pierre.

Certainly, if timing is everything in show business, then his appearance before the glittering audience of five hundred—many of whom he was personally close to—was right on the money. In the audience were Blythe Danner, Susan Sarandon, Tim Robbins,

Robert F. Kennedy, Jr., Jane Alexander, Carly Simon, Barbara Walters, and Katie Couric. Each of them had been a part of his life at one time or another.

After being driven to Manhattan in a van by a Kessler therapist, he was wheeled onstage to a prolonged standing ovation. Chris began his speech by thanking Williams for being his first hospital visitor, outside of his family, back in Virginia.

"My life was hanging in the balance and I had a fifty-fifty chance to live and I looked up and there was a guy in a blue hat and a yellow gown speaking in a Russian accent. There was Robin Williams leaping to my assistance!"

Williams, who would kiss Chris on his forehead, responded emotionally, telling the audience: "I came that day, and I'll be back a million times. This man is my family. He's the godfather of my son!"

Chris then told a joke that caused many in the audience to gasp. He remembered an English teacher he'd had at Princeton Day School who told a classmate that there was no excuse for missing class, comparing himself with the student, and saying he would have had no excuse himself if he had missed the event.

"The only excuse for nonattendance," Chris said the teacher told the class, "is having a quadruple amputation. Even then they should bring you in in a basket."

"So," he told the audience, some of whom were in tears, "I thought I'd better show up.

"I never knew how much love was pointed in my direction," Chris continued. "Since my accident I think I've heard from every single one of you. I want to thank you from the bottom of my heart. You've helped me turn my life around."

His cochair, actress Blair Brown, told a reporter before the dinner that Chris was keeping up with the goals of the organization and was on top of everything going on there.

"The first time I went to visit him [at the Kessler Institute] we were talking about the issues we were involved with. Chris was very annoyed by an op-ed piece in the *New York Times*."

Chris reminisced about the early days with Williams at Juilliard and said that the teachers there had tried to make his friend into a classical actor, laughing as he said softly, "Thank God they didn't straighten him out."

When Williams accepted the award from Chris, he didn't handle his friend with any kind of deference. After receiving the spotlight-shaped statue, he cracked, "Before we mount this headlight on Chris' wheelchair, we're going to auction off this tie [Chris' ventilator tube] he's wearing."

Then, after riffing through what seemed to be a thousand one-liners, mostly political ("The Republicans consider tobacco a vegetable for the school lunch program"), Williams praised Chris' humanitarian work and his keen mind.

"You know," he told the audience, "I'm basically the designated idiot, but this man is informed—he's like a laser."

Lest the audience think he was becoming too sentimental, Williams next looked long and hard at Chris' wheelchair and delivered another punchline.

"You're on a roll, brother—literally."

Chris concluded by making a plea for spinal cord research. It would be a theme he would repeat in subsequent appearances during the months ahead.

"Somebody's got to take the leap. Somebody's got to stand on the edge of the Grand Canyon and say that with a good enough running start we can jump this thing and cure spinal cord and other neurological problems . . . and myself and a half-million others will get up and walk in our lifetimes.

"I'm so very lucky," Chris would say, "that we're on the threshold of a cure."

15

". . . the depth of his humanity."

—DEMI MOORE

Chris left the Kessler Institute for home on an icy Wednesday in mid-December. Before he left that afternoon he spoke to the staff of the rehabilitation center, telling them, "You have set the stage for my continued journey."

Some feeling had returned to his left leg. He was getting sporadic sensations along his spine. His right arm had sensation. And he could now go fifteen minutes without the ventilator. His diaphragm was getting stronger because of the breathing exercises he had done every day. By the end of January, sitting in the right position, he would be able to go ninety minutes without the machine.

"Each day I try to get a small victory. It adds up," he told CBS's Paula Zahn of the painfully slow progress.

His garage at his Bedford home had been equipped with enough exercise paraphernalia to furnish a gymnasium. A Regis Cycle was donated to him. There was a tilt-table onto which he could be strapped and turned upright so that his legs felt his weight.

Chris told friends he was toning his unused limbs because he wanted to be ready to throw the wheelchair away as soon as the cure came. As he had convinced the world in *Superman* that the catch line "You *will* believe a man can fly" was a truism he now sought to say in every interview that he believed he would truly walk. He challenged Katie Couric on a *Today* interview to a game of tennis in the near future, and he told Paula Zahn, "Do you know what a trip it will be when I get up out of this chair and walk again—wow!"

Chris was particularly pleased to find another important feeling had returned—his libido. He became very frank in letting practically anyone who asked know that he was more than capable of fathering another child. He said he wanted to have "one or two more," and went further by candidly stating that he looked forward every day to the act of procreation with Dana.

Unlike most paralyzed people with spinal cord injuries, he said any new children he fathered could be created naturally. Usually male spinal cord victims can become erect but are not able to ejaculate. That's usually accomplished for them with electro-vibratory stimulation or, more definitively, with a probe studded with electrodes that's inserted into the rectum. Chris implied that those measures weren't needed in his case.

"[But] a little privacy ain't going to hurt," Chris said to Katie Couric just before going home.

"That's true," Dana said.

"I'm feeling like a high school senior these days," Chris said, smiling.

"Oh, really?" Couric said, "Feeling a little randy, are we?"

"This is a G-rated show, honey," Dana said, admonishing both Chris and Couric.

Speaking with Barbara Walters, Dana suggested that sex between them might have already occurred.

"It's an automatic reflex—it's part of that reflex system as opposed to the other neurological reflex system," Dana said.

"So, it would be possible?" Walters asked.

"Yes," Dana answered. "In fact, it is possible."

"In fact, it is possible?" Walters repeated.

"Yes, I'm here to tell you," Dana said. "We can, and we are able to . . ."

And Chris was even more blunt with Larry King.

"My wife walks through the room, and I'm practically leering at her. It's really embarrassing. It's an automatic reflex. So it works. You know that thing about how it has a mind of its own. That's true!"

In a more demure interview, Dana told *Ladies' Home Journal* that their plans to have more children were "a year and a half away."

On another front, Chris had a new problem that was nearly as serious as his health—money. Despite earning millions of dollars during his two decades as a highly paid actor, the high-maintenance lifestyle on two continents, some bad investments, and the fees he had paid to agents and publicists had left him with no nest egg savings of any great size. The Kessler Institute alone had cost more than $250,000, largely covered by the insurance plan he had purchased years before from the American Federation of Television and Radio Artists—one of the many acting unions to which he belonged.

His at-home care still required an around-the-clock nurse and a visiting physical therapist. First-year costs were estimated to be about $400,000 a year. (Robin Williams, in noting Chris' turnover of nurses, began referring to the firm that sent them as the "Care Less Agency," whose slogan was "Leave it to us, we'll be fine and you'll be flat line.") Chris' insurance had a "cap" of $1.2 million, which was still twenty percent higher than that of the average disabled person. His insurance payments are expected to run out by late 1997.

He began selling assets. One of the first items to be disposed of was Eastern Express. Chris asked $25,000 for the horse. He renamed it Buck to avoid any stigma that the thoroughbred might carry from the accident.

A media story started making the rounds that Robin Williams had agreed to pay for all of Chris' medical expenses. A London paper claimed that the two had made a secret pact while at Juilliard, pledging to each other in blood that they would come to the rescue if one of them were ever in serious need of help. That certainly was denied, but Williams—whose net worth has been estimated at $100 million—has helped Chris in minor ways financially, but it's far less significant than the tabloid headlines have claimed.

"A year or two ago we seemed to be well off," Chris told a *Washington Post* reporter in January 1996 as he lobbied from home, trying to get Congress to raise private health insurance lifetime caps to a minimum of $10 million. "Now my picture has changed. And there are so many other people who are in this situation whose positions are even worse."

Dana confessed she'd become depressed by the insurance predicament, saying: "When I really got into depth looking at the policy's cap, to be quite honest, it was as horrifying to me as when Chris first had his accident. It was one of my worst days when I realized what our financial situation would be and what Chris' care would cost."

Chris wrote a letter which was mailed under his name to every U.S. senator. It asked them to change the cap. He asked them to require every insurance plan to *begin* with a minimum $10 million cap for catastrophic injuries and diseases. A new health reform law was being pushed by senators Nancy Kasse-

baum, a Kansas Republican, and Edward Kennedy,
the veteran Massachusetts Democrat. Chris' friend,
James Jeffords, a Vermont Republican senator,
attached an amendment to it which included the $10
million cap.

One of Chris' arguments was that passing the
amendment would ease the costs of Medicaid. He
pointed out that a third of all Medicaid payments
went to disabled people even though they only made
up only fifteen percent of the recipients.

"[But] you're mistaken if you think I can support
costs of $400,000 a year unless I find work," Chris
lectured one reporter, explaining that he too was one
of those needing help.

Chris even invoked the name of his great-
grandfather on his father's side of the family—the
one who'd once been an executive officer of the
Prudential Insurance Company.

"I remember him saying they felt an obligation to
their customers from cradle to grave," he said. "It's
the proper humanitarian and economic thing to do.
All people in my situation are desperate not to be a
burden to their families, to the government, or to the
insurance companies.

"If [my great-grandfather] knew what was going
on with the insurance companies today, he'd spin in
his grave," Chris concluded.

An official of a powerful insurance lobbying group
trying to block the amendment told the *Washington
Post* that while he had "profound sympathy" for
Chris' "extraordinary tragedy . . . limits are a regret-
table part of many health plans. Without them, many
employers—those who are voluntarily providing
health care benefits to their employees—wouldn't be
able to provide health care at all."

Chris countered the lobbyist's argument by citing
a neutral Price-Waterhouse study which showed the
higher cap would cost an average of just eight dollars

more a year for each policy (Jeffords used the figure of one percent or $19). Relentless in his pursuit of the amendment passing, he recorded a radio commercial that pushed Jeffords' legislation. The spot, funded by the Creative Coalition, soon seemed to run every hour on Washington news and talk stations. It began, "Hello, this is Christopher Reeve. Most health insurance plans limit your benefits. I unfortunately, had to find this out firsthand. . . .

"It's part of my obligation to help push the public and the private sectors to work together," Chris told Paula Zahn as he made the media rounds lobbying for the bill.

USA Today, in a lead editorial, endorsed Chris' concerns:

"Believe it or not, things could have been worse for actor Christopher Reeve, left paralyzed after breaking his neck in a riding accident last May," the newspaper began. "His health insurance has a $1.2 million lifetime payment cap. That's small comfort and it won't last long. Reeve's care runs about $400,000 a year, with no end in sight. After his benefits are exhausted, his insurance company will wash its hands of his care."

They went on to point out that the $1 million cap that most insurers currently offered hadn't been raised for twenty-five years, and thus had eroded ninety percent due to inflation. Summarizing, the paper said that increases in insurance caps were necessary because "without it, millions of Americans—movie stars, workers, and taxpayers alike—are exposed to ruinous costs."

The Jeffords amendment on insurance caps was first debated by the Senate on April 18, 1996, losing 52–46 and then tabled. A spokesperson for the Vermont senator told the author that the Kassebaum-Kennedy bill, with Chris' catastrophic cap adjustment, could be signed into law "with some adjustments" before the end of the year. Unwilling to give up, he did similar radio ads in New York State which protested cuts in Medicaid there.

Chris' visibility in pushing for more research funds for spinal cord victims soon brought results from an unexpected quarter. An Orange County, California, philanthropist, Joan Irvine Smith, pledged $1 million as seed money for a spinal cord research center at the University of California in Irvine. Her reason for giving the gift was a surprise. As a lover of horses, Smith said she gave the money because Chris had not destroyed Eastern Express after the accident and because he had never blamed the thoroughbred publicly for his fall.

Smith handed university officials a check for $250,000, and told them they'd get the remaining $750,000 as soon as they raised $2 million on their own. The total amount of the endowment that the center is seeking, already named the Reeve-Irvine Research Center, is $5 million.

By early May 1996, the center had donations totaling nearly $1 million. Chris was thrilled by the project, saying that the facility would certainly "enhance the chances for recovery of function." It will be located inside the school's College of Medicine, and will focus on Chris' primary theory for a cure—developing treatments that will repair and regenerate neurological functions.

Chris also allowed himself to be elected to the board of directors of the American Paralysis Association, a nonprofit organization in New Jersey. The APA has sought a cure for spinal cord injuries since 1981 by awarding grants to scientists and raising research money. It recently formed a worldwide consortium of scientists to meet and trade information on spinal cord injuries. On virtually every television talk show Chris did after that, he would make sure that the organization's telephone number (1-800-225-0292) was flashed several times.

Even Matthew and Alexandra, now teenagers, made a rare public appearance for their father in England. They helped to launch Push 2000, a project of the International Spinal Research Trust, in London in January 1996. At the inaugural function, held inside a Planet Hollywood restaurant, the press swooned over his children's movie star good looks, speculating on whether or not a show business career for Matthew was possible.

Less than a month after returning home, Chris seemed to be in full attack mode. Every day he worked earnestly in his garage, undergoing the painful physical exercises that promised to improve his condition. At the same time he was raising research money which he believed would hasten a cure. It was much the same way he had attacked the mountains of Vermont for fifty miles pedaling his bicycle summers ago.

When a spinal cord injury made the news—such as that of Travis Roy, the Boston University freshman hockey player who was paralyzed seconds into his first college game—Chris was on the phone to buck the person up, giving advice on what to expect during the rehabilitation phase. He flew to Green Springs, Ohio, in March to christen an $18 million spinal cord treatment center. His first words were, "I'm glad to be here. Actually, I'm glad to be anywhere!" before getting serious and adding, "We stand on the threshold of full recovery. It can happen. The scientists are ready, willing, and able. With support, they will do it."

To show the world he was trying to lead a "normal" family life, he made forays to public events like a matinee performance of the Big Apple Circus during the first week of 1996. He allowed himself to be photographed with Will, calling him his "sunshine," and letting him snuggle in his lap as they watched the clowns.

Was he attempting too much, too soon? Soon after the trip to the circus Chris awoke with blurred vision and a severe headache. After measuring his blood pressure and finding it had soared during the night, he told Dana, "Get me to the hospital, now." He was experiencing "autonomic dysreflexia," which sometime occurs among recovering spinal cord victims because of a urinary infection or constipation. If left untreated, he would have likely experienced a stroke.

Dana dialed 911. An ambulance was dispatched to rush him to nearby Northern Westchester Hospital Center, eight miles away.

"My case was clearly due to an impaction of the colon, which affects high quadraplegics like myself," Chris said in a matter-of-fact statement a few days later from the hospital. "My blood pressure has been stabilized, and I am in no danger."

He added that it could happen again for other reasons like "the lack of drainage from the bladder or even something as simple as an ingrown toenail, or clothing or shoelaces that are too tight."

After being released from the hospital, Chris developed a blood infection which prevented him from exercising for more than a week. There were times at night when his ventilator tube would pop out of his throat as he slept and he would be unable to breathe. An alarm would be triggered which brought a nurse rushing to his bedroom. Although he knew that lying on his back without the ventilator gave him just three minutes to live, Chris joked about it by saying that all his nurses should start "wearing sneakers."

Determined not to allow himself to become down from the setbacks, he stubbornly began telling his TV interviewers: "I deny these limitations. I'm going to fight for the cure. I'm going to fight for funding. I'm going to fight for change."

The good news was that for the first time in years, Chris had far more offers to act, direct, or otherwise offer his talents than he could have handled before his accident. James Ivory offered him a starring role in a new film, then later asked him to direct it by using a video monitor. Keith Samples, an executive with Rysher Entertainment, which had coproduced *Above Suspicion*, told Chris he could still direct the romantic comedy that Chris had been scheduled to begin just after his accident. To prove his intentions, Samples took out a large display ad in *Variety* pledging that the job was being held until Chris was ready.

Chris still had his voice, and old friends were willing to pay him for its use. Warner Brothers, for whom he had made several hundred million dollars with the *Superman* movie series, gave him the part of King Arthur for a full-length animation feature it was producing, *The Quest for Camelot*. He did inspirational speaking at one-day "Success" seminars, at a fee estimated to be as much as $50,000, appearing on the same platform with former New York governor Mario Cuomo and Olympic gold medalist speed skater Bonnie Blair.

He would gladly act appearing in his wheelchair, he said, if his character was "positive." There had already been several offers to do wheelchair parts, but Chris refused, saying the character he had been asked to play was either "a villain" or "someone who's pathetic.

"What we need is more parts like Jon Voight's in [the Academy Award–winning] *Coming Home*—a person of dimension," he told Larry King.

Chris has started writing an autobiography with the help of essayist Roger Rosenblatt. For the project the author began to visit Chris each Friday, interviewing him for an hour. Currently, the book is scheduled to arrive in bookstores by late 1998.

He also agreed to be master of ceremonies at the

August 1996 Paralympic Games in Atlanta. The eleven-day sports event for the physically challenged was scheduled to be broadcast by CBS television.

Dana too has been in demand. She filled in for Chris at the Renew America Honors dinner in New York, at which she presented the Christopher Reeve Environmental Leadership Award to a Sonoma County, California, group. She appeared at Drew University in New Jersey in the state's Shakespeare Festival as Julia in *Two Gentlemen of Verona*. She has begun weighing television acting offers, trying to juggle the jobs with the commitment she has to her husband and Will. Taking a weekend break in February 1996, she managed to find time to teach the youngster the basics of skiing at a Vermont resort.

Dana has called her new dual role "a little daunt-ing," saying Chris and she had "debated for a long time" over a partial resumption of her career.

Chris decided to attend the 68th annual Academy Awards in Los Angeles in January 1996, more than three months before the worldwide broadcast was scheduled to take place. It was a difficult decision, because unlike the interviews he had given to Barbara Walters, Katie Couric, Paula Zahn, and Larry King, there would be no taped delay, and thus no margin for error. When he had done the other shows, the shots of the nurse adjusting the ventilator, or attend-ing to him during commercial breaks, were all ex-cised. One fear was that his legs, which had been suffering involuntary spasms, might begin convuls-ing, unsettling the audience. This time Chris would be onstage, totally alone, and live before more than a billion people worldwide.

The project required meticulous planning. The ef-fort of transporting him from New York to Los Angeles was both arduous and costly. The potential air pockets and turbulence that could occur while jetting five hours across the country could destabilize his condition, and there would be no hospital nearby at thirty thousand feet. Thus, the travel insurance policy alone that was needed for the trip was reported to have cost more than $100,000. To maximize his safety, a team of doctors and nurses developed a plan to monitor his health every step of the way, including a seventy-five-page booklet that offered solutions in case Chris' health faltered or even if his wheelchair broke down.

Fortunately, nearly all the costs of the trip were absorbed by Warner Brothers, who provided one of its corporate jets for the trip. Chris boarded it strapped onto a gurney, lying on his back, with Dana, doctors, and nurses in tow. His respirator, a heart monitor, and other life-support equipment was wheeled into the plane after him.

As an actor, Chris knew that the drama created by his appearance at the Academy Awards would be heightened even more if it was a total surprise to both the audience and the television audience at home. So after arriving in Los Angeles he secluded himself in a suite at the Beverly Hills Hilton, where he received a group of close friends—Robin Williams and his wife, Marsha, and Emma Thompson. A local radio station revealed his planned appearance early that evening, but it occurred as most of the guests were headed toward the Dorothy Chandler Pavilion, site of the ceremonies. The appearance by Chris was more of a rumored buzz than a certainty.

Producer Quincy Jones wanted to bring Chris onstage to John Williams' *Superman* theme music, but Chris vetoed the score, not wanting to be associated with the one film that had both begun and hampered his acting career. He also told them to be sure to include a scene of Jon Voight in his wheelchair from *Coming Home*.

The 1996 Oscars were a night of high drama that exceeded anything in memory. Supporting-actress winner Mira Sorvino's thanking of her father, Paul, the camera capturing his weeping, was followed by a speech-impaired Kirk Douglas. The veteran actor, recovering from a stroke, made a poignant figure as he accepted a lifetime achievement award while the cameras cut back and forth between him and his four teary-eyed sons. The subject of the Best Documentary Short Subject winner, Gerda Weissmann Klein, further moved the audience by recounting some of her personal memories of the Holocaust. Then, just before the end of the evening, a voice simply intoned, "Ladies and gentleman, Christopher Reeve." A curtain was raised, and Chris appeared alone onstage in front of a thousand peers.

Again, as at the Creative Coalition dinner, there was prolonged, tearful applause. As Dana and his medical team watched nervously from the wings, Chris began speaking about the clips with the theme of "Hollywood Tackles the Issues."

"I wouldn't have missed this kind of welcome for the world," he began before telling a self-deprecating joke: "What you don't know is that I left New York last September. I just arrived here this morning."

Chris then got serious by lauding serious films like *Platoon* and *Philadelphia*, reminding everyone, "The film community can do this [social relevance] better than anyone else."

He told the celebrity-filled audience that "when I was a kid, my friends and I went to the movies just for fun. But then we saw Stanley Kubrick's *Dr. Strangelove*, which started us thinking about the madness of nuclear destruction. Stanley Kramer's *The Defiant Ones* taught us about race relations. It was then we began to realize that films could deal with social issues."

Afterward, Chris and Dana attended the Governor's Ball dinner and were seated between Robin Williams and Donald Trump. Eyebrows were raised at Trump's easy rapport, unaware of the admiring detente Trump had sought with him when the flamboyant billionaire had been opposed by Chris on Trump City.

Actors that included the likes of Demi Moore were moved to rare eloquence. She told a reporter after the ceremonies that "his tremendous courage, his depth of humanity and strength, is something that we should all be so lucky to find."

Mel Gibson, the evening's big winner, clutched his two Oscars from *Braveheart* and adamantly told anyone who would listen what the world was beginning to believe:

"The attitude he's got—he'll walk. I have no doubts about it!"

FILM, TELEVISION, AND THEATER ROLES PLAYED BY CHRISTOPHER REEVE

MOTION PICTURES

GRAY LADY DOWN, 1978, Universal

Director: David Greene

Charlton Heston, David Carradine, Stacy Keach, Ned Beatty, Ronny Cox, Dorian Harewood, Rosemary Forsyth, William Jordan, *Christopher Reeve*

SUPERMAN: THE MOVIE, 1978, Warner

Director: Richard Donner

Marlon Brando, Gene Hackman, *Christopher Reeve*, Ned Beatty, Jackie Cooper, Glenn Ford, Trevor Howard, Margot Kidder, Jack O'Halloran, Valerie Perrine, Maria Schell, Terrence Stamp, Phyllis Baxter, Susannah York, Jeff East, Marc McClure, Sarah Douglas, Harry Andrews, Larry Hagman, John Ratzenberger, Rex Reed

SOMEWHERE IN TIME, 1980, Universal

Director: Jeannot Szwarc

Christopher Reeve, Jane Seymour, Christopher Plummer, Teresa Wright, Bill Erwin, George Vaskovec, Susan French, John Alvin

SUPERMAN II, 1981, Warner

Director: Richard Lester

Gene Hackman, *Christopher Reeve*, Ned Beatty, Jackie Cooper, Sarah Douglas, Margot Kidder, Jack O'Halloran, Valerie Perrine, Susannah York, Clifton James, E. G. Marshall, Marc McClure, Terrence Stamp

DEATHTRAP, 1982, Warner

Director: Sidney Lumet

Michael Caine, *Christopher Reeve*, Dyan Cannon, Irene Worth, Henry Jones, Joe Silver, Tony DiBenedetto, Al LeBreton, Stewart Klein, Jeffrey Lyons, Joel Siegel

MONSIGNOR, 1982, Twentieth-Century Fox

Director: Frank Perry

Christopher Reeve, Genevieve Bujold, Fernando Rey, Jason Miller, Joe Cortese, Robert Prosky, Joe Pantoliano, David Mills, Ritza Brown

SUPERMAN III, 1983, Warner

Director: Richard Lester

Christopher Reeve, Richard Pryor, Jackie Cooper, Marc McClure, Annette O'Toole, Annie Ross, Pamela Stephenson, Robert Vaughan, Margot Kidder, Gavan O'Herlihy, Nancy Roberts, Graham Stark, Henry Woolf

THE BOSTONIANS, 1984, Merchant-Ivory

Director: James Ivory

Chirstopher Reeve, Vanessa Redgrave, Madeleine Potter, Jessica Tandy, Nancy Marchand, Wesley Addy, Barbara Bryne, Linda Hunt, Nancy New, John Van Ness Phillip, Wallace Shawn

THE AVIATOR, 1985, MGM/UA

Director: George Miller

Christopher Reeve, Rosanna Arquette, Jack Warden, Sam Wanamaker, Scott Wilson, Tyne Daly, Marcia Strassman

STREET SMART, 1987, Cannon

Director: Jerry Schatzberg

Christopher Reeve, Kathy Baker, Mimi Rogers, Jay Patterson, Andre Gregory, Morgan Freeman, Anna Maria Horsford, Frederic Rolf, Erik King

SUPERMAN IV: THE QUEST FOR PEACE, 1987, Warner

Director: Sidney J. Furie

Christopher Reeve (also cowriting and second-unit directing credits), Gene Hackman, Jackie Cooper, Marc McClure, Jon Cryer, Sam Wanamaker, Mark Pillow, Mariel Hemingway, Margot Kidder, Clive Mantle, Robert Beatty, David Garth, Susannah York, Matthew Reeve, Alexandra Reeve

SWITCHING CHANNELS, 1988, Tri-Star

Director: Ted Kotcheff

Kathleen Turner, Burt Reynolds, *Christopher Reeve*, Ned Beatty, Henry Gibson, George Newburn, Al Waxman, Charles Kimbrough, Fiona Reid

NOISES OFF, 1992, Touchstone

Director: Peter Bogdanovich

Carol Burnett, Michael Caine, Denholm Elliott, Julie Hagerty, Marilu Henner, Mark Linn-Baker, *Christopher Reeve*, John Ritter, Nicollette Sheridan

MORNING GLORY, 1993, Academy

Director: Steven Stern

Christopher Reeve, Deborah Raffin, Lloyd Bochner, Nina Foch, Helen Shaver, J. T. Walsh

THE REMAINS OF THE DAY, 1993, Columbia

Director: James Ivory

Anthony Hopkins, Emma Thompson, James Fox, *Christopher Reeve*, Peter Vaughan, Hugh Grant, Tim Pigott-Smith, Patrick Godfrey, Peter Eyre, Brigitte Kahn

SPEECHLESS, 1994, MGM

Director: Ron Underwood

Michael Keaton, Geena Davis, *Christopher Reeve*, Bonnie Bedelia, Ernie Hudson, Charles Martin Smith, Gailard Sartain, Ray Baker, Mitchell Ryan

VILLAGE OF THE DAMNED, 1995, Universal

Director: John Carpenter

Christopher Reeve, Kirstie Alley, Linda Kozlowski, Michael Pare, Mark Hamill, Peter Jason, Karen Kahn, Buck Flower

---

TELEVISION SERIES

LOVE OF LIFE (Ben Harper) 1974–1976, CBS-TV

EARTH JOURNEYS (Host/Narrator) 1993–1994, The Travel Channel

TELEVISION MOVIES AND MINISERIES

ANNA KARENINA, 1985, CBS-TV

Director: Simon Langston

Jacqueline Bisset, *Christopher Reeve*, Paul Scofield, Anna Massey, Judi Bowker, Joanna David, Ian Ogilvey

THE GREAT ESCAPE II: THE UNTOLD STORY, 1988, NBC-TV

Directors: Jud Taylor (part one), Paul Wendkos (part two)

Christopher Reeve, Judd Hirsch, Anthony Denison, Charles Haid, Michael Nader, Ian McShane, Mijou Kovacs, Derek McLint, Donald Pleasance, Andrew Bicknell, Manfred Andrae

BUMP IN THE NIGHT, 1991, CBS

Director: Karen Arthur

Meredith Baxter-Birney, *Christopher Reeve*, Geraldine Fitzgerald, Shirley Knight, Wings Hauser, Richard Bradford, Anne Twomey, Terrence Mann, Travis Swords, Corey Carrier

THE ROSE AND THE JACKAL, 1990, Turner Network Television

Director: Jack Gold

Christopher Reeve, Madolyn Smith Osborne, Kevin McCarthy, Carrie Snodgrass, Granville Van Dusen

DEATH DREAMS, 1991, Lifetime Cable Network

Director: Martin Donovan

Christopher Reeve, Marg Helgenberger, Fionula Flanagan, Taylor Fry, George Dickerson, Conor O'Farrell, Pat Atkins

MORTAL SINS, 1992, USA Cable Network

Director: Bradford May

Christopher Reeve, Roxanne Biggs, Francis Guinan, Weston McMillan, Phillip R. Allen, Lisa Vultaggio

THE LAST FERRY HOME, 1992, WCVB's Family Works

Director: Fred Barzyk

Christopher Reeve, Josef Sommer, Roxanne Hart, Lois Smith, Mako, Billy L. Sullivan

NIGHTMARE IN THE DAYLIGHT, 1992, CBS-TV

Director: Lou Antonio

Jaclyn Smith, *Christopher Reeve*, Tom Mason, Eric Bell, Wren T. Brown, Christina Pickles, Glynnis O'Connor

THE SEA WOLF, 1993, Turner Network Television

Director: Michael Anderson

Christopher Reeve, Charles Bronson, Catherine Mary Stewart, Len Cariou, Marc Singer, Clive Revill

ABOVE SUSPICION, 1995, HBO Cable Network

Director: Steven Schachter

Christopher Reeve, Joe Mantegna, Kim Cattrall, Edward Kerr, Finola Hughes, Dana Reeve

BLACK FOX, 1995, CBS-TV

Director: Steven Stern

Christopher Reeve, Tony Todd, Raoul Trujillo, Kim Coates, Janet Bailey, Nancy Sorel, Chris Wiggins, Kelly Rowan

(Note: *Black Fox* was a trilogy of films broadcast over a three-week period during the summer of 1995.)

SELECTED THEATER PRODUCTIONS

A MATTER OF GRAVITY, 1976, Broadhurst Theater, New York

Director: Noel Willman

Katharine Hepburn, Charlotte Jones, Robert Moberly, *Christopher Reeve,* Elizabeth Lawrence, Paul Harding, Wanda Bimson, Daniel Tamm

MY LIFE, 1977, Circle Repertory Company, New York

Director: Marshall W. Mason

William Hurt, Nancy Snyder, *Christopher Reeve,* Claire Malis, Roger Chapman, Jeff Daniels, Tanya Berezin, Douglass Watson, Jo Henderson

FIFTH OF JULY, 1980, New Apollo Theater, New York

Director: Marshall W. Mason

Christopher Reeve, Jeff Daniels, Jonathan Hogan, Swoosie Kurtz, Joyce Reehling, Amy Wright, Mary Carver, Danton Stone

THE GREEKS, 1981, Williamstown Theater Festival, Massachusetts

Director: Nikos Psacharopoulos

Celeste Holm, Edward Herrmann, Blythe Danner, Carrie Nye, *Christopher Reeve*, Kate Burton, Maria Tucci, Dwight Schultz, Gwyneth Paltrow, Donald Mofatt, Roxanne Hart, Tony Goldwyn, Pamela Payton-Wright, Chris Kavanaugh, Derek Evans, Judith Anna Roberts, Jane White, Roberta Maxwell, Josef Sommer

HOLIDAY, 1983, Williamstown Theater Festival

Director: Nikos Psacharopoulos

Blythe Danner, Ken Howard, Marisa Berenson, *Christopher Reeve*, Jerome Dempsey, Edmond Genest, Jennifer Harmon, Mary Tharp, Christian Clemenson, Chris Weatherhead, Peter Herrick, James Morgan

THE ASPERN PAPERS, 1984, Theatre Royal, London

Director: Frith Banbury

Vanessa Redgrave, *Christopher Reeve*, Wendy Hiller, Tony Robins, Francine Morgan, Joseph Long

THE ROYAL FAMILY, 1985, Williamstown Theater Festival

Director: Edward Payson Call

Christopher Reeve, Maria Tucci, Karen Allen, Ruth Nelson, Joseph Maher, Robin Strausser, Louis Beachner

THE MARRIAGE OF FIGARO, 1985, Circle in the Square, New York

Director: Andrei Serban

Anthony Heald, *Christopher Reeve*, Mary Elizabeth Mastrantonio, Louis Zorich, Carol Teitel, Caitlin Clarke, James Cahill, Dana Ivey, Debbie Merrill, William Duell

SUMMER AND SMOKE, 1986, Williamstown Theater Festival

Director: James Simpson

Christopher Reeve, Laila Robins, Ann Reinking, Stephanie

Zimbalist, Joe Ponazecki, Meg Mundy, Joshua Pilot, William Swetland, Frances Helm, Tisha Roth, David Beecroft, Doug Fields, Edouard Desoto

THE ROVER, 1987, Williamstown Theater Festival

Director: John Rubinstein

Stephen Collins, Harry Groener, Edward Herrmann, *Christopher Reeve*, Ann Reinking, Cameron M. Smith, Kate Burton, Tisha Roth, David Purdham, Jeffrey Rose, Jennifer Van Dyck, Robin Strasser, Myra Taylor

SUMMER AND SMOKE, 1988, Ahmanson Theater, Los Angeles

Director: Marshall W. Mason

Christopher Reeve, Christine Lahti, Carol Potter Eastman, Carol Barbee, Michael Chieffo, Lois de Banzie, Wand De Jesus, Russel Lunday, Richard Seff, Leo Carranza, Jacque Lynn Colton

THE WINTER'S TALE, 1989, Public Theater, New York

Director: James Lapine

Mandy Patinkin, *Christopher Reeve*, Alfre Woodard, Jennifer Dundas, Graham Brown, MacIntyre Dixon, Tom McGowan, Rocco Sisto, Albert Farrar, Diane Venora, Rob Besserer, Graham Winton, James Olson, Michael Cumpsty

JOHN BROWN'S BODY, 1989, Williamstown Theater Festival

Director: Peter Hunt

Christopher Reeve, Robert Lansing, Laurie Kennedy

LOVE LETTERS, 1990, Wilbur Theater, Boston

Director: John Tillinger

Christopher Reeve, Julie Hagerty

DEATH TAKES A HOLIDAY, 1990, Williamstown Theater Festival

Director: Peter Hunt

Christopher Reeve, Maria Tucci, Blythe Danner, George Morfogen, John Franklyn-Robbins, Calista Flockhart, Jenny Greenberg, Robert Brolli, Patrick Boll, Robert Hogan, Giulia Pagano

THE GUARDSMAN, 1992, Williamstown Theater Festival

Director: Michael Bloom

Christopher Reeve, Anne Twomey, Ron Holgate, Anne Pitoniak, Leonard Tucker, Arija Bareikis, Patricia Jones, Jay Apking, Allegra di Carpegna, Annette Ricchiazzi

THE SHADOW BOX, 1993, Temple of Music and Art, Tucson, Arizona

A nondirected dramatic reading

Christopher Reeve, Mercedes Ruehl, Estelle Parsons, Blair Brown, Robert Sean Leonard, Michael Tucker, Jill Eikenberry, Harry Hamlin, Michael Alvarado

MISCELLANEOUS CREDITS

The Muppet Show (guest), 1981, ABC
I Love Liberty (participant), 1982, ABC
Celebrity Daredevils (host), 1983, ABC
Faerie Tale Theater (Prince Charming), 1983, Showtime
Vincent, a Dutchman (host), 1984, PBS
Juilliard at Eighty (host/narrator), 1985, CBS
Night of 1000 Stars (participant), 1985, ABC
American Portrait, Robert Goddard (host), 1985, CBS
Dinosaur! (host/narrator), 1985, CBS
Future Flight (host), 1987, syndicated
Superman's Fiftieth (participant), 1988, CBS
World's Greatest Stunts (host), 1988, CBS
Valvoline Driving Test (host), 1989, ABC
The Reporters (participant), 1989, FOX

11th Annual ACE Awards (presenter), 1990, HBO
44th Annual Tony Awards (role), 1990 CBS
Black Tide (narrator), 1990, Discovery
Tribute to Vaclav Havel (role), 1990, PBS
Carol & Company (guest), 1990, NBC
The Road from Runnymede (host/narrator), 1991, PBS
Earth and the American Dream (participant), 1993, HBO
Tales From The Crypt (role), 1994, HBO

ACKNOWLEDGMENTS

This book could have never been written without the help of hundreds of people who shared their time and information.

The Richmans—Alan, Kelli, and Matthew—were my eyes and ears in New York and New Jersey. Dorothy Wolfe in Newark was of great help in researching the Reeve family history. Also, a special thanks to the staff of the Mudd Library archives at Princeton University, in particular, Nanci Young and Monica Ruscil.

In Williamstown, Massachusetts, the help of Shawei Wang of Williams College is fondly remembered, as is the cooperation of Mark Rondeau at *The Advocate*, and Jeffrey Borak at the *Berkshire Eagle* in Pittsfield. Anne Lowrie of the Williamstown Theater Festival helped me track down some of the many plays in which Christopher Reeve has appeared.

In Washington, special thanks are due to Elias Savada, one of the foremost experts on the history of the Hollywood motion picture, and also to Robert Nelson, Ph.D., who patiently answered my questions about the American stage at all hours of the day and night. Leslie Eckard, who was my Merchant-Ivory expert, filled in important gaps there.

To Robert Taylor, Phil Bunton, and Brian J. Williams—whose names rarely appear in succession—thanks for the deluge of information.

Rosemary Hanes of the Motion Picture division of

the Library of Congress deserves a special mention, as does Jacob Wind, who was part of the book's genesis.

In Charlottesville, Virginia, Marguerite Beck was very patient with my repeated queries, faxing me reams of information. David Burds of the Spinal Cord Network in Arlington, Virginia, gave freely of his expertise.

And a special thanks to the dedicated people who have enthusiastically given aid "beyond the call of duty" at the following institutions: Billy Rose Theater Collection of the New York Public Library at Lincoln Center, and the Performing Arts division of the Library of Congress.

Thanks also to Virginia Cohen at the National Endowment for the Arts and Paula Vogel of AP/Wide World Photos in New York.

Finally, Brenda Atkins' sharp eye for manuscript errors has always been appreciated. And I would be remiss in not mentioning Jane Dystel and Miriam Goderich, who are both literary agents *extraordinaire*.

More Fascinating Biography from Headline

MICHAEL DOUGLAS ACTING ON INSTINCT

John Parker

Michael Douglas is Hollywood's man of the moment. His image is sexy, violent. He earns $10 million-plus a picture. He is recognised as a real Nice Guy, whereas his father Kirk was once voted the Most Hated Man in Hollywood.

During his early years Michael fought to escape his father's overpowering image but his niceness hindered his acting career. He turned to producing and made *One Flew Over the Cuckoo's Nest*, which won five Oscars, including one for himself. He finally broke into the big league as an actor when a darker side of his persona emerged in mid-life with controversial movies like *Fatal Attraction*, *Wall Street*, *Basic Instinct* and *Falling Down*. Audiences cheered his beastliness.

But his fame brought his turbulent marriage to Spanish-born Diandra to a crisis. She insisted he sought help at a clinic specialising in treating sexual addiction or face the final break-up of their relationship.

It is a compelling and remarkable story: a Hollywood son who waged a very personal battle against the odds to achieve his fame and fortune.

Praise for John Parker's *Warren Beatty*

'John Parker's *Warren Beatty* is as slick as its subject. There is masses of showbiz gossip. A good racy read.' *The Times*

NON-FICTION / BIOGRAPHY 0 7472 4473 1

Denholm Elliott
Quest for Love

Susan Elliott with Barry Turner

'Susan Elliott's compulsively readable book lovingly and forgivingly records the life and work of one of our most remarkable actors.' Simon Callow, *Sunday Express*

'He was a definer of the English character, neither rural nor urban, a miniaturist of grandeur, a star-stabbing princeling among players. This is a brave and honest book. He would approve.' John Osborne, *Spectator*

'. . . this biography is critically honest and moving.' Sheridan Morley, *Sunday Times*

From *The Sound Barrier* and *The Cruel Sea* in the early fifties to *Indiana Jones* in the late eighties Denholm Elliott's career in films and on the stage brought him acclaim on both sides of the Atlantic as an actor of the very first rank.

But there was inner conflict in his life as he gradually came to recognise his bisexuality. He found an identity through a remarkably open relationship with his second wife Susan. This book is Susan Elliot's own story of his extraordinary career and of their unusual marriage and family life in London and Ibiza with their children, Jennifer and Mark, until his death, brought on by AIDS, in October 1992.

NON-FICTION / BIOGRAPHY 0 7472 4378 6

A selection of non-fiction from Headline

THE NEXT 500 YEARS	Adrian Berry	£7.99	☐
FIGHT FOR THE TIGER	Michael Day	£7.99	☐
LEFT FOOT FORWARD	Garry Nelson	£5.99	☐
THE NATWEST PLAYFAIR CRICKET ANNUAL	Bill Frindall	£4.99	☐
THE JACK THE RIPPER A–Z	Paul Begg, Martin Fido & Keith Skinner	£8.99	☐
VEGETARIAN GRUB ON A GRANT	Cas Clarke	£5.99	☐
PURE FRED	Rupert Fawcett	£6.99	☐
THE SUPERNATURAL A–Z	James Randi	£6.99	☐
ERIC CANTONA: MY STORY	Eric Cantona	£6.99	☐
THE TRUTH IN THE LIGHT	Peter and Elizabeth Fenwick	£6.99	☐
GOODBYE BAFANA	James Gregory	£6.99	☐
MY OLD MAN AND THE SEA	Daniel Hayes and David Hayes	£5.99	☐

All Headline books are available at your local bookshop or newsagent, or can be ordered direct from the publisher. Just tick the titles you want and fill in the form below. Prices and availability subject to change without notice.

Headline Book Publishing, Cash Sales Department, Bookpoint, 39 Milton Park, Abingdon, OXON, OX14 4TD, UK. If you have a credit card you may order by telephone – 01235 400400.

Please enclose a cheque or postal order made payable to Bookpoint Ltd to the value of the cover price and allow the following for postage and packing:

UK & BFPO: £1.00 for the first book, 50p for the second book and 30p for each additional book ordered up to a maximum charge of £3.00.
OVERSEAS & EIRE: £2.00 for the first book, £1.00 for the second book and 50p for each additional book.

Name ....

Address ....

....

....

If you would prefer to pay by credit card, please complete:
Please debit my Visa/Access/Diner's Card/American Express (delete as applicable) card no:

Signature .... Expiry Date ....